# IDOL OF SUBURBIA

VICTORIAN LITERATURE AND CULTURE SERIES

Karen Chase, Jerome J. McGann, *and* Herbert Tucker, *Editors*

# IDOL OF SUBURBIA

*Marie Corelli and*

*Late-Victorian*

*Literary Culture*

Annette R. Federico

UNIVERSITY PRESS OF VIRGINIA

*Charlottesville and London*

The University Press of Virginia
© 2000 by the Rector and Visitors of the University of Virginia
Printed in the United States of America

*First published in 2000*

∞ The paper used in this publication meets the minimum requirements of the
American National Standard for Information Sciences—Permanence of Paper
for Printed Library Materials, ANSI Z39.48-1984.

Library of Congress Cataloging-in-Publication Data
Federico, Annette, 1960–
    Idol of suburbia : Marie Corelli and late-Victorian literary culture /
Annette R. Federico.
        p.      cm. — (Victorian literature and culture series)
    Includes bibliographical references and index.
    ISBN 0-8139-1915-0 (cloth : alk. paper)
    1. Corelli, Marie, 1855–1924—Criticism and interpretation.
2. Feminism and literature—England—History—19th
century.   3. Women and literature—England—History—
19th century.   4. Authors and readers—England—History—19th
century.   5. Popular culture—England—History—
19th century.   6. Suburban life—England—History—19th
century.   7. Women—England—Books and reading.   I. Title.
II. Series.
PR4505.F43    2000
823'.8—dc21                                                              99-39131
                                                                              CIP

*For Joseph A. Federico*
*1949–1998*

# Contents

# Illustrations

# Acknowledgments

Two research grants from the College of Arts and Letters at James Madison University, in 1996 and 1998, supported summer travel to consult archival materials on Marie Corelli at the Beinecke Rare Book and Manuscript Library at Yale University, the University Archives and Special Collections at the University of Detroit Mercy, and the Shakespeare Birthplace Trust in Stratford-upon-Avon. I am grateful to Christine Yancy at the University of Detroit Mercy, who patiently and with good humor monitored my protracted readings of the Severn correspondence, and to Dr. Robert Bearman, Mairi Macdonald, and Eileen Alberti for their help in sorting through the Corelli archives at Stratford. Images are reproduced with the permission of the Shakespeare Birthplace Trust in Stratford-upon-Avon and the National Portrait Gallery, London.

A different version of chapter 1 appeared originally as "Literary Celebrity and Photographic Realism: Marie Corelli and Late-Victorian 'Picture Popularity,'" in *Nineteenth Century Studies* 11 (1997): 26–50; of chapter 2 as "Marie Corelli: Aestheticism in Suburbia," in *Women and British Aestheticism,* edited by Talia Schaffer and Kathy Alexis Psomiades (Charlottesville: University Press of Virginia, 1999); and of chapter 3 as "'An Old-Fashioned Young Woman': Marie Corelli and the New Woman," in *Victorian Women Writers and the Woman Question,* edited by Nicola Diane Thompson (Cambridge: Cambridge University Press, 1999).

# IDOL OF SUBURBIA

# Introduction

In February 1886, against the advice of its readers, Richard Bentley and Son published in two volumes a strange novel about Chaldean mysticism and electric religion called *A Romance of Two Worlds* by an unknown writer named Marie Corelli. The few reviewers who condescended to notice the book were merciless in their disapprobation. "Miss Corelli would have been better advised had she embodied her ridiculous ideas in a sixpenny pamphlet," wrote one critic. Another stamped the novel with words hostile reviewers would apply to Corelli for the next twenty years: "it is pure bosh."

Despite critical indifference, *A Romance of Two Worlds* became tremendously popular—to use Corelli's words, the book was "successfully launched on the sea of public favour"—and so began a publication record without parallel. In five years Corelli published five more novels with Bentley, all popular successes: *Vendetta, or: The Story of One Forgotten* (1886), *Thelma: A Society Novel* (1887), *Ardath: The Story of a Dead Self* (1889), *Wormwood* (1890), and *The Soul of Lilith* (1892). Reviewers and the literary elite continued to ridicule her (Edmund Gosse dismissed her as "that little milliner"), but such treatment had no effect on her mass appeal. Her audiences crossed all class lines, and she was admired by men as well as women. Queen Victoria requested that all of Corelli's novels be sent to Balmoral, and the Prince of Wales invited her to dine, proclaiming, "You are the only woman-writer of genius we have." William Gladstone called her "an earnest woman-thinker" and advised her to resist "trivialities in fiction. Fiction is a powerful factor in the education of the people." Although one critic ironically anointed her "the idol of Suburbia" (and truly she was), Corelli was also admired, at least for a time, by some of the literary and theatrical lights of London: Oscar Wilde asked her to write for *Woman's World,* she was introduced to Robert Browning and Algernon Charles Swinburne, Ellen Terry adored her, and Lillie

Langtry asked to perform in dramatizations of her novels. Corelli broke all publishing records: on average, a Corelli novel sold 100,000 copies a year. At the turn of the century sales averaged 175,000 copies, and in 1906 *The Treasure of Heaven: A Romance of Riches* achieved a first-day record of 100,000. In their biographies Eileen Bigland and Brian Masters tend to make her appear either neurotic or quaint, yet both testify amazement at Corelli's celebrity. Bigland writes, "In two short years Marie had made such a name for herself that as a topic of conversation she ran the Prince of Wales and Mr. Gladstone pretty close" (103). Masters simply claims, "While Queen Victoria was alive, Miss Corelli was the second most famous Englishwoman in the world; afterwards, there was no one to approach her" (6).

In this book I hope to return Corelli to conversations about the late-Victorian and Edwardian literary world. My approach falls somewhere between literary criticism, women's studies, and cultural studies. I am impelled less by an evangelical urge to rescue a once popular writer from oblivion than by a curiosity about a woman whose fame at the turn of the century was unsurpassed and yet who by the end of the twentieth century had become only a name vaguely, and pejoratively, connected with Victorian popular fiction. Corelli is interesting as a cultural icon and a barometer of Victorian taste, and certainly my intention is to study her books against their social background. But she also shows some surprising innovations as a novelist. Her books cross genres, mixing the conventions of romance, gothic, historical, and society novels. She invented stories that anticipate feminist science fiction, mixed bodice-ripper sex with transports of spiritual ecstasy, and daringly rewrote biblical history. These strange fictional encounters are central to my reading of Corelli's novels: she offers a rich field for interpreting the way gender informed a changing aesthetic of the melodramatic at the end of the century; her manipulation of almost every feature of literary decadence challenges antithetical genres, styles, audiences, and sexualities; her dislike of New Woman fiction does not preclude her use of independent female geniuses as heroines; and although she called herself an old-fashioned idealist, she experienced moods of profound disillusionment and sought to reconcile scientific theories with her spiritual longings and religious faith.

Such literary and philosophical departures are part of a set of intriguing paradoxes and ambiguities. From the start of her career Corelli was scorned by reviewers yet adored by readers, a paradox she flaunted in author's notes, in letters to the press, and in articles she wrote in her own defense; she was a highly successful woman who insisted publicly on women's intellectual equality in a competitive book market controlled by men, yet she cultivated an image of hyperfemininity and abhorred the New Woman; she was unmarried and lived intimately with another woman her entire life, yet her books dwell on displays of heterosexual passion, sometimes to the point of erotic frenzy; she was anti-intellectual yet wished to appear well educated in history and modern languages. Corelli's novels attack or expose Victorian vice, hypocrisy, and injustice with all the fire and brimstone the public could crave, yet they also indulge the pleasures of social, moral, and sexual transgression. These contradictions, no doubt, contribute to Corelli's fascination. Contrary energies, what Rebecca West has called her "demoniac vitality," are the makings of a best-seller (321).

I address the question of *why* Corelli's novels were so popular, and the contradictions listed above are central to my reading of her place in turn-of-the-century English society. But I have many corresponding questions. How does Corelli participate in literary decadence, in feminism and New Woman fiction, and in emerging technologies of self-representation and self-advertisement? How seriously should we take her aesthetic, that is, her overt claims for her novels and her methods of writing, her style, and her literary influence? Why does heterosexual love seem pathological in so many of her novels, and relatedly, how valid are biographical and psychoanalytic explanations about Corelli's celibacy, her lifelong companionship with another woman, her efforts to conceal her illegitimacy, her elaborate self-mythology?

The story of Corelli's life is extremely interesting, and I have relied heavily on information in the biographies by Bigland and Masters. I am especially indebted to Masters's *Now Barabbas Was a Rotter: The Extraordinary Life of Marie Corelli* (1978), although a more sympathetic (and more feminist) biography would give a very different picture of Corelli's life.[1] In sketching out Corelli's career in this introduction, I will emphasize episodes that are suitable to my approach to her work in the chapters that follow.

"Marie Corelli" was the pseudonym of Mary "Minnie" Mackay, but "Marie Corelli" was much more than a pen name; it was an identity.

Her family background was a mystery for years, but it seems probable that she was the illegitimate daughter of Charles Mackay, a journalist, poet, and balladeer who never satisfied his literary ambitions. Her mother was Charles's second wife, Mary Elizabeth Mills, who was probably a servant in the Mackay household at the time Marie was conceived. Throughout her life Corelli referred to Charles Mackay as her "adopted father." She was born 1 May 1855 (although she made herself ten years younger when she got into print) and raised at Fern Dell, near the village of Mickleham, in Surrey; the Mackays' close neighbor was George Meredith, who was enchanted with little Minnie's spontaneity. As a child, she was, by several accounts, precocious, determined, ambitious, confident, dreamy, vain, and lonely. There is an unusually frank letter written by Corelli in the Records Office at Stratford-upon-Avon (where she lived from 1901 to 1924), which gives some idea of the emotional life of her childhood. The letter is addressed to William Meredith (the son of George Meredith and his second wife, Marie Vulliamy), whose parents moved to Box Hill in 1865: "I do not remember the 'breaking through the bridge,' but I remember *you,* chiefly because you seemed to be a very happy boy, while I 'on the other side of the bridge' was a *most* lonely and miserable girl! The days of my childhood are days of such intense and bitter suffering, that I never willingly look back to them, nor can I be reminded of them without indescribable pain." This letter was written on 9 April 1905, when Corelli was almost fifty and a very famous woman. Perhaps she feared that certain unsavory constructions would be given to this candid expression of childhood grief, for she continued: "My position was in itself uncomfortable—for to know that my parents were dead, and that I was adopted by good Mr. Mackay out of the sheer kindness of his heart and his old associations with those dead parents, and to have no brothers or sisters of my own, and no companions, and nothing to look forward to in the world, was enough, so I thought, to make anyone miserable—and indeed I was so *very* unhappy that I never care to think of it now." Heartfelt sentiment and self-pity are combined through the reference to "good Mr. Mackay" and the (perhaps) self-protective fabrication of the poor orphan—a familiar Corellian blend of genuine feeling and melodramatic invention.

Her education was unconventional and undisciplined. Charles Mackay encouraged her vivid imagination and gave her the run of his

extensive library. A series of governesses fled from her intellectual exhi-
bitionism and her intimidating sense of her own brilliance, and eventually
she was sent to a convent school (she claimed in France or Italy, but more
likely it was in England), where she concocted private theatricals about
love and murder. Corelli adored her father and was much attached to her
stepbrother, Eric, who was twenty years her senior and living in Italy,
where he was trying to establish a reputation as a poet. Both Bigland and
Masters describe her mother as a shadowy, inconsequential woman, and
Corelli has very little, if anything, to say about her. When Corelli returned to Fern Dell after her schooling was ended, she found her home
melancholy and lonely: her father's health was poor, they were constantly
short of money, and Eric was getting into disgraceful scrapes in Italy.
When Corelli was twenty-one, her mother died, and a friend her own
age, Bertha Vyver, moved into the house; the two women remained
companions for the rest of Corelli's life. In 1884, after Charles Mackay
was left semiparalyzed from a heart attack, Eric, now forty-eight, returned from abroad, and the family moved to Longridge Road in Earl's
Court, London, hoping for brighter prospects.

The picture of the household as presented by Corelli's biographers
is one of sexual repression, frustrated ambition, and contested power.
Practically an invalid, Charles Mackay was autocratic and egotistic, and
his son was much the same. Eric was adept at flattery, and he reawakened
Corelli's adolescent longings for love and recognition. His European experiences were romantic dreams come true, and the fact that he had published some flaccid verse led Corelli to believe the family's creative and
artistic gifts must find a venue. She tried a career as a pianist, giving several recitals, where she displayed her skill at improvisation. She was well
received, but there was never enough money to pay for proper musical
training. When her hopes for a musical career collapsed, she wrote poetry
and was encouraged by both her father and Eric to try to sell something
as soon as possible. From the very beginning Corelli's strained romanticism and sensuous responsiveness to music and art were joined with financial necessity. Desperate for some kind of recognition, in 1885, at the
age of thirty, she sent a manuscript she had been writing about "personal
electricity" (originally titled "Lifted Up") to Richard Bentley and Son
under her romantic-sounding pseudonym.

Although George Bentley, the head of the firm, recognized the novel's faults and predicted that it would "provoke much adverse criticism," he shrewdly saw that its extravagant assertions and bold style would appeal to some readers. "I think," he wrote to Corelli, "it will be considered by some as the production of a visionary" (Bigland 73). He was right. Corelli received fan letters from readers interested in theosophy and psychical research, from an "earnest seeker after Truth," from a clergyman who was saved from suicide by reading it, and from an atheist who was converted to Christ. With the zeal of a prophet and the acumen of a publicist, Corelli printed the letters and her explanations of the "Electric Creed" in an appendix to subsequent editions of the novel (*A Romance of Two Worlds* 337–48).

The success of her first book led to some embellishments in the construction of "Marie Corelli" the author: she told George Bentley she was only nineteen years old and the daughter of a Venetian who could trace her ancestry back to the Renaissance musician Arcangelo Corelli. She was under five feet tall and grew stout later in life, but she always adopted a hyperfeminine, almost girlish, style of dress. Many of her novels contain portraits of petite, golden-haired, rosy young Englishwomen who happen also to be intellectuals or artists. The negotiation between her public image and her private identity was of vital importance from the very beginning.

Corelli's first book apparently called out a widespread longing for moral certainty and spiritual assurance that had been left unfulfilled by the morbid frankness of new fiction and New Women novelists, as well as by male fantasy and adventure writers such as Rudyard Kipling, H. Rider Haggard, the young H. G. Wells, and Hall Caine. By coincidence, Caine was one of the readers for Bentley who had recommended against publishing *A Romance of Two Worlds,* and he reappeared in Corelli's life as both her arch rival and her male alter ego. He was her nearest competitor in sales; Corelli sold a hundred thousand novels a year on average, Caine forty-five thousand, Mrs. Humphry Ward thirty-five thousand, Wells and Arthur Conan Doyle only fifteen thousand each (Scott 233). Corelli did not see herself as belonging strictly to any class of modern fiction, but she tended to insist that her writings honestly exposed the shallowness and sinfulness of modern society. She took pride in her writing, and indeed her books are undoubtedly unique, ardent, and thoroughly sincere. "I *must* be myself," she wrote to George Bentley in

March 1887, "and if I write at all, I must be allowed to handle a subject my own way."

Her own way was good enough for the British reader. Her sales continued to soar, and statistically she reigned supreme. *Barabbas: A Dream of the World's Tragedy* outsold all previous Corelli novels in 1893, the year it was published, and went into seven editions in seven months; the single-volume edition sold ten thousand copies in one week (Masters 130). Then on 21 October 1895 Methuen published *The Sorrows of Satan,* which had an initial sale greater than any previous English novel, even though Corelli, fed up with the critics, refused to send out copies for review. The novel sold twenty-five thousand copies in one week and fifty thousand in seven weeks (Feltes 123). It was the first modern best-seller, and it was read by everyone, from noblemen to scullery maids. At Corelli's death in 1924 *The Sorrows of Satan* was in its sixtieth edition and had been translated into almost every European language and adapted both to the stage and to film.[2]

By 1895 Corelli appeared unstoppable. Certain of a hit, Hutchinson in 1896 advertised a first edition of an incredible twenty thousand copies of *The Mighty Atom* (Scott 44). Corelli published almost a novel a year and in 1900 reached astonishing heights of fame with *The Master Christian,* which sold 160,000 copies in two years (Masters 165), and was followed by the success of *Temporal Power: A Study in Supremacy* (1902), which her 1903 biographers T. F. G. Coates and R. S. Warren-Bell called "the most talked-about book in the world" (247).

In 1901 Corelli settled for good in Stratford-upon-Avon with Vyver as her companion, buying a distinguished old brick house on Church Street called Mason Croft (it now houses the University of Birmingham Shakespeare Institute). She was financially secure, famous, sought-after by celebrity hunters, and invited to lecture at literary functions and to preside at ribbon-cutting ceremonies. Corelli was a local legend, riding about town with her cart and ponies or gliding down the Avon in her authentic Italian gondola (with an imported Venetian gondolier, until he had to be replaced by a more reliable English gardener). She became a fierce protector of Shakespeare's birthplace, getting involved in several ugly controversies with trustees, citizens, and benefactors. In less than twenty years Minnie Mackay had transformed herself into the morally imperious yet femininely gentle Marie Corelli, and she would go to great lengths to defend the construction of that brilliant persona. In an age of mass media Corelli refused to give interviews and fled from cameras. She wanted control of her celebrity, and for the most part she got it.

Vyver features prominently in the story of Corelli. She is an example of a woman who fashioned her life around her love, and although there is no evidence that she and Corelli were lesbian lovers (Lillian Faderman calls close female relationships "romantic friends"), both women were stigmatized as frustrated spinsters (213–15). There is no doubt that Vyver was Corelli's partner in life, a devoted and supportive companion who took care of their home and stayed out of the limelight, a friend with whom Corelli shared the happiness and misery of her struggles and her fame. The relationship became strained but never broke. Even when, at the age of fifty-one, Corelli fell miserably in love with the painter Arthur Severn and pestered him with her effusions until he and his wife had to break off relations with her, Vyver remained an ally and a sympathizer. Several of Corelli's books are dedicated to Vyver, whose hagiographic *Memoirs of Marie Corelli* was published in 1930.

After World War I (when she was scandalously and falsely accused of food hoarding), Corelli was regarded by the public "more as a curiosity than as a novelist who wrote books anyone wanted to read" (Bigland 265). She died of a heart attack on 21 April 1924. Vyver, who inherited Mason Croft and Corelli's entire literary estate, died in 1942. Their graves are side by side in the cemetery at Stratford-upon-Avon.

### Literary Culture and Modernity

Corelli's inescapable celebrity from 1886 until the beginning of World War I and her almost total erasure from cultural memory after her death in 1924 present questions about literary taste and how it is formed (and unformed), about the vicissitudes of the late-Victorian literary market, and about the limitations and advantages of being a woman writer during a period of feminist agitation. My interest in Corelli originates in an interest in fin-de-siècle literary culture: she seems an underappreciated contributor to the ongoing debates about literary value, class, and gender, a writer whose fame alone suggests myriad possibilities for interpreting the reading activities of the British at the turn of the twentieth century. Her life and her novels place the ideological contradictions of the period in bold relief: the opposing artistic claims of realism, naturalism, and romance; the ubiquitous arguments over feminism, marriage, and sexual equality; and especially the perceived power and elitism of the literary world given the demands of middle-class consumers.

Although the title of this book stresses the late-Victorian era because that period represents the height of Corelli's fame, her relationship with the modern period, and with modernity and high modernism, is also important. The distance between high and popular art had become wider by 1900, and Corelli's fame presented a challenge not only to British cultural authority but to the social and political life of English citizens. One way of understanding modernism is to ask how high art and popular fiction overlap, and a good way to begin such an inquiry might be to ask which authors high modernists read in their formative years. The name Marie Corelli turns up in some unexpected quarters. At the turn of the century James Joyce was apparently fascinated with Corelli, whose style he appropriated in segments of *Ulysses* and *Finnegans Wake* (Kershner, "Joyce" 213–16). Among men of letters, V. S. Pritchett read Charles Dickens, Marcus Aurelius, Thomas Hardy, John Ruskin, and Marie Corelli as a boy (Angell). The narrator of George Orwell's autobiographical novel *Coming Up for Air* (1939) recalls a turning point in his intellectual life when, at the age of eighteen, in 1910, he "suddenly turned highbrow, got a ticket for the County Library, and began to stodge through books by Marie Corelli and Hall Caine and Anthony Hope" (99). Betty Smith's *A Tree Grows in Brooklyn* (1943) details a similar coming-of-age when, in 1912, the eleven-year-old heroine, Francie, follows an alphabetical reading schedule at the city library: "After that came Browning. She groaned, anxious to get to the C's where there was a book by Marie Corelli that she had peeped into and found thrilling. Would she *ever* get to that?" (24). William Stuart Scott's memoir of Corelli includes a comparable account of his working-class childhood in Ireland, when he would race to the library to see if her books had been returned by other avid borrowers. And just as Scott's father disapproved of his son's sordid reading matter, Willa Cather's antagonism toward her mother is coded in terms of reading tastes. Cather's mother was a fan of the "trashy romantic novelist Marie Corelli," whereas Cather yearned for higher things (Acocella 68). At the turn of modernism, sometime around 1910, Corelli was *both* "trashy" and "highbrow."

*Reassessments*

In a long review of *The Sorrows of Satan* in 1895, the editor of the *Review of Reviews*, W. T. Stead, declared:

> (453)
>
> *If, after she has achieved her success, sold her scores of thousands, and avenged herself to her heart's content upon her critics, she would then be so good as to take the book, tone it down, omit her superlatives, and cut out every solitary word that relates to reviews, reviewers, and other women novelists, she will have produced a book which will live long after much of the ephemeral literature of the day is forgotten. Otherwise* The Sorrows of Satan *will be sunk by the sorrows of Marie Corelli which, however interesting they may be to our little contemporary world, cannot be expected to be entertaining or edifying to posterity.*

This characterization has ostensibly held for three quarters of a century, but Corelli never completely disappeared. In the field of contemporary critical theory, literary historians, Victorian and early-twentieth-century scholars, feminists, and students of mass culture are now beginning to find her work "interesting" and, paradoxically, for the very reasons Stead dismissed it—her preoccupation with Victorian "reviews, reviewers, and other women novelists." Several useful reconsiderations of Corelli have appeared since Janet Galligani Casey's 1992 essay "Marie Corelli and *Fin de Siècle* Feminism." R. B. Kershner has argued that Corelli's characteristic blend of the sexual and the spiritual, her use of myth and allusions within a present-day narrative, her attitude of persecuted artist, and her high moral claims for art make her a "Modernist hybrid." For Kershner the "lines of demarcation drawn by the major Modernists are as much mystification as clarification," for the distinctions between high and popular art have definite political agendas ("Modernism's Mirror" 83).

In *Literary Capital and the Late Victorian Novel* N. N. Feltes applies a materialist analysis to Corelli's novels, looking at the empirical details of publishing history to account for her extraordinary popularity. Although Feltes insists on the importance of Methuen's weekly broadcasts of how fast *The Sorrows of Satan* was selling, he admits that these factors are "massively overdetermined" by the cultural preoccupations of the book itself: the contemporary ideologies of the new fiction and the New Woman (127).

Finally, Rita Felski in *The Gender of Modernity* devotes a chapter to Corelli, relocating her fiction at the turn of high modernism. Felski sees Corelli as an example of "the popular sublime," evoking the significance of transcendence as an impetus to modern mass culture. Her feminist treatment underscores the aesthetic binarisms of high and popular art with an analysis of gender binarisms. Although she sees Corelli as an "ideal candidate for rediscovery," a writer who invites a counterreading of such epithets as *vulgar, sentimental,* and *melodramatic,* Felski rightly questions the "assumption that the noncanonical text must be legitimated as subversive in order to be considered worthy of study" (142). Just as popular status does not necessarily reflect dominant ideology, it does not necessarily resist it.

These reassessments have emerged from affiliated critical practices: historical materialism, feminism, cultural studies, and a self-reflexive interrogation of categorical or oppositional accounts of literary history. Each approach conscientiously avoids simplifying the context for reading Corelli, and each recognizes this writer's immense popularity and vigorous self-promotion.

In my readings of Corelli and late-Victorian culture, I have not been constrained by a single theoretical paradigm. In *Mixed Feelings: Feminism, Mass Culture, and Victorian Sensationalism* Ann Cvetkovich writes that "the conflicting claims of Marxism, feminism, Foucauldianism, and psychoanalysis can be negotiated without assimilating any of them to a master-narrative provided by a single theoretical framework" (44). I find this a reassuring articulation of my own instincts in approaching the work of a writer who, despite the apparent simplicity of her books and their generic features, defies reflexive categorization. Although each chapter and its theoretical approach may seem to compartmentalize Corelli or conveniently subdivide her oeuvre, I try throughout this book to emphasize the profuseness of her imagination and the variety of directions she offers for modern literary and cultural studies. I hope that my eclectic approach will give other readers and scholars of Victorian culture a starting point for their own inquiries about Corelli and her contemporaries in the turn-of-the-century literary market.

In a way, this book seeks to honor Corelli's protean ambitions. Chapter 1 focuses on her literary celebrity and the late-Victorian fascination with authors' personal lives. Corelli hated to be photographed and often hid from Victorian paparazzi who waited in the shrubbery around her house in Stratford. In 1906 she commissioned an official portrait that was touched up to make her appear young and ethereal. I use Roland Barthes's essay on the photographic image and the work of marxist critics Guy Debord and Pierre Macherey to analyze Corelli's struggle to control her image at the moment of expanding consumerism, the development of mass media, and changing interpretations of the author.

Throughout this book I am interested in the ways Corelli participated in literary trends of the 1880s and 1890s, broadly labeled the aesthetic movement or literary decadence. My subject in chapter 2 is Victorian mass culture, in particular the tension between the democratic strain of aestheticism—how it is manifested in home decoration, popular satires, and mass fiction—and the aesthete's often explicit scorn for bourgeois education, tastes, and modes of living. I want to emphasize the often positive interdependence of apparently antithetical cultural positions. Corelli's unpublished letters to George Bentley between 1886 and about 1894 are useful documents in this regard, for they reveal her need to establish her originality while working up many popular genres to suit her own moral convictions. In my argument for her revision of the myth of the artist and in my reading of *Wormwood* as a decadent text, for instance, I want to suggest that Corelli's participation in the cultural life of her time was highly creative, combative, and contradictory; I devote a large part of this discussion to how *The Sorrows of Satan* exploits many recognizable features of decadence while ostensibly condemning the immorality of effeminate aesthetes and unhealthy New Women.

In chapter 3 I explore Corelli's often contradictory efforts to negotiate a feminine aesthetic against the radically politicized debates about gender and literary merit at the turn of the century. Linda Alcoff's essay on cultural feminism and poststructuralism serves as a touchstone for Corelli's rough maneuvers toward a consistent view of women. Her ideologically reflexive invocations of motherhood and female beauty often coexist with angry and bitter examples of drudgery and unfulfilled lives. Corelli also was an adept deconstructionist, redefining masculine values to suit her own political purposes. I do a somewhat close reading of the novella *My Wonderful Wife* to demonstrate how she moved stylistically and politically between antifeminism and pro-woman feeling. At the end of the chapter I turn to how female biology was involved in feminine writing and feminist politics for Corelli and how she later came to revise the earlier figures of the virgin and the femme fatale in her science-fiction fantasy *The Young Diana: An Experiment of the Future* (1918).

Feminist theorists have argued that a modernist aesthetics of impersonality may be handled differently by women writers. I begin chapter 4 with this suggestion and think also about the role Corelli's religious beliefs, her metaphysics, played in her utopian vision of sexual equality and the transcendent powers of love. This chapter has two parts, both involved with female subjectivity. I study the uses of the subjective in the context of modernist strictures against self-expression by focusing on two "texts": Corelli's unpublished correspondence with Arthur Severn and the imaginative version of their relationship, which was published by Vyver the year after Corelli's death as *Open Confession: To a Man from a Woman*.

Finally, in chapter 5 I look at cultural readings of Corelli in the decades after the Victorian age. Unlike a biographer, I am not interested in uncovering the facts or arguing from incomplete evidence about her life. I want to look chiefly at how the next two generations understood the Victorian phenomenon called Marie Corelli and how her identity and reputation were construed in various public forums; my sources range from obituaries to biographies, memoirs, letters, and literary reviews.

Several recent books about New Woman fiction, melodrama and sensation fiction, high and low modernism, and literary production from a materialist perspective offer provocative reevaluations of the late-Victorian period that have been crucial to my own investigations. I have tried to integrate the historical and theoretical approaches garnered from other scholars with the mass of information I have uncovered about Corelli. Although my work has borrowed from the practices and assumptions of cultural studies, I privilege Corelli's novels with close readings, something that other scholars who have focused on Corelli as a cultural marker have not done. I believe we can only arrive at some understanding of Corelli's popularity by being friendly to her art and taking it seriously, recognizing that her more than twenty-five novels represent a real achievement during a period when cultural antagonisms did not do much to ease the transition into the modern world of the twentieth century.

# I

## The Queen of Best-Sellers
## and the Culture of Celebrity

*Marie Corelli has many admirers. She is the ruler of a public that buys her books by the hundred thousand. She treats the Press with a hauteur the mere thought of which sends the less fortunate author into a tremor. She is, with the possible exception of Mr. Hall Caine, the greatest genius of self-advertisement produced by our century.*

Westminster Review, December 1906

*I would also suggest that the details of a man's or woman's private life should be considered sacred, and out of the pale of journalism altogether.*

Marie Corelli, "Manners, Gentlemen!"

MARIE CORELLI LIVED in an age of publicity, mass media, and spin. By the time of Charles Dickens's death in 1870, the book business had escalated to such an extent that images and biographical sidelights were more than promotional mechanisms in the book trade; they defined the book trade. Margaret Stetz has described how publishers were forced to find "aggressive techniques for generating public interest in both literature and its makers" and how it became a matter of course to ask writers to supply "tit-bits" or "chit-chat" about their private lives (172). Henry James, for one, lamented "this age of advertisement and newspaperism, this age of interviewing" (quoted in Salmon 159), for the proliferation of literary interviews at the turn of the century "bore witness to the increasingly pervasive definition of authors as celebrities" (Salmon 160).

By the 1890s developments in photographic technology and photomechanical reproduction meant that the interviewer was usually accompanied by the photographer. Readers were now able to see the "real life" of a famous author, in her library, tending her garden, writing letters. Such regular features as the *Idler*'s "My First Book," a series started in 1892 in which authors described their road to literary fame, and journalistic photographs of writers' homes and haunts offered "a comforting reassurance as to the essentially bourgeois character of modern authorship" (Salmon 174). Although most of these journalistic snapshots were posed, they had more immediacy and intimacy than mid-Victorian studio portraits. Author iconography was becoming standard in the late-Victorian publishing industry.

Not only had publishing become a highly competitive industry, but the place of literature was being increasingly contested in a society bombarded with images. As Gerard Curtis has argued in a fascinating essay on Dickens, "the visual system, and not the word, was considered the universal language of Victorian culture. . . . Pictorial realization . . . was the dominant and desired mode of expression in Victorian (and, to an extent, European) writing, drama, and art" (225). What Curtis calls the "visual market" aggressively participated in what other critics have called "print culture," "literary sociology," or "the sociology of texts" (Jordan and Patten 1–18). Authors' images as well as their texts were being read by middle-class consumers, and both were tied to a competitive literary market.

Corelli's participation in the culture of celebrity reveals a great deal about her personality, ambition, and canniness as a woman in a male-dominated industry. Her letters to her first publisher, George Bentley, and the all-out war she waged with journalists and photographers for more than twenty-five years offer an intimate angle, an author's-eye view, on the politics of publicity at the turn of the century. In this chapter I first examine Corelli's apparently contradictory attitudes toward a book market she inadvertently took by storm when she published her first romance in 1886 and then focus on how she struggled to own the image that would be projected to her growing audience.

This chapter will also address the significance of Corelli's self-mythology. The elaborate pose she created is typical of fin-de-siècle culture. Richard Ellmann has observed that "the notion of selfhood changed drastically during the nineteenth century. If the self is binary or double-decked, whatever one's conceptions of the two parts may be, we may expect writers to anthropomorphize each part" (*Masks* 72). Ellmann believes that this explains the popularity of the pseudonym, which "symbolized the duality which resulted from the dissociation of personality," and that even the verbal distinction at the end of the century between "personality" and "character" suggests a preoccupation with a synthetic or invented self (*Masks* 73, 72). In reading the self-mythology of "Marie Corelli" against Ellmann's theory of the split self, I want to suggest that although her maneuver is typical of the ethos of the decade, the authenticity of the self she created makes hers an exceptional case of authorial anthropomorphizing. Her strict defense and preservation of a carefully designed image are attached to her love of romance and her distaste for literary realism. Ultimately, her battle with the media is about truth telling and the assertion of a subjective version of reality over the ostensible facts of journalistic investigation or photographic evidence.

### "Is This Authorship?"

Corelli was ambitious in her scope from the very beginning and disliked being pinned down as a type. While the six books she published with Bentley between 1886 and 1892 may be stylistically similar, they are generically distinct. Her first novel, *A Romance of Two Worlds* (1886), is a supernatural romance, but she had no intention of establishing her reputation along those lines. *Vendetta, or: The Story of One Forgotten* (1886) is a lurid revenge melodrama set in Italy; *Thelma: A Society Novel* (1887) is a sentimental story about a Norwegian girl in decadent London; *Ardath: The Story of a Dead Self* (1889) is an esoteric tale about reincarnation; *Wormwood* (1890) is a sermon against absinthe-drinking bohemians in Paris; and *The Soul of Lilith* (1892) is a science-fiction story about a mystic's obsession with dominating other people's souls and psyches (Brian Masters calls it "a kind of Women's Liberation of the Soul" [113]). All of these novels have subplots that usually involve women artists. Even the novels Corelli published with Methuen after 1892 are generically different, from the controversial *Barabbas: A Dream of the World's Tragedy* (1893), a retelling of the Crucifixion, to *The Mighty Atom* (1896), a critique of modern atheistic education, to her crashing best-seller *The Master Christian* (1900), which takes on the Roman Catholic Church, Christian socialism, and masculine envy for female genius in a story about Christ's return to the modern world as a little child. Corelli absolutely stuck to her early claim to Bentley in 1887: "for as the 'Daily Mail' has sagaciously observed that I am a descendant of [Ann] Radcliffe (!) I wish to prove that I am capable of more than one style of novel, and that the simply sensational will form but a very small part of my future work. In brief, I have resolved that no two books of mine shall be in the least alike, so that neither the critics nor the public shall know what to expect from me" (1 January 1887).

If eventually the critics and the public learned what to expect, it was because Corelli tutored them. She was her own spin doctor and refused to have an agent, claiming that "authors, like other people, should learn how to manage their own affairs themselves" ("My First Book" 252n). Nevertheless, she hounded George Bentley to advertise her novels lest the public forget about her. *A Romance of Two Worlds* was published in February 1886, and by March she was writing to Bentley that "the book *just now* if a taking advertisement were for a time put *prominently* before the public, with a judicious selection of one line from the press notices . . . would I am sure sell very speedily in large quantities. I am *very much in earnest* about this." And the following year, worried about promoting her third novel, *Thelma,* she wrote: "Why am I not in the list of authors enclosed just cut from The Standard? I think I have earned the right to be—and I cannot help being surprised that I seem to be persistently left out in *all* your recent advertisements. . . . Please let me know why this is not done" (October 1887). There are a great many letters of this type—written in tones that vary from the perfunctory to the pleading to the penitent—evidence that Corelli was fully prepared to exploit the advertising system.

But Corelli's early desire to be advertised and to receive paragraphs in the press (she desperately wanted it to be known, for example, that the queen had ordered all her books to be sent to Balmoral) came up against the wisdom and experience of George Bentley, who was "averse to associate your name or mine with a system of vulgar exploitation" (Corelli-Bentley Correspondence, 28 January 1892). Bentley asked, what did the great Victorian writers such as Dickens, Anthony Trollope, and William Makepeace Thackeray owe to exploitation? Corelli replied, "In the days of the great authors you quote, there were not so many in the field, and there was less necessity for 'push' or exploitation" (30 January 1892). She

## MARIE CORELLI'S NEW ROMANCE.

*Messrs. METHUEN will publish this month a New Romance, in ONE VOLUME,
crown 8vo. price 6s., by MARIE CORELLI, entitled*

# THE SORROWS OF SATAN.

### OR, THE STRANGE EXPERIENCE OF ONE GEOFFREY TEMPEST, MILLIONAIRE.

*As the Publishers anticipate a very large demand for this Book, they request that
orders should be sent in as soon as possible.*

"Alike the most reviled, the best praised, and the widest read book of the day."—WORLD.

*Messrs. METHUEN announce that the Seventeenth Edition being exhausted, an* **EIGHTEENTH EDITION**
*is now ready.*

# BARABBAS.

## A DREAM OF THE WORLD'S TRAGEDY.

### By MARIE CORELLI.

*The following are the various Editions published since October, 1893 :—*

### ENGLISH EDITIONS.

| | | | | | |
|---|---|---|---|---|---|
| FIRST EDITION | In 3 vols. | October 13, 1893. | TENTH EDITION | In 1 vol. | July 26, 1894. |
| SECOND EDITION | ,, | November 14, 1893. | ELEVENTH EDITION | ,, | September 18, 1894. |
| THIRD EDITION | ,, | December 9, 1893. | TWELFTH EDITION | ,, | November 12, 1894. |
| FOURTH EDITION | In 1 vol. | March 22, 1894. | THIRTEENTH EDITION | ,, | December 5, 1894. |
| FIFTH EDITION | ,, | March 24, 1894. | FOURTEENTH EDITION | ,, | March 2, 1895. |
| SIXTH EDITION | ,, | March 28, 1894. | FIFTEENTH EDITION | ,, | May 2, 1895. |
| SEVENTH EDITION | ,, | March 30, 1894. | SIXTEENTH EDITION | ,, | June 17, 1895. |
| EIGHTH EDITION | ,, | April 25, 1894. | SEVENTEENTH EDITION | ,, | July 23, 1895. |
| NINTH EDITION | ,, | June 1, 1894. | EIGHTEENTH EDITION | ,, | September 21, 1895. |

### FOREIGN EDITIONS.

| | | |
|---|---|---|
| **AMERICAN EDITION** ... | ... | Messrs. Lippincott & Co., Philadelphia, U.S.A. |
| **CONTINENTAL EDITION** | ... | Baron Tauchnitz, Leipzig. |
| **FRENCH EDITION** ... | ... | Translated by C. BERNHARD DEROSNE, and published by Gautier, Paris. |
| **GERMAN EDITION** ... | ... | Translated by J. HUMMEL, and published by Messrs. Lutz in Stuttgart. |
| **SWEDISH EDITION** ... | ... | Translated by E. KULLMANN, and published by Skoglund Brothers in Stockholm. |
| **IN HINDUSTANI** ... | ... | Translated by KUNIVAR SHIVANATH SINGH (Barrister-at-Law), and published at the State Press, Lucknow, India. |
| **IN GUJURATI** ... | ... | Translated by M. C. MURZBAN, and also published in Lucknow. |

"The tender reverence of the treatment and the imaginative beauty of the writing have reconciled us to the daring of the conception, and the conviction is forced on us that even so exalted a subject cannot be made too familiar to us, provided it be presented in the true spirit of Christian faith. The amplifications of the Scripture narrative are often conceived with high poetic insight, and this ' Dream of the World's Tragedy ' is, despite some trifling incongruities, a lofty and not inadequate paraphrase of the supreme climax of the inspired narrative."—*Dublin Review.*

### London: METHUEN & CO. 36, Essex-street, W.C.

Fig. 1. After Corelli broke with Richard Bentley and Son, she joined Methuen, a firm unafraid
of "vulgar exploitation." Methuen's advertisement for *The Sorrows of Satan* in the *Athenaeum*
stirred interest in the novel several weeks before its publication on 21 October 1895.

did not like being outdone by other authors' publicity stunts, and eventually she split with Bentley, writing rather spitefully in 1894, "I think it not unnatural on my part that I should experience some astonishment to find Mssrs. Methuen's figures for the sales of one book of mine . . . exceeding the sale of all my other popular novels in *your* hands" (9 June 1894). Corelli felt that she knew what the public wanted and that she could write to the interests and issues of the moment but that she needed the help of her publisher's publicity agents. "I am anxious to appear again before the public—they so soon forget one in these 'fast' days" (Corelli-Bentley Correspondence, 3 February 1887). Understandably, she wanted to strike while the iron was hot.

Despite her concern about publicity, Corelli was frequently uncomfortable with some of the demands from the media. She wanted control. Although she was anxious to see her books advertised in the daily and weekly papers, she disliked autograph seekers, interviewers, and especially photographers. In a letter written to Bentley in 1889 she seems astonished that John Strange Winter (Henrietta Stannard) had a stall at a carnival in the Albert Hall, "where she is *selling her own novels* and *her own autograph!:*—is this authorship? because to me it seems degradation! But perhaps I am too proud . . . and I may be wrong in sending away 'interviewers'" (15 March 1889). She sarcastically refers to "Celebrity at Home" articles and in the persona of a neglected author says, "I ought, by all the modern rule and plan, to be 'interviewed' as—well, let me modestly suggest, as a 'Coming' person, perhaps? Lots of fellows are 'Coming,' according to the press, who never arrive" (*Silver Domino* 162). She also bitterly disliked critics and reviewers, whom she called "press cliques" and accused of "log-rolling" and "booming" books by certain authors. She viewed herself as a persecuted genius and a woman maligned by a male press that felt threatened by her mental independence. Corelli vented her anger in private letters, in magazine articles, in novels, and in an anonymously published satire of the literary world called *The Silver Domino, or: Side Whispers, Social and Literary* (1893), in which even kind Mr. Bentley was not spared her wrath.

The record of Corelli's anger is stunning, and her belief in the injustice of press reviewers forced her into a position of aloof superiority to all journalists. She wrote to Bentley, who was a man of letters as well as a gentleman of business, "Now, my dear friend, has the 'Press' ever lost an opportunity to 'come down' on me as it is? Was not the 'Romance' scouted as *'a farrago of nonsense'*—'Vendetta' as *'a brutal compound of villainy and immorality'*—'Thelma' as *'a ridiculous heroine'*—'Ardath' as *'an outrageous compound of venal sentiment and blasphemy'*? After this, after such wilful abuse and gross misunderstanding of my work, can you think for a moment that I care for press opinions?" (8 September 1890). Corelli's emotional attacks on the press, for which she acquired as large a reputation as she did for her novels, have been interpreted as paranoia, but in fact her feelings about journalism were a part of controversial debates throughout the 1890s. William Scheick has argued that "journalism was at the forefront of cultural consciousness as the nineteenth century approached its end and the next century commenced" (13). The cultural opposition between art and journalism surely contributed to Corelli's stormy reactions to the press. "Any novelist who writes magazine serials is simply committing literary suicide," she wrote (*Silver Domino* 205). This attitude was prevalent throughout the decade: Oscar Wilde's well-known jokes at the expense of journalists are only the wittiest of many critiques of "newspaperism."[1]

Corelli also felt newspaper reviewers had much more power than they deserved and that they barely read the novels they wrote about, worked in cliques, were merely commercial businessmen, and were all in a conspiracy against women writers. She felt she was justified in exposing the corruption within this system. In an article titled "Press Cliques" (probably from 1892), she lashed out against the "dangerous and dishonest form of 'clique' which is being here and there formed between *journalists* and *publishers*." She wrote from the point of view of a reviewer in this send-up in *The Silver Domino:* "This is how we generally manage. A Three-volumer comes in 'for review,' nicely bound, well got up; we look at the title page, and if it is by some individual whom we know to be a power in one or other of the cliques, we pay strict attention to it, cover its faults, and quote platitudes as epigrams. But if it is by someone we personally dislike, or if it is by a woman, we never read it. We simply glance through it in search of a stray ungrammatical sentence, a misprint, or a hasty slip of the pen" (296–97).

Although Corelli's suspicions are probably exaggerated and not always justified, many reviews of her novels were dismissive or mean-spirited. She was out of tune with the taste for realism and new fiction, and her belief in romance and idealism seemed so much feminine "bosh" to literary men and press critics. Corelli's resistance to journalistic judgments is emphatically connected with her resistance to prosaic or materialistic interpretations of all kinds, and in this sense she was very much a part of the Victorian debate over objective fact and subjective impressions, realism and romance, scientific truth and imaginative make-believe. All of these binarisms are easily transferred from the arena of literary criticism to the expanding world of images in the visual market. Carol Christ and John Jordan identify two critical accounts of the nine-teenth-century visual imagination: "One has stressed the predominance of the realist modes of representation, culminating in photography and, in the twentieth century, the cinema. The other has emphasized a break with realism, an increasingly subjective organization of vision leading to modernism" (xxi). These alternative perspectives belong as much to Victorian writers and artists as they do to modern theorists, for "neither an exclusively subjective nor an exclusively objective model provides a sufficient explanation for the Victorian idea of perception. Rather, the Victorians were interested in the conflict, even the competition, between objective and subjective paradigms for perception" (xxiii).

Images of popular authors in photographs, frontispieces, postcards, and portraits sold books for publishers, and authors were expected to co-operate in the commodification of their faces, bodies, pets, houses, and favorite haunts, all in the name of art, if not of profit. Certainly the public appetite for images was not new, and, as Linda Shires has pointed out, there was a demand for portraits of and gossip about well-known novelists and poets from the time of the French Revolution. But with the rise of photography and photojournalism during the Victorian period, self-management for literary celebrities became an issue that required some vigilance. By the turn of the century even the most high-minded artist could hardly escape the pressures of the visual market.

*Lady Novelists*

At the turn of the century this conflict was about more than epistemic and aesthetic paradigms. As widely available merchandise—by the 1890s in a single-volume, cheap format—books had to be advertised and au-thors exposed to publicity, and these strategies could be tied to the gender of authors and readers. N. N. Feltes has explained that over the course of the nineteenth century British publishing transformed itself from a

"petty-commodity" to a "patriarchal/capitalist" literary mode of production: "modern publishing is a *structure,* determined not only by the
practice of the publisher and the author, but by the practices of publishers' readers and authors' agents. Moreover it is a *gendered* structure, and
one which produces as a commodity either an addition to a publisher's
'list' or a book to be 'boomed' as a 'bestseller'" (16−17). Feltes rightly
insists on the articulation of gender in discussing late-Victorian literary
capital, citing Margaret Shaw's argument that reviewers "worked, wit-
tingly or unwittingly, to 'construct' an image of the 'literate woman,' of
her appropriate habits of reading and writing" (52). Hostile stereotypes
of the woman writer's physical unattractiveness or sexual abnormality circulated during the 1880s and 1890s, usually in illustrations caricaturing
her "masculinity" or her neglect of domestic responsibilities. Elaine
Showalter and others have discussed the implications for literary history
of "edging women out" and the struggles of women writers whose
voices have been heard chiefly in the context and amid the clamor of
sexual competition and misogynist accusations or erasures.[2]

In this section I am interested less in images of the lady novelist
or the literate woman as a class than in the individual woman writer at
the turn of the century. Given the stereotypes, what strategies of self-
advertisement and self-display were available to her, and how did she
control the circulation of public images, such as photographs, frontispieces, sketches, and cartoons? Unlike other public women—suffragettes
and protesters, lecturers and society hostesses—the woman writer could
be heard without being seen. Yet late-Victorian mass media dominated
virtually all modes of discourse, and the innovations of photojournalism
made image control of greater importance than ever before. What self-
marketing strategies did a woman writer have to undertake who wished
to understand herself as a subject, an author, but who also accepted her
cultural role as a spectacular object, an *auteur?*

Despite her flamboyance and literary vanity, Corelli demanded control over the image projected to her adoring fans. She carried on a public
fight not only with the newspaper critics who "slashed" her novels and
laughed at her pretensions but with the periodical press that published
photographs without her permission and with enterprising marketers
who circulated postcards and caricatures to a curious public. From the
very beginning of her career, Corelli recognized the stereotype of the
unattractive, unsexed, and half-educated authoress and earnestly worked

to contradict it. I do not think she was paranoid; assumptions of a literary woman's absurd or repulsive appearance existed and were widespread. After meeting her for the first time in 1894, the publisher and columnist Edmund Yates told her, "You are not the least like what I fancied you might be. . . . You don't look a bit literary. . . . You've taken us all in! We expected a massive strong-minded female with her hair divided flat on each side and a cameo in the middle of her forehead . . . like a sign-board on the brow; a sort of 'enquire within' for intellectual qualities. Well I'm glad you're not that sort of person. I'm afraid I should never get on with a real 'bluestocking'" (Corelli, "Last Days"). In 1903 T. F. G. Coates and R. S. Warren-Bell wrote, "For many are the 'surprises' that have been given to those expectant of meeting in the novelist a severe liter-ary woman with spectacles and a bilious complexion" (315–16). These stereotypes no doubt inspired Corelli's many remarks in her novels, often interjected rather superfluously, in defense of the literary woman's physi-cal attractions. Her novel *The Murder of Delicia* (1896), for example, car-ries a heated preface in defense of intellectual women: "If a woman does anything out of the common in the way of art and literature, she is im-mediately judged by men as being probably without tenderness, without permanence in her work, and certainly without personal beauty. . . . it is not a *sine qua non* that a clever woman must be old and must be ugly. It sometimes happens so,—but it is not always so" (12–13).

Corelli began to work on her image when she, her father, and Bertha Vyver moved to London in 1884. In April 1883 and January 1884 she had published three sonnets as Marie di Corelli, and she gave several piano recitals at her home in Longridge Road as the Signorina Corelli (Masters 48–49). She embellished this new identity for George Bentley when he asked about her background after publishing *A Romance of Two Worlds:* she took ten years off her age in order to appear the young lady in need of guidance, affected cosmopolitan tastes rather than appear a bluestocking, and created a foreign ancestry with ties to aristocracy. Not only did she tell Bentley she was Venetian and could trace her lineage back to Arcangelo Corelli, she also gave herself a godfather in Rome, claimed an intimate acquaintance with Queen Margherita, and explained that she was living *en famille* with the Mackays, referring to "Miss Mackay" as a "sweet friend to me." As *The Romance of Two Worlds* sold and sold, as hundreds of letters arrived from admiring readers, male critics continued to ignore or ridicule her work. Minnie Mackay began to see what she was up against, and she polished her weapons. Her defensiveness attests to the sexism she faced as a woman in a patriarchal and competitive book market, but it is also tied to the increasingly invasive attitude of both readers and journalists in the 1890s. She urged her publisher to keep her name before the public, worrying that "people are on the high road to forgetting my very existence" (Corelli-Bentley Correspondence, October 1887), but at the same time she sidestepped all requests to trade on her appearance: "Your son [Richard Bentley] has very kindly written to me to suggest my appearance in 'Men and Women of the Day'—but I have resisted the temptation! Did you ever meet a young woman before who could resolutely refuse to have her portrait admirably produced for the edification of the public? Give me credit for true heroism, in this age of notoriety-hunting!!" (Corelli-Bentley Correspondence, 6 May 1888).

Heroic or not, by the turn of the century Corelli's celebrity was inescapable. In 1906 J. M. Stuart-Young (under the pseudonym Peril) wrote in the *Westminster Review* that Corelli was "the greatest genius of self-advertisement produced by our century," and by that date many commentators were accusing her of manipulating the media (680). She always denied it: "I have never written anything in my life with a desire to be praised for it. And I never, though often accused of doing so, 'advertise myself.' The press does all the advertising for me lavishly and gratuitously, and then finds fault with itself for its own action" ("Manners, Gentlemen!" 13–14). Nevertheless, by the early 1890s pressure from eager interviewers was becoming too great to withstand, and Corelli found herself swept up in the fashion for interviews and "Authors' Homes" that she had mocked, whether coyly or acerbically, at the start of her career.

A few examples will suffice to fill out the contours of her career as a public spectacle. The *Strand* published a lengthy illustrated interview in 1898, in which the interviewer, Arthur H. Lawrence, proudly referred the reader to the accompanying photographs illustrating "the scene of many walks and talks which I was subsequently privileged to have with the charming novelist" and especially to a *very* charming photograph of the author herself in one of the Winter Garden lounges at Woodhill Spa, in Lincolnshire (18). The pictures of walks and houses are very nice, but the personal portrait is a different story (fig. 2). At Corelli's feet is her little dog, Czar, and at her side is a woman, her lifetime friend and intimate companion, Bertha Vyver; but the photographer is so far away from

Fig. 2. Posed snapshot of Marie Corelli and Bertha Vyver for an author's interview in the *Strand*. (*Strand* 16, no. 91 [1898]: 17–26)

his subject that the reader can only make out that Corelli is posing as a very sweet young lady. This photograph is iconographic rather than documentary. The caption is written in Corelli's characteristically bold script, and the pen is almost mightier than the image.

In 1893 the *Idler* published an article by Corelli in its series of authors' accounts of their first books, which included essays by Morley Roberts, David Christie Murray, John Strange Winter, Jerome K. Jerome, and Bret Harte. Corelli's is the only article in the year's series unaccompanied by either a photograph or a drawing of the author opposite the title page. According to Masters, Corelli sent her stepbrother, Eric, to the *Idler's* offices to remonstrate against their intention to publish a photograph. Hers is the only story in the series that includes a large facsimile of the author's signature, just as the *Strand* interview included a facsimile of a whole page of manuscript in her handwriting. These are clues to Corelli's later claim for the primacy of words over pictures in the press's manipulations of public identity. Her ornate signature was published at least twice as often as pictures of her face and was even embossed on the covers of her later novels.

Finally, in 1897 Corelli agreed to sit for her portrait (fig. 3). The massive oil painting by Helen Donald-Smith was rejected by the Royal Academy and subsequently exhibited at the Graves Art Gallery in Pall Mall. It is now in the National Portrait Gallery, although it was cut down because it was too large. A framed photogravure of the entire painting hangs unceremoniously in Corelli's former home at Stratford, Mason Croft, which now houses the University of Birmingham Shakespeare Institute. It is a romantic portrait of Corelli in flowing robes in a setting that is vaguely reminiscent of Joshua Reynolds or Thomas Gainsborough, with stone urns, crawling ivy, and a serene background of rolling hills. Corelli's expression is one of mild contentment, and her eyes, like those of so many of her heroines, are large and lustrous.

According to Coates and Warren-Bell, this portrait "was at once made the subject of personal and abusive attacks, not on the artist, but on Marie Corelli herself for being painted at all! Some journalists went so far as to accuse her of 'taking the gate-money' and 'speculating in her own portrait'" (314–15). Corelli received none of the percentages allowed on the photogravure, and she withdrew the picture altogether from the public after the exhibit.[3] As if to underscore Corelli's modesty, her affectionate biographers insist that she agreed to sit only because she was seriously ill (she was) and did not expect to live. She "wished to leave some resemblance of herself to her dearest friend, Bertha Vyver" (314).

These episodes in Victorian publicity must be understood in the context of Corelli's recognizable prose—and her enormous sales. In his chapter "The New Fiction" in *The Eighteen Nineties,* Holbrook Jackson

Fig. 3. Oil painting of Marie Corelli by Helen Donald-Smith, 1897. The full-length portrait was cut down because it was too large. (By courtesy of the National Portrait Gallery, London)

has merely to invoke "the name of Marie Corelli" to identify a kind of fiction, implying that her identity was itself part of the traffic in commodities, as was, of course, "the species of sensationalism" to which it was attached (26). By 1895 a novel with her name on it was called simply "a Marie Corelli." By thus situating the different yet conflated

categories of woman and legend—Marie Corelli and "Marie Corelli"—
we can interrogate interpretations of value in late-Victorian culture: the
value of authorial subjectivity and autonomy in relation to the exchange
value of books and commercial iconography. The contest is also, however, connected with the cultural antagonism suggested by Christ and
Jordan—the claims of subjective and objective ways of seeing, perceiv-
ing, knowing.

In *A Theory of Literary Production* Pierre Macherey notes that an author's desire "to please the crowd" is not artistically suspect. Appropriately, he uses a novel by Ann Radcliffe—"a naive, spontaneous text, the
most uncomplicated novel imaginable"—to show how even popular
works are not "innocent" and possess an "inside" and "outside" that deserve critical scrutiny (27). For Macherey a "book is neither reality nor
experience, but artifice. The artifice is not a riddle, but an authentic mystery which lives entirely in the trajectory of its resolution" (37). Macherey's theory is applicable not only to Corelli's romantic and speculative
novels but to the romantic construction of her authorial identity. If, as
Macherey argues, popular forms such as melodramas and mysteries demonstrate the progression of narrative by the inhibition of truth, then it is
feasible that both Corelli's fiction *and* her public image present a paradoxical narrative of inhibition and self-display, authenticity and simula-
tion, concealment and disclosure.

### *"A Photograph of a Lady Who Will Not Be Photographed"*

In 1905 the paparazzi of the English publishing world captured the best-
selling novelist of the period emerging from a London cab. The photograph was published, without the subject's approval, in the *Sketch,* with
the caption, "A photograph of a lady who will not be photographed: A
snapshot of Miss Marie Corelli leaving her cab at the Portland Rooms to
attend the Shaksperean [*sic*] Bazaar" (fig. 4). There is more text in smaller
print under the caption, explaining why the publication of the photograph is an event in itself: "Miss Marie Corelli has a great aversion to
photographers, and steadfastly refuses to sit to them—hence the particular interest of this snapshot. The popular novelist was one of those who
received Princess Henry of Battenberg on Her Royal Highness's arrival
for the opening of the bazaar." The photograph is an action shot that
shows Corelli at the age of about fifty, short and stout, smiling under a

Fig. 4. Unauthorized snapshot of Marie Corelli emerging from a London cab on the cover of the *Sketch,* 1905. (By courtesy of the Shakespeare Birthplace Trust, Stratford-upon-Avon)

wide-brimmed Edwardian-style hat and holding up her large skirt to expose her buckled shoes. The editor of the *Sketch* must have anticipated "particular interest" in this snapshot: it takes up the *entire* front page of the paper, which is about seventeen inches by twelve inches.

I agree with Corelli's biographer William Stuart Scott that there is something very likable about this picture. Corelli obviously loves being involved in the whole affair: she is a famous and wealthy woman, mixing with royalty, honoring her beloved Shakespeare, having a gay time. But the photograph did not please her, despite her love of flattery and fame. Although she kept her name constantly before the public, extravagantly displayed herself in print, put in plenty of social appearances, and even gave several lectures in prestigious forums, Corelli was sensitive to the perceptual mastery of the camera. Apparently this was not just the price of fame. Ronald Thomas has described how the dry-plate, fixed-focus photographic process replaced the wet-plate process developed in 1851 and enabled "amateurs and journalists alike to take instantaneous candid snapshots of people without their consent." He explains that "the *Weekly Times* and *Echo* applauded the formation of a 'Vigilance Association' in 1893 whose sole purpose was the 'thrashing of cads with cameras who go about in seaside places taking snapshots of ladies emerging from the deep'" (147).

Just what these cads intended to do with their photographs is open to speculation: there appears to be something mildly pornographic going on. Clearly the widespread cultural surveillance of *women* that the camera represents is connected to Corelli's attitude of self-protection, and this is true even of women who consent to be photographed. Corelli did not approve of ladies exhibiting themselves in photographs displayed in shop-windows. In 1900 she wrote:

> *Bitten by the same tarantula-craze for notoriety, our married women of honourable position will permit their photographs to appear in shop windows, side by side with those of the latest stout and more than half nude "variety" dancer. Their sense of modesty has grown to be so tough and pachydermatous a thing that it is not even pricked when the Fleet Street penny-a-liner labels them in print as "beauties," valued at so much per head, per face, per eyes, per hair, and carries their portraits in his dirty pockets to show to his fellow-pensters, and say they were "gifts" to him for his perspicacity.*

(*Social Note on the War* 10–11)

The female body represented in these photographs is nothing more than an assemblage of marketable fetishized parts that a grubby journalist carries in his "dirty pockets" and passes on for the visual delectation of other men. If a capitalist society requires a culture based on images and the supervision of class identities, as Susan Sontag argues in *On Photography*, and if patriarchy requires a culture based on the surveillance and exchange of women, getting a peep at Marie Corelli effectively participates in the construction of ideology through representation. There can be no such thing as a woman "who will not be photographed" because she is culturally defined as something to be looked at, as a sexual object to be scrutinized. Corelli tried to negotiate the necessity of having a public image that is sexual and descriptive and an identity that is inaccessible outside the act of reading her books, an identity chiefly semiotic or symbolic. But she wanted the impossible. A woman writer could not be presented to nineteenth-century society as a page of manuscript, a brassy signature, a disembodied mind that wrote books! Publishing images was both a commodification of the woman writer and a form of discipline in a culture where women had to have bodies as well as books. This was different from women's public appearances on the London streets, in department stores, or at rallies and lectures, which Judith Walkowitz has discussed.[4] Visual representations of women performed an ideological function: "Representations are not just a matter of mirrors, reflections, key-holes. Somebody is making them, and somebody is looking at them, through a complex array of means and conventions. Nor do representations simply exist on canvas, in books, on photographic paper or on screens: they have a continued existence in reality as objects of exchange; they have a genesis in material production. They are more 'real' than the reality they are said to represent or reflect" (Kappeler 3). Photographic realism, especially, involves "a thematization of the act of looking— of voyeurism, peeping, leering, examining, adoring" (Steiner 43–44). Sexual appropriation seems implicit in the act of taking photographs. According to Andy Grundberg, "Almost from the moment of the medium's birth in 1839, photographers have been fascinated with the contradictory but inherent eroticism of the camera's disembodied gaze" (quoted in Steiner 44). The eroticism is not experienced equally by photographer, subject, and audience. In Corelli's case there is not even the added tension of the subject's role as victim or accomplice, as a woman coerced or deriving erotic pleasure from being looked at. Given the invasiveness and implied sexual proprietorship of press photographers who stalked Corelli waiting for their chance to snap a picture, it is no wonder she called the newspapers that printed unflattering portraits "the dirties" (Masters 219).

It was not that Corelli disliked being the center of attention, but she condemned the appropriation of her image by the photographic press. Although snapshots and cartoons appeared in abundance before 1906, she never sanctioned their publication. Masters relates incidents of newspaper photographers hiding in the shrubbery at her home in Stratford-upon-Avon or surreptitiously snapping pictures of Corelli and Vyver as they rowed in her gondola on the Avon or laid flowers at Shakespeare's grave. Masters's explanation for Corelli's dislike of this kind of guerrilla publicity is consistent with the patronizing tone of what is otherwise a very lively and detailed biography. He explains, "The fact was, Marie Corelli was no longer the ethereal beauty she had striven so long to project, and the only way to maintain the fiction was never to be seen at all. . . . She was, in truth, a fearsome looking woman" (219–20).

This is far too simplistic an explanation; Masters assumes that Corelli's feelings are nothing more than female narcissism. Possibly Corelli disliked the implications involved in all forms of masculine scrutiny, for she had a very different attitude about women's involvement in professions involving spectatorship. It is notable that she chose a woman to paint her portrait (there was a portrait painted by a man, Ellis Roberts, which has disappeared), and Vyver was a gifted amateur photographer who took pictures of Corelli and published them under the pseudonym F. A. Adrian. Furthermore, Corelli elected to have a female surgeon perform an operation (probably a hysterectomy) in 1897: Dr. Mary Scharlieb, the first woman to graduate with an M.D. from London University and the first woman to hold a staff position at a general hospital. Women doctors were considered scandalous in the 1890s, so Corelli's choice suggests both boldness and confidence in women's abilities. Masters attributes her going to a woman doctor to sexual hysteria. Yet choosing Scharlieb to perform the operation is consistent with Corelli's dislike of perceived appropriations of her body by men, in both art and life—hardly a transparent symptom of female neurosis. There is another possible explanation for her dislike of such appropriations: after her stepbrother, Eric, died in 1898, rumors of an incestuous relationship were circulated (Masters 154–59). Eric was twenty years older than she, and the Mackays' was an adamantly patriarchal and emotionally overwrought Victorian household. Although there is no proof of incest, it is interesting to note Louise DeSalvo's theory that Virginia Woolf's "looking-glass complex" was related to her sexual victimization (13). Like Corelli, Woolf hated to be photographed, and sitting for her portrait was a form of torture. All of this is speculation, of course, but it is certainly more generous than Masters's view of Corelli as simply a vain, ugly old woman.

Furthermore, we cannot simply oppose Corelli's maintaining a fiction of her youth and beauty to her concealing the truth of her age and unattractiveness. Possibly she did not wish to be photographed because she suspected that photographs were counterfeit truths. She feared not the camera's realism but its realistic liabilities. Her notion of realism, in her novels and in her life, comprehends much more than her biographers have allowed and exposes the fault lines in the Victorian realist aesthetic, especially in its claims for moral edification. Corelli participated in late-Victorian debates about the virtues of literary realism exemplified in the challenges to Henry James by romance writers such as Robert Louis Stevenson and H. G. Wells and in protests in Victorian periodicals against "Zolaism." But, paradoxically, she also had something in common with aestheticism. "Facts . . . are usurping the domain of Fancy, and have invaded the kingdom of Romance. Their chilling touch is over everything," Wilde declared in "The Decay of Lying" (226). "I have put myself into literary harness," Corelli wrote, "and am once more on the track of imaginative romance, a relief from the horrible 'realities' of life that sicken and weary one's soul" (Corelli-Bentley Correspondence, 1 October 1888). It is not all that surprising that Wilde was one of Corelli's early admirers, for both writers saw imaginative self-creation as more than an aesthetic project: it was a soul-preserving and socially militant necessity. George Bernard Shaw concluded his "Memories of Oscar Wilde" with the statement, "He held fast to his pose to the very last, because it was an honest pose. For that very reason it has been unspeakably annoying to English morality which, too, is a pose, but without the benefit of the excuse of being an honest one" (Shaw 32). To those literary men who occupied their own high moral ground, Corelli's "honest pose" could be similarly annoying. In his autobiography Mark Twain relates an anecdote that is instructive in this regard.

*Marie Corelli and Mark Twain*

Mark Twain took an immediate dislike to Corelli when they met at a dinner party in Germany in 1892, but when he received a "warm, affectionate, eloquent, persuasive letter" from her while he was on a tour of England in 1905, he agreed to visit her home in Shakespeare's Stratford (Twain 350). The occasion was excruciating to Twain: "the most hateful day my seventy-two years have ever known" (353). Corelli went out of her way to make arrangements, even ordering a special train to bring him to Stratford, but Twain interpreted every attempt at hospitality (she wished to show him Shakespeare's church and Harvard House, for example) as nothing more than unwelcome publicity, the "self-advertising scheme" of "a conscienceless fool" (350). Twain's repeated allusions to Corelli's "advertisements" in his autobiography are striking, given her many denials of self-promotion, and probably she was overly gregarious, excited to host such a famous man. But his impression of her physical appearance offers the more interesting angle on the intersections of gender, publicity, and the subject at the turn of the century: "She is about fifty years old but has no gray hairs; she is fat and shapeless; she has a gross animal face; she dresses for sixteen, and awkwardly and unsuccessfully and pathetically imitates the innocent graces and witcheries of that dearest and sweetest of all ages; and so her exterior matches her interior and harmonizes with it, with the result—as I think—that she is the most offensive sham, inside and out, that misrepresents and satirizes the human race today" (351).

"Mark Twain," of course, was the product of Samuel Clemens's personal mythology, and his physical image, self-constructed as a dapper southerner, was so widely circulated as to be immediately recognizable even to those unfamiliar with his books. "Marie Corelli" was likewise the self-mythology of a middle-class woman named Minnie Mackay, whose physical image (unlike Twain's) was so fiercely protected that "for twenty years, while she was at the height of her fame, no one knew what she looked like" (Masters 3).

Twain did not like Corelli and found her overbearing. Still, he was disgusted not by Corelli's duplicity but by the integral unity of her "interior" and "exterior": she really was as she appeared, paradoxically a "sham" both "inside and out." Several of her contemporaries, as well as later biographers, remarked with amazement on Corelli's utter sincerity.

Her novels are often direct statements of her beliefs, a quality that challenges the idea that there is a "real" text buried somewhere, that "the secret of every work" can be discovered by literary critics and biographical sleuths (Macherey 38). Indeed, some readers admired the fact that Corelli "lets her reader know, before she has covered many pages, precisely what her book is to be about" (Coates and Warren-Bell 127). In 1902 the editor of the *Manchester Chronicle* asked, "What manner of woman is this most popular novelist of the hour . . . ? Until lately she was thought to be a mystery. One has only to marvel why. For Marie Corelli does not shroud herself in obscurity, does not affect the life of the recluse, does not pretend to be other than she is—a winsome, warm-hearted, sunny-natured woman" (quoted in Coates and Warren-Bell 347–48).

Corelli's physical—and textual—appearance as a sweetly feminine lady novelist was not an affectation. For a woman with a moral mission, looking the part was essential to gaining converts (and readers), especially given the mass circulation of mechanically produced images in modern culture. The woman who wrote books aimed at exposing the myth of masculine superiority, the degradation of society marriages, political corruption, religious hypocrisy, and rotten reviewers had to look sweet and solemn, charming yet wise, feminine but self-assured. Mark Twain was being sarcastic, but such a woman did have to harmonize inside and outside.

Corelli dealt with this very issue in two novels published within a year of each other, *The Sorrows of Satan* (1895) and *The Murder of Delicia* (1896). Both confront sexist stereotypes, but *The Sorrows of Satan* deserves attention here since reviewers ridiculed the character of Mavis Clare, a sweetly feminine popular novelist, as an idealized self-portrait of the author. Corelli angrily denied "being so *conceited* as to draw *my own picture* in that ideal conception" (quoted in Masters 143). Still, there was plenty of gossip; David Christie Murray devotes several pages to the question in his book *My Contemporaries in Fiction* (1897), concluding that even if we accept Corelli's disclaimer, she "has fallen into a serious indiscretion" (142). I will discuss *The Sorrows of Satan* in more detail in the next chapter, but the Mavis Clare issue is relevant to this discussion of self-image and portraiture. A pure and much loved novelist, Mavis appears in a book where male condescension to female writers is exposed as vitriolic jealousy of women's success in the book wars. Men's mean-spirited stereotypes of intellectual women abound. But given Corelli's campaign against image appropriation, the creation of Mavis Clare can be seen as a curious form of cultural resistance, through words rather than pictures. Mavis is a blatant retort to the hero of the novel, a viciously competitive male writer who has to buy fame and who has a firm hatred of women novelists. When he hears about Mavis Clare, he pictures a "dyspeptic, sour, savage old blue-stocking" and is surprised to meet "a fair-haired girl in a white gown" whose "small head was surely never made for the wearing of deathless laurels, but rather for a garland of roses (sweet and perishable) twined by a lover's hand" (217). It is bad enough to find that this woman is not a revolting bluestocking, but it is even more upsetting to learn that Mavis Clare is not even a cover-up for a revolting bluestocking. She is exactly as she appears. Satan (he passes as an aristocrat named Lucio Rimânez) calls himself "a personified lie" but says of Mavis, "This woman-wearer of laurels is a personified truth!—Imagine it! she has no occasion to pretend to be anything else than she is! No wonder she is famous!" (227).

Equating fame with subjective authenticity, popularity with self-possession, is important if we accept that this assessment is close to Corelli's own confluence of the private, imagined self with a public image. She makes this connection explicitly in an article published in 1904 called "The Happy Life," in which she describes "the rewards and emoluments . . . [of] the Literary Life . . . in two sections—the outward or apparent and the interior or invisible" (75). Corelli naturally prefers the inner, invisible rewards that bring true happiness. But what is really interesting are the illustrations published with the essay. There is a full-page photograph of a very angelic-looking authoress, with the subheading "The First Published Authentic Photograph—Taken in April of This Year, 1904" (fig. 5). This is the "authentic" representation of Corelli, taken by Vyver under the pseudonym F. A. Adrian. But the essay also includes two drawings of the literary woman: in one, she sits at a writing desk; in the other, she stands, her elbow on a fireplace mantel and her foot on a fender, with a newspaper page on the floor (containing bad reviews). The caption to the latter reads, "Weary and Discouraged." These drawings look nothing like the woman in the photograph and clearly are not meant to represent Corelli. But they are not the familiar negative stereotype of the literary woman, either. Although they are visual signifiers for "woman writer," they are physically flattering and

MISS MARIE CORELLI.
THE FIRST PUBLISHED AUTHENTIC PHOTOGRAPH—TAKEN IN APRIL
*Copyright by F. A. Adrian.*]     OF THIS YEAR, 1904.     [*Entered Stationers' Hall.*

Fig. 5. Romantic photograph of Marie Corelli by Bertha Vyver in the *Strand,* 1904.
("The Happy Life," *Strand* 28, no. 163 [1904]: 72–76)

emotionally sympathetic to the woman writer's situation in a male-owned industry and so amplify, rather than contradict, Corelli's frank account of her experiences.

The fickleness of cultural signifiers is familiar to students of the many humorous illustrations of limp aesthetes (often modeled on Wilde) published in Victorian periodicals, usually in the spirit of good-natured satire. But after Wilde was tried and sentenced for "gross indecency" in 1895, it was not his pose that was satirized. Instead, his body became "a descriptive trope" for journalists and illustrators, as Ed Cohen has elaborately documented.[5] The meaning of his crime, his sexual deviance, became constituted in his physical appearance, in the details of his face and body, just as Victorian criminologists established a correspondence based on photographic evidence between criminal behavior and physiognomy. This is the kind of scientific "evidence" Corelli fought against. The idea of the literary woman as deviant or unsexed could be fortified by photographs, so that what it meant to be a writer could not be understood apart from what it meant to be a Victorian woman. In fact, meaning is already constituted in her physicality because, as a woman, her body has always been a descriptive trope. As Mary Poovey has explained, "because the 'problem' of sexuality was articulated in relation *to* women and because women's roles were given initially *by* their sex, women's investment was first of all in the representation of gender and only secondarily in other determinants of identity such as class" (43). In Corelli's case the representation of gender was indeed primary, but her suburban appeal was equally scorned by the male educated elite. A lack of sexual attractiveness would be forgiven if she were truly a woman of the upper class, a woman of intellectual sophistication, but unlike Wilde, Corelli was not an Oxonian. Unauthorized images could be used as cultural weapons to mock her pretensions to both sexual prettiness and literary brilliance.

## The Official Portrait

Not long after Mark Twain's unpleasant visit to Mason Croft, an authorized photograph of Corelli was published as the frontispiece to her novel *The Treasure of Heaven: A Romance of Riches,* which incidentally had a record-breaking first-day sale of more than a hundred thousand copies (fig. 6). Corelli required that the original photograph be retouched to

COPYRIGHT 1906 BY MARIE CORELLI

Fig. 6. Frontispiece to *The Treasure of Heaven*, 1906. This official portrait was touched up to make Corelli look young and serene.

remove signs of age and to present a figure of the novelist as a cultivated and attractive young woman. In another proof (not the one selected as the frontispiece) her pose evokes a maidenly dignity: standing on a step before a curtain (to make her seem taller), with the train of her gown delicately arranged before her and a bouquet of flowers hanging casually at her side, she holds her head upright and has a far-off gaze suggestive of womanly tenderness combined with moral seriousness (fig. 7). There is no doubt that personal vanity motivated Corelli to polish her image, but considering the prevailing stereotypes of women writers as masculine, shabbily dressed, shriveled, and lank-haired and the misogynistic attacks on her works by male reviewers who laughed at her lack of education and literary sophistication, Corelli may also have sought a reply to the social stigma placed on women novelists as unfeminine and, like Corelli, unmarried. But her decision to visit G. Gabell's London studio—she used the name Bertha Vyver, not wishing to reveal her identity even to the photographer—may also be construed as a refusal to acknowledge the truth function of photography. She capitulated to the demand for a literary iconography, but she did not accept the prevailing faith in photography as factual representation, what Roland Barthes called the "mechanical analogue of reality," the belief that the camera does not lie ("Photographic Message" 197). For example, in 1903 she wrote a furious letter (apparently one of many) to the *Manchester Despatch* after it published a picture of her that, she said, "makes me out old and hideous. . . . The two *purposely made* deep dents in the face are like the marks on the countenance of a woman of sixty! and insult is added by calling it an excellent likeness!!!" (quoted in Masters 219). If flaws can be purposely made, they can be purposely unmade. She sent back the proofs of the official portrait to Gabell with lines drawn around the waist and wrote on it "Why this stoutness?" (quoted in Masters 220). Why this literalness? Why be wedded to mere "fact" (fig. 8)?

The frontispiece, which Corelli and Vyver controlled from start to finish, was brought about only by public pressure to issue an official portrait and put an end to spies and speculations. This was a big deal: Corelli wrote a lengthy "Author's Note" prefacing not the novel but the photograph. In it she proclaims her reluctance to publish the frontispiece at all and says, "I am not quite able to convince myself that my pictured personality can have any interest for my readers, as it has always seemed to

Fig. 7. Retouched photograph of Marie Corelli by G. Gabell of Eccleston Street, London. (By courtesy of the Shakespeare Birthplace Trust, Stratford-upon-Avon)

Fig. 8. The unretouched photograph by G. Gabell. (By courtesy of the Shakespeare Birthplace Trust, Stratford-upon-Avon)

me that an author's real being is more disclosed in his or her work than in any portrayed presentment of mere physiognomy." She continues:

> But—owing to the fact that various gross, and I think I may say libellous and fictitious misrepresentations of me have been freely and unwarrantably circulated throughout Great Britain, the Colonies, and America, by certain "lower" sections of the pictorial press, which, with a zeal worthy of a better and kinder cause, have striven by this means to alienate my readers from me,—it appears to my Publishers advisable that an authentic likeness of myself, as I truly am to-day, should now be issued in order to prevent any further misleading of the public by fraudulent inventions. . . . I may add, in conclusion, for the benefit of those few who may feel any further curiosity on the subject, that no portraits resembling me in any way are published anywhere, and that invented sketches purporting to pass as true likenesses of me, are merely attempts to obtain money from the public on false pretences. One picture of me, taken in my own house by a friend who is an amateur photographer [Vyver], was produced some    (vii–viii) time ago in the Strand Magazine, The Boudoir, Cassell's Magazine, and The Rapid Review; but beyond that, and the present one in this volume, no photographs of me are on sale in any country, either in shops or on postcards. My objection to this sort of "picture popularity" has already been publicly stated, and I here repeat and emphasise it. And I venture to ask my readers who have so generously encouraged me by their warm and constant appreciation of my literary efforts, to try and understand the spirit in which the objection is made. It is simply that to myself the personal "Self" of me is nothing, and should be, rightly speaking, nothing to any one outside the circle of my home and my intimate friends; while my work and the keen desire to improve in that work, so that by my work alone I may become united in sympathy and love to my readers, whoever and wherever they may be, constitutes for me the Everything of life.

Here Corelli exhibits the modesty worthy of a woman who sees herself as merely attendant on the public. The press is vilified because it seeks to "alienate" her loyal readers; she reassures her fans that she does not take advantage of her celebrity and gets her picture taken as an "ordinary stranger." More important, Corelli gently directs attention away from the age's rampant "picture popularity," images, and toward her "work," texts. This reassertion of her texts, and even of her textual self—"an author's real being is more disclosed in his or her work than in any portrayed presentment"—may be read as a reaction to modern industrial culture's elevation of images over texts. Barthes writes, "In other words, and this is an important historical reversal, the image no longer *illustrates* the words; it is now the words which, structurally, are parasitic on the image" ("Photographic Message" 205). This is true of the paradoxical caption that accompanies the surreptitious snapshot of Corelli getting out of a cab; the text cooperates with the "photographic message," and the two structures remain separate from each other, but the photograph's "analogic perfection," its literal and objective reality, privilege its denotative meaning ("Photographic Message" 195). But Corelli subordinates her prearranged and professionally polished portrait to a text—to two texts, actually, the explanatory "Author's Note" and the novel, *The Treasure of Heaven,* where it may well be forgotten once reading has begun.

The authorized "authentic likeness" was retouched to make Corelli appear at least twenty years younger. But it is the context of the publication, rather than its faked content, that opposes the picture to the "fictitious misrepresentations" published without her permission, which, because they are photographs, assume an authority and authenticity equal to Corelli's discourse. I am by no means insisting on some straightforwardly subversive intent. Corelli had a formidable ego. Nevertheless, she managed to dismantle her society's faith in realism as an index to the truth in her control of her own visual image, just as she did in her unapologetic belief in the efficacious effects of her romances. "The portrait was entirely false," states Masters. "She knew that the libellous snapshots to which she took objection represented the truth, and this invented likeness represented an idealized version of herself" (220). It is possible, however, that this official portrait represents Corelli's attempt to contest journalists' versions of the "truth" and her skepticism about the truth-value of photographic representation, as evidenced in her accusations that sneaky photographers exaggerate her flaws and in her asking Gabell to touch up the proofs. Obviously, this visual "truth" could be manipulated and reshaped to harmonize with one's own fiction, one's personal mythology. And perhaps it should be. Corelli was not the only celebrity in the 1890s to rely on artificial constructions of selfhood and the importance of the pose; to experience one's life self-consciously as art, to idealize oneself, may offer a more meaningful relationship to the world for those "who do not enjoy the privileges of subjecthood in reality" (Felski, *Modernity* 121).

In a sense, Corelli reveled in her life and all its artifice. Although she suspected actors of immorality, she loved the theater, and she adored going to fancy-dress parties; on one occasion she and Vyver each posed for the camera in their costumes and then had the prints retouched, although they were never published (figs. 9–12). There is something both playful and earnest about these pictures, just as the frontispiece to *Poems* (1925), another photograph taken by Vyver, is a perfect arrangement of romantic tropes.

Corelli's ideas about composition and retouching are in keeping with Victorian reassessments of the function of photography. Henry Peach Robinson, a prominent member of the Royal Photographic Society, emphasized that photographs must not be understood as objective reproductions of fact. In an essay of 1896 Robinson interrogates the realist aesthetic in ways Corelli would surely have approved. He attacks new fiction as well as trends in photography, asserting, "A passion for realism is the affectation of the hour in art and literature, and is making some of our novels so dirty—in the name of art—that one scarcely likes to mention even the titles of them" (92). Robinson quotes with approval a writer in the *Nineteenth Century:* "To be real and true is the first great quality; but to conceive and superadd the highest possible ideal is also indispensable if we would ever hope to reach perfection which is, indeed, in this world unknown, but which, in a world to come, may yet be found attainable" (97). To this end, Robinson has nothing against retouching, which "is not in itself . . . condemnable, but the *bad* retouching, at present almost universal, which turns the human face divine into a semblance of marble busts or, still worse, turnips or apple dumplings" (97). *Good* retouching can make real human faces look more beautiful. What is wrong with that? Photographers, artists, and writers should pursue perfect, ideal forms in which to represent reality. This is a cultural challenge Corelli understood, for she wrote ardently again and again about the social and moral efficacy of romance: "Some of our fellow-creatures there

Fig. 9. Unretouched photograph of Marie Corelli in fancy dress. (By courtesy of the Shakespeare Birthplace Trust, Stratford-upon-Avon)

Fig. 10. Retouched photograph. (By courtesy of the Shakespeare Birthplace Trust, Strat-ford-upon-Avon)

Fig. 11. Unretouched photograph of Bertha Vyver in fancy dress. (By courtesy of the Shakespeare Birthplace Trust, Stratford-upon-Avon)

Fig. 12. Retouched photograph. (By courtesy of the Shakespeare Birthplace Trust, Stratford-upon-Avon)

are in these days who can only be reached through the medium of 'romance.' . . . I have tried to raise the great art of *romance,* i.e., the art of idealizing a given subject like a sculptor or painter, by means of words—to something higher than a mere story of love-making, murder, and money-trouble. I have been able to persuade people to pause awhile and *think.* . . . The world is too good and beautiful for men to give themselves over to despair and suicidal mania" (Corelli-Bentley Correspondence, 24 November 1893). Corelli again detached herself from a genre associated with Ann Radcliffe or sensation novels and sought to raise the romance to a greater moral, as well as artistic, level. Neither her stories nor her authorized images were intended to deceive the public. Rather, they were meant to lift the spirit through their idealizations of reality, to keep before the reader a vision of a beautiful world.

Earlier I quoted from Susanne Kappeler's *Pornography of Representation:* "[Representations] are more 'real' than the reality they are said to represent or reflect" (3). Well, yes and no. Corelli's case suggests that representations have real consequences, and there is something at stake in image control for a popular woman writer at the turn of high modernism. But there are unique and peculiar contexts to visual (and textual) representations. Photojournalism, for example, is a different kind of representation from photographic art, as is the commercial studio of Mr. G. Gabell of Eccleston Street, London. Establishing and taking ownership of images are part of the ongoing struggle to form an idea of self, to find some meaningful identity, and they are especially important for sexually marginalized groups, as feminism and the gay-rights movement have shown. Jeffrey Weeks has argued, "Identity is not a destiny but a choice. . . . Identities are not expressions of secret essences. They are self-creations, but they are creations on ground not freely chosen but laid out by history" (209). Barthes also insists that photographic meanings, codes, or connotations are "neither 'natural' nor 'artificial' but historical, or, if it be preferred, 'cultural' " ("Photographic Message" 206).

The historical and cultural particularities shaping the case of Marie Corelli include changes in late-Victorian publishing and advertising, the rise of photojournalism, feminism, and new aesthetic binarisms based on education, gender, and class. In the paradox of flaunting the sincerity of a carefully constructed image for public consumption, Corelli met the requirements of a spectacular and commodifying society. But she inserted

"Marie Corelli" between her subjective, disembodied, and authoritative voice—the voice received from the private act of reading her autonomous works—and the public pictures of the woman who owned it. The caption "A photograph of a lady who will not be photographed" apparently names the triumph of representation over the subject: a woman, Marie Corelli, is "captured" on film. But as Alan Sinfield has asserted, "representation is always involved in contest" (10). The caption may also imply that there is no lady to represent. She has declined the assumptions of truth or knowledge in this technology.

By 1919, with the dawn of moving pictures, Corelli was even more conscious of the dominance of images in society. Asked by an American newspaper if she feared the cinema would divert public interest from reading, Corelli replied that it probably would and that this was not a movement forward in civilization, but deeply retrogressive. People were being "thrust back by a greedy commerce into old savage ways of ignorance, when 'signs' or 'pictures' were the only ways of making them understand events" (Carroll 1). Appropriately, the newspaper page on which this interview appears consists of large illustrations of five British authors (Corelli's is a drawing, not a photograph), which take up at least four times the amount of space as the text. It would seem that, ultimately, images belonged to the public, absorbed in the scopophilic function of an expanding media. As Guy Debord asserts in *The Society of the Spectacle,* "the spectacle corresponds to the historical moment at which the commodity completes its colonization of social life. It is not just that the relationship to commodities is now plain to see—commodities are now all that there is to see: the world we see is the world of the commodity" (29). Among the commodities generated by the "Corelli cult," as Stuart-Young called it (680), were "The Marie Corelli Calendar," which offers quotations from her works for every day of the year, and *The Marie Corelli Birthday Book,* with original drawings of Corelli heroines by Ernest Prater and G. H. Edwards.[6] Corelli also wrote several patriotic pamphlets, which suggest she was willing to use her celebrity to serve propagandistic or nationalist agendas: *The Greatest Queen in the World, The World in Tears, A Tribute to the Grand Fleet and the Grand Fleet's Commander,* and *Is All Well with England?*[7] In lending her name to spin-offs and boosterism, she may not have been able to resist her historical moment. But she seems to have understood what was at stake for a woman celebrity in the era of commodities, and she tried energetically to interfere with the cultural assertions of images over words.

In the next chapter I continue to read Corelli in the context of literary culture. Although I am always concerned with her position as a woman writer, and feminist theories inform my approaches to both her life and her novels, in chapter 2 I shift the discussion to include class issues. Victorian critics were anxious to pin down Corelli's reading constituency, which suggests that an author's audience determined her cultural and artistic value. But Corelli's cross-class appeal made her impossible to locate. She challenged antithetical categories based on art, class, and gender in ways that baffled men who felt they knew their society's tastes and reading habits. An ardent supporter of democracy and "the people," Corelli seemed to represent the decline of literary taste among the newly enfranchised British reading public.

# II

Aestheticism in Suburbia

> *Yes, I maintain (and in my opinion this should be a*
> *rule of conduct for an artist) that one's existence should*
> *be in two parts: one should live like a bourgeois and*
> *think like a demi-god.*

Gustave
Flaubert, let-
ter to Louise
Colet, 1853

> *The actual* love *of art for its own sake is to some*
> *persons perfectly incomprehensible.*

Marie Co-
relli, letter
to George
Bentley, 1888

IN THIS CHAPTER I am interested in the ways Marie Corelli participated in literary trends of the 1880s and 1890s broadly labeled the aesthetic movement or literary decadence. My focus is primarily on mass culture and the tension between the democratic strain of aestheticism—how it is manifested in home decoration, popular satires, or mass fiction—and the aesthete's often explicit scorn for bourgeois education, tastes, and modes of living. In using the word *aestheticism* I am asking for a very inclusive interpretation of fin-de-siècle literary culture, one that embraces decadence, New Women novels, and the new fiction (including naturalism). According to William Scheick, "such expressions as *aestheticism* (including *decadence*), literary *realism* (including *naturalism*), and *subjectivism* (including *modernism*) . . . were employed time and again at the end of the nineteenth century and the beginning of the twentieth century to refer to various modes of fiction," although none seems to have been able to capture the diversity of each type of fiction (18). But apparently antithetical cultural positions are often interdependent. In my argument for Corelli's revision of the myth of the artist, and in my reading of *Wormwood* (1890) as a decadent novel, for instance, I want to suggest that her participation in the cultural life of her time was highly creative, combative, and contradictory. I also devote a large part of this discussion to her best-seller of 1895, *The Sorrows of Satan*. In this novel the treatment of literature versus commercial art is complicated by gender politics, and I make a considerable divergence into New Woman fiction and its intersection with decadence and with class stratification. Corelli's letters to George Bentley between 1886 and about 1894 are fascinating evidence of how "Marie Corelli," as a newcomer on the scene, had to cut a path through the meshes and quagmires of patriarchal literary circles while thinking through the competing claims of art, Victorian readers, and the commercial market. Very few writers at the turn of the century spoke with such fervor and sincerity in defense of "the masses" or with such faith in the public's taste and reading habits. Corelli's contentious battles with critics, reviewers, literary cliques, and journalists document forcibly how the new spirit of equality infringed on the rapidly changing literary world of the 1890s.

### Bohemians, Aesthetes, and Starving Artists

In *Five Faces of Modernity* Matei Calinescu explains that "the alienation of the modern writer" began with the romantic movement, especially as it was manifested in Germany and France, where "the object of hatred and ridicule is *philistinism,* a typical form of middle-class hypocrisy" (43). The artist's resistance to mercantilism, industrialism, and utilitarianism was fundamentally linked to class, and this is reflected in a shift in the cultural meanings of *bourgeois* and *artist.* If the laughingstock of the neoclassical period was the pedant, who was mocked for his academic priggishness, the satiric target of the 1830s was the bourgeois, who was "defined mainly by his class background, all his intellectual attitudes being nothing but disguises of practical interests and social concerns" (44). The famous formula *épater le bourgeois* was thus the artist's "aristocratic creed in a time of egalitarianism" (55), and it was followed up decisively by Gustave Flaubert's claims for the artist as an exquisite stylist, a high priest, a martyr who is separated alike from ordinary bourgeois morality and from politics and social change.

Flaubert's artistic independence, Charles Baudelaire's emphasis on the pursuit of beauty as a spiritual adventure, Théophile Gautier's notorious preface to *Mademoiselle de Maupin* (1835), with its call for *l'art pour l'art,* and the Goncourts' naturalistic stance of the coldly detached artist—all of these tendencies in French literature influenced British aestheticism in the 1880s and 1890s. The cultural and literary effects of *l'art pour l'art* in England were so various, though, that one critic has suggested we dismiss *aestheticism* altogether, since any attempt to give the subject "the substance and stability of a noun . . . is to miss the point completely" (Weir 70). Indeed, literary culture in these decades was highly diverse. Holbrook Jackson's *The Eighteen Nineties,* which was published in 1913, is still one of the best overviews of this "period of a thousand movements" (30). This was a time "when people went about frankly and cheerfully endeavoring to solve the question 'How to Live'" (30). Jackson neatly characterizes decadent literature by its perversity, artificiality, egoism, and curiosity and identifies the dandy as the figure most representative of the aesthete's love of town life. He also points out that the fin de siècle had its own mass media: "the interpreters of the hour—the publicists, journalists and popular purveyors of ideas of all kinds—did not fail to make a sort of traffic in the spirit of the times" (20). The dominant idea was newness, especially in literature. The realism of New Women novels and the portrayals of sex in the new fiction ushered in a new frankness, but it was matched by a new romantic spirit that, according to Jackson, "did not scruple about using many mediums for its purpose" (227). The fin de siècle, then, was a hybrid period, though with certain recognizable features.

Many of these features were appropriated by the middle class in highly imaginative ways. Popular, satiric treatments of the aesthetic movement in the 1880s and 1890s—George Du Maurier's drawings of the aesthete Maudle in *Punch,* William Gilbert and Arthur Sullivan's operettas, and the countless advertisements, ballads, songs, and novels aimed at Oscar Wilde and his followers—confirm that for all its snobbishness, aestheticism was a regenerative force in Victorian society. Indeed, Lionel Lambourne has claimed that the most "remarkable thing about the satirical comment upon the Aesthetic Movement is that it is remembered more vividly than the subject satirized" (114). Such industrious appropriations of aestheticism by philistines demonstrate Victorian self-consciousness and resilience. They also show the adeptness of an advanced consumer society in transforming an oppositional art movement into commodities. Yet aestheticism undoubtedly raised popular awareness about the growing distance between utilitarian and commercial concerns and the world of beauty, intellect, and emotion. The complex relationships between literature and commerce, design and production, art and life created by industrial and technological progress were rendered visible and accessible to many people because of the flamboyance of aesthetes, dandies, decadents, and New Women.

Aestheticism's success may be marked by the many ways its tenets were absorbed by the Victorian middle class. In *The Aesthetic Movement in England,* published in 1882, Walter Hamilton approvingly cites an anonymous essay published in July of the same year:

> *This improvement is rapidly spreading through all classes of society—good taste is no longer an expensive luxury to indulge in—the commonest articles of domestic use are now fashioned in accordance with its laws, and the poorest may have within their homes, at the cost of a few*
>
> (126–27) *pence, cups and saucers and jugs and teapots, more artistic in form and design than were to be found twenty years ago in any homes but those of the cultured rich.*
>
> *And to whom are we indebted for these advantages? Why, to the aesthetes, the fools and idiots of Philistine phraseology.*

The tone of this passage is as instructive as its content: aestheticism's democratic function is praised, yet a note of haughtiness remains, for the movement helped to mythologize and circulate a mystique of the aesthete as a poor bohemian who was a martyr to beauty or as a cultivated aristocrat with taste. The word *genius* is often summoned to evoke the extraordinary talent and vision of the *artiste,* who is inevitably misunderstood by commoners and only appreciated by an informed elite. This is the image of the artist, always defined against the philistine, that is distinctly linked with aestheticism.

It is not surprising, then, that after more than fifty years of democratic reforms, *aestheticism,* for some people, carried negative connotations of political disengagement, arrogance, and affectation. Linda Dowling relates that when William Morris announced his conversion to socialism in 1883, "such terms as *Aestheticism, art for art's sake,* and *Culture* had become synonymous . . . for the apparent betrayal of art and beauty into the hands of a self-nominated and supercilious elite" (75). Yet Walter

Pater and Wilde each hailed Morris as one of the leaders of the very movement he ostensibly scorned. This example demonstrates that the antithesis of bourgeois and *artiste,* or of social pragmatism and aesthetic uselessness, was not clearly defined. Nevertheless, the romantic myth of the self-sacrificing and misunderstood artist continued to have a powerful hold on many ambitious young writers, and there was a definite stigma attached to writing books that were popular with middle-class readers. Joseph Conrad, for example, who was Corelli's almost exact contemporary, was extremely ambivalent about writing for a wide audience, confessing in a letter of 1897 the desire for "a little reputation, and the rest of my life devoted to the service of Art and free from material worries." Conrad blames his situation on both literary profiteering and the impossibly stupid taste of the public. In his letters he refers broadly to the despised "masses," the "beastly bourgeois," the "Philistines," and the "respectable (hats off) part of the population" and deplores the passing of the Third Reform Bill in 1885 as the enfranchising of "idiots" (1:16). Still, even Conrad hoped for more public interest in his books. In 1900 he watched the rate of subscriptions for *Lord Jim* hopefully, writing, "It isn't exactly like Marie Corelli's but let us hope it will improve" (2:298).

In a way Conrad perfectly illustrates the modern "artistic" author who desperately wants to make money and must generate sales but who despises the populace who would buy his books. His position represents the predicament of many writers born in the 1850s and 1860s, the second generation of Victorians—including Rudyard Kipling, H. G. Wells, Wilde, George Moore, John Galsworthy, George Gissing, Arnold Bennett, H. Rider Haggard, Arthur Conan Doyle, Robert Louis Stevenson, and Olive Schreiner—all of whom at some point in their careers were occupied with balancing personal politics, financial necessity, and a commitment to art. Democratic reforms, in particular the Education Act of 1870, made the spread of "culture" among the middle classes a matter of fact, while serial publication and the triple-decker were beginning to give way to cheaper forms of publication and to more experimentation in fictional technique and subject matter. For the novelist of the 1880s and 1890s, to serve art and to make a living was to strike a delicate balance, especially if he or she wished to avoid the suspiciously bourgeois stigma of popularity.

Unlike Conrad, and unlike most of her competitors in the literary market of the fin de siècle, Corelli was able to reconcile the unruly trinity of artistic integrity, money, and popularity. The love of art for its own sake was entirely compatible with finding a mass audience. In fact, for Corelli reaching the public was a virtuous aspiration for a writer and every bit as worthy as pursuing her vocation for the sake of literature. "For indeed I love my work for its own sake," she wrote to Bentley in 1886, "while as far as the public goes, I want to make it also feel rested, invigorated, and rendered for a time oblivious of its troubles in the perusal of my pages. A high aim!—but it is always better to try for the best" (13 November 1886). From the very beginning of her literary career, she held herself to the highest standards of artistic integrity.

Corelli is an interesting mediator in these ideological contradictions. As a best-selling novelist, she would appear the antithesis of aesthetic style: the astonishing sales of her romances surely disqualify her from being either avant-garde or decadent, bohemian or aesthete. Her immense popularity was consistently identified with the zeal and directness with which she spoke to the democratic feeling of the British middle class. She believed she had a genuine affinity and commitment to what she called "the people." Yet for all her moral confidence, Corelli's passionate interest in sin and sexuality, literature and commercialism, death and the afterlife struck some critics as more than melodramatic excess. Her popularity was seen by some as evidence of the triumph of the "degeneration of the last twenty years," and she was even accused of plagiarizing the works of one "French decadent" and another "degenerate writer of Paris" (Stuart-Young 689, 687). She was astounded to report to Bentley in 1893, after the appearance of *Barabbas,* that the Ealing Public Library had "dismissed *all* my books, Thelma included, and the 'Romance' as 'highly *immoral*—' (!)" (6 November 1893). This accusation is interesting because Corelli repeatedly expressed her disgust with literary decadence and the French school of art, and throughout her career she was openly laughed at by the majority of English critics, who thought her tawdry, unsophisticated, and even ungrammatical.

In *British Literary Culture and Publishing Practice, 1880–1914* Peter McDonald uses Pierre Bourdieu's idea of the "literary field" to approach Edmund Gosse's rhetorical ploys in an 1892 essay on the death of Alfred, Lord Tennyson, arguing that Gosse's tone may be variously interpreted as manipulating the rhetoric of class interest, of political dogma, or of gender bias. It is an instructive and interesting analysis, for in the 1890s these agendas seem to converge in an alarmist rhetoric of class war, and it is virtually impossible to ignore the subtexts of many emotional articles that appeared in Victorian periodicals. For example, in an essay published in the *Fortnightly Review* (1890) called "Literature: Then and Now," Eliza Lynn Linton deplores the "cartloads of absolute rubbish," the "appalling amount of trash," the "grotesque . . . sensationalism" and "vapid senti-mentalism" of the current literary market. This appalling state of decay is, unfortunately, tied to the achievements of democratic reformers: "The democratic wave which has spread over all society—and washed down some things which had better have been left standing—has swept through the whole province of literature. The spread of education among the people demands literature cheap enough to at once suit their pockets and meet their wants" (527). The result is incompetence, unoriginality, and the degradation of a literary profession that is forced by the market to amuse the half-educated classes.

Linton was not alone in expressing anxiety about the menacing en-croachments of popular taste. The tone in many articles and reviews at the turn of the century is scornful, if not panicked, about the quality of popular fiction and the implications for the body politic. A writer in *Blackwood's* in 1895 directly connected bad art with social anarchy: "Hysteria, whether in politics or art, has the same inevitable effect of sapping manliness and making people flabby. . . . The sturdy Radical of former years, whose ideal was independence and disdain of Govern-mental petting, is being superseded by the political 'degenerate' who preaches the doctrine that all men are equal, when experience proves precisely the opposite" (Stutfield 843). Or as the *Westminster Review* put it, the "cloying sentimentalism" of popular literature "trains up a nation of criminals and weaklings. . . . It is the artist, whether he paints in oils [or] words or have stone as his material, who is responsible for the state of his country" (Stuart-Young 691–92).

If politics and ideology were attached to a respected English literary tradition associated with robustness, sanity, humor, and truthfulness, low-status mass fiction was undermining the cultural establishment. Far from being innocuous amusement for the middle class, art and literature were seen as vital to the nation's political health, an idea that surely owed something to aestheticism. But allusions to degenerates, criminals, and weaklings invoke fear of the hedonistic and possibly homosocial attitudes associated with Wilde and the "cult of beauty," the doctrines of which had infiltrated the imaginations of even the sturdy middle classes. Likewise, references to hysteria and sentimentalism suggest the sexism underlying many of these cultural alarms, a fear that society was becoming effeminate and "flabby." As Andreas Huyssen has persuasively argued, mass culture at the turn of the century was frequently inscribed as feminine, an identification that conflated women and the masses as social threats.

The effects of democracy on art intersect with the effects of art on the body politic: consumers of literature and the men and women who produce literature share accountability for cultural and social ills. So Gosse, in 1893, blamed "those charming, fresh, ingenuous, ignorant, and rather stupid young ladies, the English and American publics," for the mediocrity of modern fiction (137–38). But he also blamed writers who pay too much attention to the public: "necessary to write down to a wide audience," "obliged to supply the kind of article demanded," "women the only readers catered for" are the excuses made by novelists who write for the mass market (23). Gosse had no problem reducing the "public" to a homogeneous mass of half-educated females. At least Wells realized that there were different markets for different genres, though, in 1896, he also connected democratic reforms and literary mediocrity:

> *The passing of the Education Act in 1870 and the coming to reading*
> *age in 1886–1888 of multitudes of boys and girls have changed the con-*
> *ditions of journalism and literature in much the same way as the French*
> *Revolution changed the conditions of political thought and action. . . .*
(74)
> *And while the male of this species has chiefly exerted his influence in*
> *the degradation of journalism, the debasing influence of the female, re-*
> *inforced by the free libraries, has been chiefly felt in the character of fic-*
> *tion. 'Arry reads* Ally Sloper *and* Tit-Bits, *'Arriet reads* Trilby *and*
> The Sorrows of Satan.

Both *Trilby* and *The Sorrows of Satan* are popular novels that exploit the public fascination with art and artists stimulated by aestheticism. *Trilby* (1894), the highly successful novel by George Du Maurier about English artists in bohemian Paris, is set in the 1850s, but it is as much a novel of 1890s aestheticism as *The Picture of Dorian Gray* (1891)—in fact, the American painter James Abbott McNeill Whistler threatened Du Maurier with a libel suit (Purcell 63). *The Sorrows of Satan* (1895) was Corelli's eighth best-selling novel and had an initial sale greater than any previous English novel, even though Corelli, fed up with the critics, refused to send out copies for review. It is about a struggling male novelist who falls under the spell of an aristocratic Satan and is exposed to the destructiveness, greed, and immorality of the late-Victorian publishing world. He is finally redeemed by the honesty and sweetness of his rival, the popular novelist Mavis Clare, whose books radiate goodness and truth instead of atheism and despair.

Wells's claim that Corelli's principal audience was "''Arriet of the Board-school'' needs further scrutiny, however. As we know, Corelli gained the admiration of quite a few celebrities. This extraordinary attention baffled journalists and literary men who confidently classified her fiction as low art. Critics and writers who thought they understood their society's tastes and reading habits stood bewildered by the Corelli phenomenon. "The questions which I have asked myself with marked insistence have been, 'Who are chiefly Miss Corelli's admirers?' 'Why is she so popular?' and 'What relation does the popularity of an author bear to the quality of the writer's books?'" wondered a writer in the *Westminster Review* in 1906 (Stuart-Young 681). The *Daily Mail* asked, "What is the secret of Miss Corelli's wonderful success? Why do the public return with unabated zest to the perusal of her works? The problem is worth probing" ("Miss Marie Corelli"). And, writing anonymously in *Blackwood's Edinburgh Magazine* in 1895, Mrs. Humphry Ward pondered: "Miss Marie Corelli's 'Barabbas' has sold—how many million copies? heaven (or another place) and the publisher only knows" (914). And then there is the long and appreciative profile of Corelli in the *Bookman* in 1909:

> *The superiority of your very superior literary person depends upon his being able to maintain that literature is not for all the world, but is a sort of exotic that can only be cultivated and appreciated in select holes and corners. In the interest of this gospel—for popularity is an offence to those who cannot obtain it— no living author has been more persistently maligned and sneered at and scouted by certain sections of the Press—by the presumptuous and struttingly academic section of it particularly—than has Miss Marie Corelli, and none has won (by sheer force of her own merits, for the press has never helped her), a wider, more persistently increasing fame and affection among all classes of that* (Adcock 59–60)

*intelligent public which reads and judges books, but does not write about them. "Yes," say her detractors, "she is the idol of Suburbia—the favourite of the common multitude. . . . She is suburban and the delight of Suburbia"; so that when you find, on making inquiries, that everything she has written has been translated many times into so many varied languages and dialects, that there are some five or six hundred translations of her books selling all over the world, you can only ask yourself, if this is suburban, which one of our novelists may be regarded as approximately cosmopolitan?*

Sorting out the differences between suburban and cosmopolitan, the "mass culture/modernism dichotomy" (Huyssen 19), has been an important project for materialist and sociological approaches to studying literature and culture. Clearly, it was important to Victorian critics and writers, too, who simply did not understand the dynamics of public taste. Arnold Bennett wrote that the whole aim of his collection of essays *Fame and Fiction* (1901), was "to explain to the minority why the majority likes or dislikes certain modern novelists" (6); he includes a chapter on Corelli's 1900 blockbuster, *The Master Christian*. Gosse, in an otherwise sanguine essay titled "The Influence of Democracy on Literature," probably best sums up the exasperation of the man of letters when confronted with the enigma of popularity:

(62–63)

*But a novel may be utterly silly, be condemned by every canon of taste, be ignored by the press, and yet may enjoy a mysterious success, pass through tens of editions, and start its author on a career which may lead to opulence. It would be interesting to know what it is that attracts the masses to books of this kind. How do they hear of them in the first instance? Why does one vapid and lady-like novel speed on its way, while eleven others, apparently just like unto it, sink and disappear? How is the public appetite for this insipidity to be reconciled with the partiality of the same readers for stories by writers of real excellence? Why do those who have once pleased the public continue to please it, whatever lapses into carelessness and levity they permit themselves? I have put these questions over and over again to those whose business it is to observe and take advantage of fluctuations in the book-market, but they give no intelligible reply. If the Sphinx had asked Oedipus to explain the position of "Edna Lyell," he would have had to throw himself from the rock.*

Gosse could have had Corelli in mind as much as Edna Lyell. His confusion is representative of literary men of his class and education, and it invites some questions: What were some late-Victorian constructions of "suburban" taste and sensibility, and how do these assumptions contribute to fears about the decline of literature? Are reading habits accurate indicators of social class? How do judgments about literary value reflect expectations based on gender as well as class?

Corelli offers an exceptionally interesting case for studying the way these questions were approached by writers, literary men, and consumers in the 1880s and 1890s. She is a curious example of cultural crossover not just in her appeal across classes but in her literary works, where the virtue of simplicity is extravagantly dramatized through the vices of the upper crust and the interests of artists and writers are played against the narrowness of the "aesthetic" critics and reviewers she knew from personal experience.

In *Literary Capital and the Late Victorian Novel* N. N. Feltes discusses Corelli's success in the context of late-Victorian publishing, pointing out that she was frequently attacked for her mistakes, her "vulgarities," her ignorance of languages, history, and grammar and that these attacks imply a "patriarchal/class judgment" (125). This is certainly true, and as we saw in chapter 1, Corelli was not afraid to accuse the critics of sexism and clubbish snobbery. Her most sustained and vicious attack is *The Silver Domino,* published anonymously in 1893. Corelli's sarcasm and invective are ruthless, but she defends the "B.P." (short for British Public) from the snobbery of critics, with their "Oxford and Cambridge pets and [their] heavy men," who give no foothold "to the 'vapid' feminine climber [who] wantonly attempts to scale Parnassus, . . . a mountain exclusively set apart for the masculine gender" (298, 301). Her anger, hurt, and resentment are even more apparent in her private letters to Bentley. "Rudyard Kipling is a young mushroom growing on the roots of the Savile Club, and this is why he is elevated into a sudden 'Genius'—though of genius he has none," she wrote bitterly on 30 April 1890, and on 8 September, "the 'Savile Club' knows me not, and Andrew Lang of sixteen newspapers detests me, and now that I know how criticism is done, I care not a jot for it! See how they paragraph Rudyard Kipling!—Andrew Lang's work again." Corelli blamed a corrupt reviewing process for Kipling's success because his appeal was as incomprehensible to her as her own fame was to men such as Gosse. But she was right to be suspicious of the old-boy literary network. John Gross has described Victorian intellectual circles as "remarkably small and tightly-knit: everyone knew everyone else, and was somebody else's brother-in-law" (100). The Savile Club was one of many male writers' clubs, such as the Omar Khayyám Club, the Athenaeum, the New Vagabonds Club, the Rhymers' Club, and the Rabelais Club; its members included Kipling, Stevenson, George Saintsbury, and W. E. Henley—all writers who, incidentally, contributed to the revival of male romance in the 1880s.[1]

Corelli's bitter letters must have been hard on Bentley, who was not to blame for Andrew Lang's dynasty or Kipling's popularity, and they may come across today as paranoid, megalomanic, or both. But consider how unusual it was for a woman writer in 1890 to express this kind of frustration to her publisher, to identify bias and protest against it. It is strange to encounter so many references to Kipling as the archenemy, but in a pamphlet on the Boer War, Corelli explains that what she really dislikes about his writing is its sexism: "We do not know whether Mr. Kipling considers it a 'small duty' to think of mothers and sisters, sweethearts and wives; but we do know that the popular rhymester's contempt for women, as displayed in his stories, not one of which includes a lovable or sympathetic feminine character, is not a code of the British Army" (*A Social Note on the War* 6). For Corelli it was perfectly legitimate to evaluate a work of fiction on the basis of its portraits of women. But as I have already suggested, her situation as an outsider was as much about her class background as about her gender.

### Shopkeepers and Kings

That literary critics felt compelled to locate Corelli's audience suggests they believed that a consistent demographic profile of readers could neatly identify an author's merit. The name Marie Corelli was sometimes used to suggest the taste and intelligence of the kind of person who read her novels.[2] But the problem was that Corelli had no consistent reader base. For example, a hostile critic wrote that her readers were from the "unthinking classes," "undoubtedly . . . members of her own sex, in middle-class society, and from the working classes—shop girls and young men of the large towns" (Stuart-Young 683); but a sympathetic journalist claimed, "many of her most enthusiastic admirers are men of the professional classes—doctors, barristers, lawyers, writers, men of education and intelligence" (Adcock 78). Corelli was acutely conscious of how reader demographics could affect her position in the eyes of her publisher. After the success of *A Romance of Two Worlds* she told Bentley, "I have much *very* much to say to women especially" (15 November 1886), but two years later she reassured him that a "clever and distinguished" man told her, "*Men* read your books, Miss Corelli, as well as women—for the reason that you not only tell us a story, but you give us something to *think about*" (5 March 1888). Of course, in 1889 she wrote effusively to Bentley about the prime minister's surprise visit to her home in Earl's Court. William Gladstone, an ardent Liberal, appreciated the ideological work of fiction, but he took a more pro-democratic view than the writers in *Blackwood's* and the *Westminster Review*. His advice to Corelli, as she recounted it to Bentley, unites fiction and mass education in a much more positive way: "You are I see very earnest and sincere, do not put up with trivialities in fiction. Fiction is a powerful factor in the education of the people, let those who read it find great examples, and fine thoughts" (5 June 1889).

Democracy, class allegiance, fiction, gender politics: the intersection of these concerns encroaches on any single definition of *the people* or any monolithic claim for art. While one corner asserted that a Corelli novel appealed only to readers in Camberwell and Brixton, Corelli countered by insisting, "Camberwell and Brixton must be included in the London radius; and I believe the Prince of Wales, who has always been most kindly in his appreciation of my books, has property there!" (quoted in Arthur Lawrence 24). Once we discuss shopkeepers in the same breath as royalty, suburbia begins to look indeterminate or, as the historian H. J. Dyos has written, "a curious blend of romantic idealism and hard-headed realism" (23). The suburban dweller wanted the Englishman's castle and the pleasures of the countryside but also affordable lodging and a location convenient to his work. Thus the suburban sensibility is divided between a desire for privacy and a love of ostentation, for "individual domesticity and group-monitored respectability" (Thompson 159). As a contributor to *Architect* wrote in 1876, "A modern suburb is a place which is neither one thing nor the other" (quoted in Thompson 151). And according to John Carey, "intellectuals were, of course, in no position to generalize about the suburbs, since the subject was too various for categorization. Like 'masses,' the word 'suburban' is a sign for the unknowable" (53).

Given this identity crisis, it is fitting that the most famous account of late-Victorian suburban life was called *The Diary of a Nobody,* written by George and Weedon Grossmith and published serially in *Punch* in 1892. Along with describing the comical mishaps at the Pooters' Hollo-way villa (and the popularity of aesthetic decor among the suburban middle class—the Pooters have Japanese pictures, muslin curtains over the folding doors, and an arrangement of fans on the mantelpiece), *The Diary of a Nobody* testifies to the perceived gulf between middle-class philistinism and aesthetic sensibility. "Our lives run in different grooves. I live for MY ART – THE STAGE. Your life is devoted to commercial pursuits," Mr. Burwin-Fosselton tells Pooter. "Cannot even you see the ocean between us?" (107). And when a savvy American, Mr. Hardfur Huttle, makes a speech equating middle-class respectability with "miserable mediocrity," he asserts that such a man "will spend the rest of his days in a suburban villa with a stucco-column portico, resembling a four-post bedstead. . . . That sort of thing belongs to a soft man, with a soft beard, with a soft head, with a made tie that hooks on" (172). What is wonderful about *The Diary of a Nobody* is that the satire is directed as much at affected aesthetes as at the Pooters' suburban Eden. Both of these cultural polarities are exposed as ridiculous.

Despite *The Diary of a Nobody*'s evenhandedness, with the rise of the aesthetic movement (the Grosvenor Gallery had its first exhibition in 1877) the suburbs became "objects of ridicule and even contempt" and were "associated less with a geographical expression than an attitude of mind and a species of social as well as economic behaviour" (Dyos 26). The suburban mind was considered petty, unimaginative, and without social, cultural, and intellectual interests, in direct contrast with the cosmopolitan emphasis on art, variety, and sophistication. This reduction relies less on economic status than on cultural emphasis: untalented amateurs without a shilling can become alienated artists in the hands of French decadents, but they become something else in the hands of British middle-class readers—they become Little Billie and the Laird in *Trilby*. The cosmopolitan-suburban construct privileges aestheticism, which is associated with young men, explorations of life, and "the wizardry of cities" (Jackson 107), rather than suburbia, which is associated with feminine domesticity, homogeneity, and the delights of nature (or at least of a small garden). This opposition was commonplace by the 1890s, and it became more polarized in the twentieth century as automobiles and large-scale building firms combined to create even more sprawl. The cultural consequences were inimical: "the massive expansion of suburbia, and the antagonisms, divisions, and sense of irrevocable loss it generated were major shaping forces in twentieth-century English culture. They exacerbated the intellectual's feeling of isolation from what he conceived of as philistine hordes" (Carey 50). There are also gender divisions evoked by the cosmopolitan-suburban split. Among intellectuals the suburbs were the site not only of weak-brained materialists but of "specifically female triviality" (Carey 52).

Though it was supposedly upheld by those "presumptuous and struttingly academic" male reviewers, the dichotomy I have described was anything but clear-cut, and in fact most modern critics agree that aestheticism was "essentially a middle-class movement" (Lambourne 13). In *Idylls of the Marketplace* Regenia Gagnier explains that although aestheticism was "an engaged protest against . . . the whole middle-class drive to conform," it was not simply about the separation of art and life or of art and politics (3). Gagnier urges "a theory of aestheticism from the point of view of consumption, or of the different publics that, in different ways, consumed it" (7). Similarly, Jonathan Freedman claims that Wilde's service to aestheticism was to bring the movement to the marketplace. In *The Picture of Dorian Gray* Wilde places "Pre-Raphaelite poetry, Paterian dogma, and Huysmans's fiction alongside plot devices that he stole from Gothic horror tales, sentimental fiction, and sensation novels," thus making "the imaginative enterprise of British aestheticism available to all the various segments of the Victorian reading public" (51). And Wilde was very much aware that the public was anything but monolithic. When he was asked by an interviewer in 1895, "What is your feeling towards your audiences—towards the public?" Wilde immediately replied, "Which public? There are as many publics as there are personalities" (quoted in Dowling 93).

Audience undoubtedly affected representations of aestheticism in the 1890s. It seems as though almost any novel or play about London society published in the last two decades of the century betrays the influence of Wilde and his followers, either through absorption—imitating aestheticism as a fashion—or through satire, and these works appealed to very different readers. The pose of the dandy may have been "antithetical to the democratizing ethos of the middle-classes" (Freedman 49), but the sheer fame of the dandy-aesthete seems to have compelled the bourgeoise to adopt a pose of her own out of cultural resistance. And this is what is most interesting about the success of Corelli as the "idol of Suburbia," for in her books and in her public image she reconstructed the identity of the artist for an audience who, if they were typical suburbanites, desired both sensationalism and safety, the glow of haute couture and the convenience of the clip-on tie.

### The Reading Mob

There are different ways of constructing and sentimentalizing the artist, and it is possible to view Corelli's career as a populist crusade against male critics who wanted to keep her out of high culture. The invented story about her family connections and class background forced Corelli into an attitude in keeping with the fashion of artistic snobbery. She wrote to Bentley: "And of course I am *not* a Radical;—I see the mob call aristocrats 'toffs'—what a droll name! I suppose then I am a 'toff'—for I do not like the great unwashed at all, and have no sympathy with their imagined wrongs" (9 February 1886). One year later though, Corelli's popularity with "the mob" made this aristocratic pose unnecessary, and she could safely claim her allegiance with the masses of ordinary people who bought her books. Her attitude toward the Education Act is of fundamental importance and indicative of her class loyalties: "of all the 'signs of the times,' the one that is perhaps the most powerful and striking is the steady spread of Education among the People, and the equally steady rise of an intelligent Democracy in all corners of the world." Far from expressing artistic elitism, Corelli praised "that much abused individual, the British Working Man," who often "reads and studies much more seriously, and to wider purpose, than his aristocratic employer" with his phony pretenses to "cultchaw" (manuscript). What a different point of view *this* is from those of Linton, Wells, Gosse, and other writers and intellectuals in the 1890s. Whereas Gosse was nearly petrified by the poetry-loving mob outside Westminster Abbey after Tennyson's funeral in 1892—"I have found myself depressed and terrified at an ebullition of popularity which seems to have struck almost everybody else with extreme satisfaction" (182)—Corelli praised the "unerring good taste" of the people who purchased Tennyson's books for fifty years (*Silver Domino* ix). While obviously enjoying the company of famous writers and artists such as George Meredith, Wilde, and John Everett Millais, Corelli testified that her literary aspirations had nothing to do with social climbing. In 1887 she wrote to Bentley, "If I were a Rothschild, I should still write—and I am sure many others could be found to say the same" (1 April 1887). Corelli was appalled when "Dear, clever George Meredith informed me once through his set teeth, that he 'wrote for *porkers*' *i.e.* human pigs—whereupon I very naturally enquired—'If they are so unworthy, why do it?'—a view of things he had seemingly not considered!" (Corelli-Bentley Correspondence, 8 April 1887). "Dear, clever George Meredith" was a close neighbor in Dorking when Corelli was a child and already a grand old man when she and her family moved to Longridge Road in 1884; he may have had a slightly patronizing attitude toward the Mackay ménage, and Corelli may have felt some personal offense at his rather unkind remark—she alludes to it in *The Silver Domino* as well and goes on to say that the literary chalet Meredith built in his garden was an effort to "escape from 'domesticity' and the ways of the 'women' he is supposed to understand" (148–49). This last remark suggests that Corelli felt Meredith's condescension was sexist as well as snobbish. In any case, his comment seemed worth reporting to Bentley, probably because Corelli was still trying to establish herself as a professional writer and resented the insinuation that popularity was inconsistent with intelligence. Even a week later, she was still annoyed by Meredith's attitude and expressed disdain for his assumption of intellectual superiority: "I'm afraid I am not 'educated up' to him. I think it is quite ridiculous for any author to say he writes 'for porkers,' because a truly gifted soul should not despise the meanest thing that lives, much less his fellow creatures, no matter how densely ignorant they may be. . . . I don't believe in '*porkers*' unless we are *all* admitted to the same rough designation—authors and all!" (Corelli-Bentley Correspondence, 14 April 1887). The people may be "densely ignorant," but a writer is in no way above them morally. She gains her importance from her readers' admiration and from a moral and social commitment to literature, not from membership in educated, upper-class circles or from the praise of highbrow critics.

For twenty years Corelli negotiated images of the artist that both reflect and refute the social and literary assumptions of aestheticism: she was a sincere practitioner of her craft, a high priestess of the imagination, and a popular and commercial success. She also lived out these ambiguities, but to her they were not contradictions. This is not to say she did not urge Bentley to advertise—she did, constantly—or that she did not keep an eye on her competitors in the fiction market. But if Corelli was *artiste* enough not to give way to public taste, she was suburban enough not to collapse under the critical establishment's aesthetic values.

Most influential among these values was impressionism, associated with suggestiveness, nuance, the half tints of Whistler's nocturnes, Arthur Symons's desire to "spiritualise literature" (*Symbolist Movement* 5). Such fine distinctions are useless for a writer with a moral and democratic mission. "Have you noticed how fond some people are of the word '*subtle*'?" Corelli wrote to Bentley. "Tell them a book is *subtle* and they will rave over it instantly!" (11 May 1888). This "subtle" taste belongs to university men, not to the masses. Even reviewers recognized this dichotomy. Bennett wrote in 1901, "Size is the quality which most strongly and surely appeals to the imaginations of the multitude. . . . The attention of the whole crowd can only be caught by an audacious hugeness, an eye-smiting enormity of dimensions so gross as to be nearly physical. The unrivaled vogue of Miss Marie Corelli is partly due to the fact that her inventive faculty has always ranged easily and unafraid amid the largest things" (83). An anonymous reviewer put it more simply: "Democracy has not a discriminating taste. . . . Marie Corelli is clever enough to be a perfect literary purveyor to public taste. As an artist she paints with a brush as big as a bill-sticker's" ("Miss Marie Corelli").

Socially, too, the greenery-yallery Grosvenor Gallery foot-in-the-grave young man was Corelli's nemesis, for this parasitic Oxonian was how ordinary people had come to view literary men in light of the aesthetic movement. Corelli herself mocked the type: "I met only yesterday a limp pale young man, who is both Ibsenite and Browningite and understands neither author about whom he professes to be crazed" (Corelli-Bentley Correspondence, 16 April 1890). An offhand comment by a minor character in a minor novel by Violet Hunt, *A Hard Woman* (1895), reveals just how the cultural stereotypes of aestheticism were being spun out in the year before Wilde's trials: "It's a very common type nowadays—the decadent type—the old head on young shoulders that our grandmothers always voted an impossibility. But what can you expect? It was allowed to leave Eton at sixteen, it lay about on sofas, and read French novels, and drank absinthe. It has been everywhere, and learned nothing; done everything and enjoyed nothing; lives for itself—and the choice of a necktie" (36–37). Even the aphoristic style of this passage smacks of Wilde's influence. Corelli's project was to create a persona in opposition to both the overeducated aesthete and the starving male *artiste manqué,* for to her middle-class work ethic, these poses were simply irresponsible. The literary life can be "the most healthful and happy life in the world" if the artist, "whether male or female, is neither dyspeptic nor bilious, nor afflicted with the incurable *ennui* of utter selfishness, nor addicted to dram and drug drinking" ("The Happy Life" 76). In an 1893 essay in the *Idler* she writes:

> It is an unromantic thing for an author to have had no literary
> vicissitudes. One cannot expect to be considered interesting unless
> one has come up to London with the proverbial solitary "shil-
> ling," and gone about hungry and footsore, begging from one
> hard-hearted publisher's house to another with one's perpetually-
> rejected manuscript under one's arm. One ought to have con-    ("My First
> sumed the "midnight oil"; to have "coined one's heart's blood"      Book" 239)
> (to borrow the tragic expression of a contemporary gentleman-
> novelist); to have sacrificed one's self-respect by metaphorical
> crawling on all-fours to the critical faculty; and to have become
> aesthetically cadaverous and blear-eyed through the action of in-
> spired dyspepsia.

Corelli was proud to have done none of these things; she simply worked patiently and wrote from the heart, and the public response was warm and rewarding. Corelli was the feminine alternative to the "aesthetically cadaverous" foot-in-the-grave young man: the healthy, earnest, hardworking woman writer, clear-eyed and unashamedly populist.

## Wormwood

Bentley frequently worried that some of Corelli's novels, because of their tone and subject matter, would either offend readers with their fervid exposures of adultery and vice or invite malice from critics who found her view of reality distorted. Corelli was fiercely defensive about both the morality and the honesty of her books and took herself very seriously as a writer: "I *must* be myself," she wrote to Bentley, "and if I write at all, I must be allowed to handle a subject my own way. . . . The strange things that happen in every day life perplex me—for if I were to put them in a novel, they would certainly be termed by you 'overdrawn' or 'improbable'—yet *there* they are—*existing,* and the novelist's plain mission is to draw from life. What is to be done? I feel quite wretched about myself—still *here I am*—the public has shown its liking for what I write and desires more" (March 1887). If Bentley feared that the book (it was *Thelma*) would be condemned by the critics, Corelli retaliated by calling his attention to her "artistic" competitors (among them the "sickening" H. Rider Haggard), as she did in 1890 when she published her melodramatic attack on absinthe-drinking Parisians, *Wormwood:* "The press that deifies a 'Rudyard Kipling' and hovers between fits of ecstasy and opprobrium over Zola and Tolstoi and Ibsen, is such an utterly worthless thing now-a-days to sway an author's fame one way or the other. The 'public' is a different matter. That has forgiven me my sins always, and I hope and believe it will understand my motive in having struck the key-note of French morbidness—the partial secret of national decay" (Corelli-Bentley Correspondence, 8 September 1890).

Can there be any doubt that Corelli viewed this novel as a moral reprimand to the decadent? Yet in her directions to Bentley she sounds like a contributor to the *Yellow Book:* "The covers of the book should be pale green: the colour of Absinthe, with the title running zig-zag across it in black letters—an adder or serpent twisted through the big *W*" (5 August 1890). The antidecadent novel is packaged as the very flower of decadence, even down to the color green, which Wilde popularized as the "sign of a subtle artistic temperament" ("Pen, Pencil and Poison" 324). She even sent a copy of *Wormwood* to that celebrator of decadence, Arthur Symons, apparently because she thought it would impress him (Symons, *Selected Letters* 76).

*Wormwood: A Drama of Paris* is an excellent example of middle-class curiosity about and appropriations of decadence. The novel dwells with horrified fascination on the widespread use of absinthe among Paris art-

ists and bohemians, the morbid imaginations of French poets and paint-
ers, and the erotic dimensions of crime. The narrator, Gaston Beauvais,
becomes an "absintheur" when his beloved Pauline confesses that she is
in love with her cousin, Silvion Guidèl, an exceptionally beautiful young
man who is studying to be a priest. Beauvais's first experience with "the
Green Fairy" is on the night Pauline has broken his heart, when he meets
the poor painter André Gessonex on the Champs-Elysées and ends up
drinking absinthe with him at a café. The rest of the novel describes the
moral deterioration of the narrator under the influence of absinthe: he
commits a foul murder, coolly witnesses two suicides, takes part in lurid
scenes at the morgue and the immoral cancan rage, and experiences horrible "brain phantasms" caused by the drug, including one that involves
a leopard with green eyes following him through the streets of Paris.

Corelli's stated intention in her "Special Preface" to the authorized American edition of *Wormwood* was to bring this "fatal brain-
degradation" before French authorities and so put an end to its destruc-
tive progress (4). But even her publisher worried that the novel would be
read less as a moral tonic than as an engrossing account of the Parisian
underworld of artists and absintheurs. Despite Corelli's status as a best-
selling novelist and her ostensible missionary purpose, *Wormwood* is
completely dependent on decadent tropes. She portrays Gessonex, for
instance, as the stereotypical debauchee, with long hair, "in strict adher-
ence to true artistic tradition," and a battered hat, soiled collar, and red
flannel tie (114). He is a "genius" but cannot sell his paintings because
the ignorant masses only want representational art: "I am not to blame if
these people who want to buy pictures have no taste! I cannot paint
Dutch interiors,—the carrot waiting to be peeled on the table,—the fat
old woman cutting onions for the *pot-au-feu* . . . I can only produce grand
art!" (114–15). Gessonex's story has a predictable trajectory. He paints a
magnificent dark painting of a priest wrenching open the coffin of the
woman he once loved, whose decomposed face is just visible. Written
beneath it in blood-red paint are the words *"O Dieu que j'abjure! Rends-
moi cette femme!"* (226). Gessonex declares that he would rather "starve
like a rat in a hole" than sell the painting to philistines. Later at a café,
while drinking absinthe, he tells Beauvais he envies an artist who drew a
political cartoon in the *Journal pour Rire*. *"You* envy the foul-minded

wretch who polluted his pencil with such a thing as that?" asks Beauvais. "Assuredly," Gessonex replies. "He dines, and I do not—he sleeps, and I do not,—he has a full purse,—mine is empty!—and strangest anomaly of all, because he pays his way he is considered respectable,—while I, not being able to pay my way, am judged as quite the reverse! Foul-minded? Polluted? Tut, *mon cher!* there is no foul-mindedness nowadays except lack of cash—and the only pollution possible to the modern artist's pencil is to use it on work that does not *pay!*" (266–67). After this speech Gessonex calmly walks over to a kiosk, picks up the *Journal pour Rire,* laughs harshly at the cartoon, and shoots himself with a pistol. To guarantee his fame, he has bequeathed his masterpiece to France.

This episode is more complex than I am allowing, for throughout the novel Corelli offers competing interpretations of artists. Although Gessonex is unappreciated by the vulgar masses while he is alive, Corelli portrays his addiction to absinthe, his filthy lodgings, and his trips to the morgue as repulsive. For Corelli even aesthetic feeling cannot excuse such a life. And when Beauvais becomes obsessed with viewing Pauline's corpse at the morgue, after driving her to suicide, he ironically justifies his compulsion not as an absintheur but as an aesthete: "The girl, though dead, is beautiful! I am an artist!—I have the soul of a poet! . . . I love beauty—and I study it wherever I find it, dead or living" (321).

Like many Corelli novels, *Wormwood* is stocked with biting allusions to the school of Zola, that "literary scavenger of Paris" whose "pitchfork pen turns up under men's nostrils such literary garbage as loads the very air with stench and mind-malaria!" (280, 237). But *Wormwood* also cites appreciatively and at length the verse of French decadent writers. The most conspicuous example is that of the poet and inventor Charles Cros, a friend of Arthur Rimbaud's who reportedly drank twenty absinthes a day and died in 1888 at the age of forty-six (Barnaby Conrad 47). Beauvais recalls the first stanza of a poem by Cros:

(130)     *Avec l'absinthe, avec le feu*
          *On peut se divertir un peu*
          *Jouer son rôle en quelque drâme!*

In a book condemning the effects of absinthe, it seems peculiar to insert verse evoking its seductive powers. Even more paradoxical is Corelli's footnote about Cros, a gloss on another poem she quotes in full. There is no question that she writes here not as Beauvais but as Marie Corelli:

> *This exquisite poem, entitled "L'Archet" . . . was written by*
> *one CHARLES CROS, a French poet, whose distinctly great*
> *abilities were never encouraged or recognized in his lifetime.*
> *Young and still full of promise, he died quite recently in Paris,*
> *surrounded by the very saddest circumstances of suffering, poverty,*　(55)
> *and neglect. The grass has scarcely had time to grow long or rank*
> *enough over his grave; when it has, the critics of his country will*
> *possibly take up his book . . . and call the attention of France to a*
> *perished genius.*

Even though Corelli must have known Cros was addicted to absinthe and a follower of Rimbaud and Paul Verlaine, she was susceptible to the myth of "perished genius." And she places the responsibility for honoring Cros's genius on the critics who will gather public recognition, even though later in *Wormwood* the narrator lashes out at the so-called experts: "I ought to keep to the thread of my story, ought I not, dear critics of the press?—you who treat every narrative, true or imaginative, that goes into print, as a *gourmet* treats a quail, leaving nothing on the plate but a fragment of picked bone which you present to the public and call it a 'review!' *Ah mes garçons!*—take care! . . . The Public itself is the Supreme Critic now,—its 'review' does not appear in print, but nevertheless its unwritten verdict declares itself with . . . an amazing weight of influence" (295). The contradictions and paradoxical treatments of Parisian decadence in *Wormwood* exemplify the problems of cultural classifications, for surely in this last outburst on the "Supreme Critic" Corelli has her own ax to grind.

## The Sorrows of Satan

In 1895 and 1896 Corelli was famous enough to devote two novels, *The Sorrows of Satan* and *The Murder of Delicia,* to her views on the literary life, critics, commercial popularity, and, significantly, sexuality and gender. In both novels she does not spare the reader her scorn for the immorality of modern art and literature. *The Sorrows of Satan* is especially successful at conjuring decadence while condemning decadent tendencies, creatively playing out this fissured aesthetic in its coincidental treatment of a corrupt masculine literary world, New Women novels, and wholesome popular literature. Corelli's opinions on these literary matters are unmistakable, if not glaring. W. T. Stead, the editor of the *Review of Reviews,* wrote a twelve-page essay on the novel, asserting that half the book is about "the sorrows of Marie Corelli" as she "goes for her adversaries" in the literary market (453). There is plenty of personal outrage in the book, to be sure. But *The Sorrows of Satan* also exploits the more titillating characteristics of decadence and, by connection, the New Woman novel, since the two were often conflated in Victorian literary discourse. It accommodates sexually transgressive attitudes with startling suggestiveness. As Stead says, "it is very much uncurtained indeed, nor would it be surprising if an unthinking reader mistook 'The Sorrows of Satan' for what its author describes as 'the loathliest of the prurient novels that have been lately written by women to degrade and shame their sex'" (454). The novel irresistibly challenges apparently immutable and antithetical genres, styles, and audiences. It plays on both male aesthetes and male homosexuality and the "unwomanly" New Woman, the two "abnormal" types, according to Teresa Mangum, who were accused "of threatening the survival of the human race" with their sexual and social demands (50). On the surface, Corelli's best-seller seeks to deflate these fears and reassure readers of the essential functions of men and women sexually and socially. But it also encodes sexual dissidence as enthusiastically as more self-consciously political texts. In fact, its exploitation of sexual dissidence may be partly responsible for its status as a best-seller.

The Sorrows of Satan is a melodrama set in modern London "swagger" society, where Satan, the wealthy, handsome, and charming prince Lucio Rimânez, pulls strings in the publishing world and throws lavish parties for the English upper crust. The hero and narrator is Geoffrey Tempest, a struggling novelist, who suddenly inherits five million pounds at the same time he receives a letter of introduction to the prince. Tempest finds Lucio fascinating, if somewhat cynical, and the two become close companions as Lucio introduces Tempest into fashionable London society and helps "boom" his novel, which succeeds in making Tempest famous, though sales remain low. Lucio, a savage misogynist, arranges Tempest's marriage to an heiress, the beautiful but cold Lady Sibyl Elton, who has been corrupted by reading New Women novels. Again with Lucio's help, Tempest buys Willowsmere in Warwickshire, the childhood home of Lady Sibyl. Their neighbor in Lily Cottage is the novelist Mavis Clare, who writes wholesome books and is much loved by the masses though she is always "slashed" by reviewers: the doves in her dovecote are named "The Westminster Gazette," "The Pall Mall," and so on, and she cheerfully feeds her reviews to her dog. In the novel's most melodramatic scene Lady Sibyl declares her passion for Lucio and offers herself to him. When he brutally scorns her, she swallows poison. In her sensational autobiographical suicide note, which takes up two chapters and is partly a posthumous composition, Sibyl explains that her training for the marriage market, combined with reading new fiction and too much Swinburne at an impressionable age, blackened her soul and chilled her heart: "Between their strained aestheticism and unbridled sensualism, my spirit has been stretched on the rack and broken on the wheel" (404). Distraught by his wife's death, Tempest agrees to travel to the East with Lucio. They are on his yacht (*The Flame*) when, in the book's wildest and most overwritten chapters, Lucio reveals his identity and demands Tempest's allegiance; Tempest chooses God instead and is abandoned in the mid-Atlantic. He is picked up by an English steamer and learns that his bankers have absconded with his millions. Back in London, Tempest is again poor but chastened, doing "battle with the monster, Egotism, that presented itself in a thousand disguises" (468). A venomous critic digs out his book from Mudie's underground cellar and "slashes" it, but the capricious public suddenly finds it worthwhile and buys it by the thousands. Mavis Clare's new book is also abused in the reviews, but it is "borne along to fame by a great wave of honest public praise and enthusiasm" (468). The novel ends at the houses of Parliament, with Satan walking arm in arm with a well-known cabinet minister.

*The Sorrows of Satan* was an immediate best-seller, a fact that some critics felt portended the end of good taste among literate British subjects. Wells referred to it along with Sarah Grand's *The Heavenly Twins* and Emma Frances Brooke's *A Superfluous Woman* as a book that points to the "debasing influence of the female" in modern fiction (74). Corelli, of course, would have been appalled to find her novel grouped with New Women books by Grand and Brooke! *The Sorrows of Satan* is a self-righteous corrective to such trends and the "debasing" literature Wells and other male critics so disliked—indeed, Corelli distinctly implies that her "strong-minded" or "Aesthetic" literary competitors are directly responsible for the woman reader's damnation. At the same time, the novel is a passionate defense of women's place in the literary world, exemplified by the redemptive Mavis Clare, whose "delicate attractiveness," "golden halo," and "tender, wistful, wonderfully innocent eyes" refute sexist stereotypes about literary women and give femininity an esteemed place in the book wars (222, 252).

Corelli appears untroubled by these conflicting views of women: her disdain for the strong-minded woman does not preclude her insistence on the independence of the literary woman. In a similar way, *The Sorrows of Satan* resists assignment to a single genre. Wells groups it with *Trilby* and New Women novels not necessarily because Corelli's text belongs to either aestheticism or feminism but because it participates in the vogue for inferior books "whose relation to life is of the slightest, and whose connection with Art is purely accidental" (74). In this case, Corelli's indulgence of the late-Victorian taste for the strange and the sinful is excoriated as lurid and effeminate trash, opposed to "strong" realists such as Zola, who, says Corelli, "prostituted his powers to the lowest grade of thought" (*Free Opinions* 277).

Despite all of this, *The Sorrows of Satan* is definitely in collusion with decadence, a movement dominated by young men. One aspect of decadent literature, according to Max Beerbohm, is "a love of horror and all unusual things" (quoted in Beckson 66). Corelli's book certainly qualifies here and incorporates many other fin-de-siècle tendencies: the exotic, mysticism, dream sequences, Egyptology, French verse and phrases, strange music, eroticism (including homoeroticism), suicide, and, not least, purple prose. Just as she cites decadent French verse in *Wormwood,* Corelli describes the irreparable harm of Algernon Charles Swinburne's "Before a Crucifix" by producing four of the most offensive stanzas (394–95). The topicality of the novel is another feature that makes it similar to new fiction. It indulges the bourgeois reader's curiosity about London high society with its operas, dinners, and gambling dens, makes references to recognizable literary and dramatic people, and is very up-to-date in its use of slang.

*The Sorrows of Satan* strains after a bourgeois ethic as opposed to decadence and strains to accept Victorian constructions of gender. But the many references to women who are "unsexed" and to men who are "effeminate," as well as Corelli's use of a male narrator, undermine the novel's attempt at sexual stratification. The implicit homoeroticism between Lucio and Tempest certainly brings to mind Lord Henry and Dorian in *The Picture of Dorian Gray*. From the first, Tempest is fascinated by Lucio's beauty, especially his wonderful eyes, which are as "large and lustrous as the eyes of a beautiful woman" (82). I could cite dozens of examples: "He clapped me on the shoulder cordially and looked straight into my face,—those wonderful eyes of his . . . fixed me with a clear masterful gaze that completely dominated me. I made no attempt to resist the singular attraction which now possessed me for this man whom I had but just met,—the sensation was too strong and too pleasant to be combated" (29). One scene is particularly illustrative of Tempest's submerged desire for Lucio, and it is incidentally a good example of the decadent fashion Corelli exploits. When Lucio plays a "piercing sword-like tune" on the piano, Tempest's reaction is unmistakably sexual: "My breath failed me,—my senses swam,—I felt that I must move, speak, cry out, and implore this music, this horribly insidious music should cease ere I swooned with the voluptuous poison of it." When the music finally ends, Tempest feels that "something . . . had instilled itself into my blood, or so I fancied, and the clinging subtle sweetness of [the music], moved me to strange emotions that were neither wise nor worthy of a man" (151). To him the music suggests "Crime! You have roused in me evil thoughts of which I am ashamed." Lucio smilingly replies, "If you discover evil suggestions in my music, the evil, I fear, must be in your own nature." Tempest gazes at Lucio, and "for one moment his great personal beauty appeared hateful to me, though I know not why." The modern reader thinks she does. The reference to an unspecified crime and Tempest's humiliation at having unworthy emotions resonate in a novel published just six months after the notorious trials of Oscar Wilde. (Corelli was worried that the trials would distract interest from her latest book.) The oblique allusion is highlighted a page later when Lord Elton dismisses modern poets as "effeminate, puling, unmanly humbugs!" (153). As Alan Sinfield has explained, the Wilde trials circulated an image not only of homosexuality but of aestheticism itself as effeminate, degenerate, and aristocratic. That Corelli's suddenly aristocratic hero appears to battle homosexual desires illustrates the incipient link between wealthy, university-educated literary men and homosexual tendencies. This connection is mitigated in several ways, most obviously through the "purchase" of a beautiful and highly sexed heiress, whom Tempest displays as testimony to his virility. He also makes many manly statements, such as "A man is always a man,—a woman is only a man's appendage, and without beauty she can not put forth any just claim to his admiration or support" (42). He is most virulent when it comes to successful literary women, such as Mavis Clare, and he takes delight in "slashing" her new book, significantly titled *Differences*. He, by comparison, is a sellout and a literary whore: "My book . . . haunted my days and nights with its lustful presence" (177). To prove his masculinity he joins "in every sort of dissipation common to men of the day," which is Corelli's critique of upper-class vice but also exposes the constraints of Victorian gender ideology. Tempest gambles "solely for the reason that gambling was considered . . . indicative of 'manliness' and 'showing *grit*'" (175). He frequents low houses with "half-nude brandy-soaked dancers" "because this kind of thing was called 'seeing life' and was deemed part of a 'gentleman's' diversion" (175). His exaggerated efforts to appear manly suggest a fear of sexual inadequacy. He compares himself with "a fidgety woman" and later, after his marriage, admits that he gives way to his "brute passions" because he fears his lustful wife will sneer at him as an "effeminate milksop" were he to suggest they "reform."

Suggestions of the hero's effeminacy, of a man who must prove his heterosexuality and conform to social codes of masculinity, are counterparts to suggestions of the progressive woman's sexlessness. Corelli here engages the ongoing conversation about women's changing roles, and while she clearly disapproves of assertions about women's intellectual and biological inferiority, she deplores the sexual entrepreneurship of the New Woman, which is responsible for the erosion of Christian idealism and the degeneration of true womanly virtues. This is Satan's brand of misogyny: "And why I especially abominate them is, that they have been gifted with an enormous power for doing good, and that they let this power run to waste and will not use it. Their deliberate enjoyment of the repulsive, vulgar and commonplace side of life disgusts me. They are much less sensitive than men, and infinitely more heartless. They are the mothers of the human race, and the faults of the race are chiefly due to them. That is another reason for my hatred" (84).

Sally Ledger has explained that although New Women and decadents had little in common politically they "were repeatedly lumped together in the flourishing periodical press of the 1890s" (94); New Women writers were threatening "daughters of decadence" whose avant-garde attacks on marriage overtly challenged Victorian sexual codes (Showalter, *Daughters of Decadence* ix). Importantly, New Woman fiction creates a continuum between exclusive heterosexuality and exclusive homosexuality that suggests a threatening indeterminacy, an inability to align with either sexuality. Corelli's "decadent" New Woman, Sibyl Elton, is in *this* novel but a product of *that* fiction. Sibyl declares, "I despise men,—I despise my own sex,—I loathe myself for being a woman!" (198). Her friends recommend books that are "so dreadfully *queer*," books about "outcasts" and "the secret vices of men" (197). Sibyl's intense admiration for Mavis Clare—she has an ecstatic vision of the writer's face before she dies—and her raging heterosexuality point to an identity crisis. Sibyl suffers no moral pangs when she throws herself at the charismatic Lucio because in these days "nobody can decide as to what *is* vice, or what *is* virtue" (39). This deplorable relativism is largely due to "all the 'new' writers of profitable pruriency" (361). We should keep in mind that this "new" literature was chiefly a critique of the double standard and therefore interpreted as a subversive attack on Victorian gender roles. Nineteenth-century political and social stability relied to a large extent on maintaining the doctrine of separate spheres for men and women. Satan sees the biological consequences for the race in this disintegration of gender identities: "As for the tom-boy tennis players and giantesses of the era, I do not consider them women at all. They are merely the unnatural embryos of a new sex which will be neither male nor female" (82).

Advanced women, like aesthete men, crossed ideological gender lines, and sometimes the two types became blurred in the figuration of another freak of nature: the woman writer. Later, Tempest and Lucio return to the subject:

> "*Literary women are my abhorrence,—they are always more or less unsexed.*"
>
> "*You are thinking of the 'New' women, I suppose,—but you flatter them,—they never had any sex to lose. The self-de-* (216) *grading creatures who delineate their fictional heroines as wallowing in unchastity, and who write freely on subjects which men would hesitate to name, are unnatural hybrids of no-sex.*"

The exception to these hybrid literary creatures is the exaggeratedly feminine Mavis Clare: she is the "'old-fashioned' young woman," a paradoxical description Corelli would no doubt apply to herself. But the name of Mavis Clare's latest best-seller, as I have mentioned, is *Differences,* which strikes me as far from old-fashioned; it is a stylish 1890s title, comparable to *Cameos, Keynotes, Discords, Silverpoints, Caprices.*[3] We are never told what her novel is about, though we receive broad hints of its uplifting nature: "Clearness of thought, brilliancy of style, beauty of diction, all these were hers, united to consummate ease of expression and artistic skill" (170). The title, however, suggests a contribution to the discourse on the collapse of gender differences initiated by New Women and dandies, as well as the visibility given to homosexuality after Wilde's trials. Mavis Clare's *Differences* and Marie Corelli's insinuation that her novels are "different" from degenerate new fiction rely on the simmering tensions in the late-Victorian literary world, with its categorical oppositions of high and low fiction, of the intellectually pure male writer and the "debasing" yet popular female writer. Corelli attempts in this novel to reverse these stereotypes, but as we have seen, the text resists her polemical intentions.

Although the novel is unquestionably a conservative reaction to the prevailing ideological confusion about gender, *The Sorrows of Satan* is not simply about gender retrenchment, nor is it a simple repudiation of aestheticism and the New Woman. It is, in fact, deeply involved in the debates about sexual differences; in the context of these observations, Corelli's choice of a male narrator deserves some attention.

It was not uncommon for New Women and decadent female writers to choose the male point of view, either to comment ironically on the male perspective or to explore the male experience (Nelson 3). Rita Felski has argued that Corelli's frequent choice of a male narrator allowed her "greater narrative license to explore the erotically thrilling dimensions of feminine beauty than would otherwise have been possible" (*Gender of Modernity* 131). This suggests that the male narrator permits an expression of homoerotic fantasies for women readers. But because the grammatical gender of the narrator in a Victorian novel is ideologically constructed, Corelli's masculine, objectifying, frequently misogynistic voice itself embodies a critique of masculinity. Although Tempest's egotism, materialism, and moral cowardice are linked to his suddenly becoming a millionaire, his fierce competitiveness in the literary world, especially his absolute hatred for women writers, raises questions about cultural authority. "I never paid any attention to the names of women who chose to associate themselves with the Arts," says Tempest, "as I had the usual masculine notion that all they did, whether in painting, music, or writing, must be necessarily trash, and unworthy of comment. Women, I loftily considered, were created to amuse men,—not to instruct them" (137). Corelli, of course, inserts Mavis Clare as a rejoinder to Tempest's insufferable sexism. But if the portrait of Mavis Clare is a conspicuous and idealized self-dramatization and yet the voice of the novel is male, one could say "Marie Corelli" appears in this novel discursively as both a man and a woman (and, given the long first-person suicide note from Sibyl, even as a degenerate New Woman!). Thus instead of constituting sexual binarisms, the fluidity and constructedness of these identities ride out the indeterminacies the novel ostensibly fears.

### Art for Profit

*The Sorrows of Satan* goes after Victorian society with both barrels and not much subtlety: corrupt publishers, greedy advertisers, literary snobs, religious hypocrites and heartless atheists, aristocratic scoundrels, Darwinists, feminist extremists, and, not least, minor poets and writers of new fiction are targets of Corelli's reformist zeal. The novel seems to crave bourgeois sanity and health in this "decadent, ephemeral age" when "Art is made subservient to the love of money" (78). Much can be made of Corelli's defensiveness and personal prejudices: powerful literary men such as Andrew Lang ("McWhing") are represented as transparently corrupt; literary elitism is exposed as antidemocratic whining ("The public only cares for trash." "It is a pity you should appeal to them" [80]); the notion that legitimate literature is written only by poor and struggling authors is revealed as a self-serving fiction (81). When the devil asserts that if a writer wants to be talked about, he needs to be "a judicious mixture of Zola, Huysmans, and Baudelaire," Corelli targets not only the immorality of French decadents and their English imitators but also the depraved critics who scout them (63).

But what is equally interesting is how this novel harps on the commercialization of art: it is *The Picture of Dorian Gray* meets Gissing's *New Grub Street* (1891). The link between money, class, and artistic success is one of its controlling themes, but Corelli's concern is not with the struggling hack or the bohemian outcast. Her attempt to resolve the familiar conflict between the art value of autonomous literary texts and the money value of commodities relies on a valorization of the artist not as neglected genius, as in *Wormwood,* but as middle-class hero.

Geoffrey Tempest is a gentleman's son who emerges from Oxford with an idealistic desire for higher things, particularly the pursuit of literature. He soon discovers that society despises ardent young writers and that he cannot live by doing " 'hack work' for the dailies" (8). Starving and poor, he finds that the music emanating from a violin in the room next door appeals to "the sensuous and aesthetic part" of his nature (13). Tempest is the familiar type of the sensitive, outcast artist, even down to his ulster, which is "an artistic mildewy green" (29). When he inherits his millions, however, he decides to gain revenge on the harsh industry that rejected his work and publishes his book himself, while Satan helps "boom" it in prestigious journalistic circles. But his wealth and renown do not make Tempest happy; he has picturesque recollections of his former life: "I saw myself worn and hungry, shabbily clothed, bending over my writing in my dreary lodging, wretched, yet amid all my wretchedness receiving comfort from my own thoughts, which created beauty out of penury, and love out of loneliness" (72). Here is the familiar starving artist, poor yet hardworking and noble in spirit. Significantly, the book he writes when he is poor "propounded sentiments and inculcated theories" that he does not consciously believe, chiefly faith in God and in man's divine soul. Tempest's book seems to have been unconsciously influenced by a nobler instinct.

The crux of the problem is that starving in a garret is not the route to fame, but on the other hand, wealth can corrupt, which also makes for bad art. Tempest's atheism and literary egotism surface when he becomes wealthy, showing the moral harm caused by both the commercialization of art and the seductions of wealth. Even though Tempest wishes to win fame legitimately, Satan tells him, "You can't! It's impossible. You are too rich. That in itself is not legitimate in Literature,—which great art generally elects to wear poverty in its buttonhole as a flower of grace" (81). This is a stab at the aesthete's (and later, the modernist's) supposition that the serious artist is contemptuous of money. But economic class does not necessarily define literature; neither who buys a book nor who writes it constitutes literary value. A more cynical view underlies the obsessive conversations in this novel about art and social stratification: the literary industry is self-contained and self-perpetuating; the "six leading men who do the reviews" and their "comfortable little fraternal union" are the real cultural authorities (100, 102).

Corelli has to attack several contradictions here: middle-class society may romanticize the artist who wears poverty in his buttonhole, but this genius will not be rewarded if his works are not well received by influential publishers. On the other hand, genius cannot be secured through buying up advertisers. "I am one of those who think the fame of Millais as an artist was marred when he degraded himself to the level of painting the little green boy blowing bubbles of Pears' soap. That was an advertisement," Tempest says pretentiously (99). Obviously, the dichotomy of high and low is connected with economics as much as with aesthetics.

With *The Sorrows of Satan* Corelli began her policy of not sending out review copies; she placed a special notice on page 1: "Members of the press will therefore obtain it . . . in the usual way with the rest of the public, i.e., through the Booksellers and Libraries." She places her faith in the tastes of the middle-class public, because then success is unmediated by critics and their assumptions of readers' social status. Mavis Clare represents the provincial writer who balances commercial success and artistic worth. She is inexplicably well loved. "She always 'takes' and no one can help it," says one bookseller. "You see people have got Compulsory Education now, and I'm afraid they begin to mistrust criticism, preferring to form their own independent opinions; if this is so, of course it will be a terrible thing, because the most carefully organized clique in the world will be powerless" (207–8). The seditious assumptions in this remark suggest that much is at stake—recall Wells's comparing the effects of mass education with those of the French Revolution. But with all of its decadent borrowings and allusions to the end of the world, its fierce attacks on wastefulness and privilege, its anguish at the gulf between rich and poor, and its criticism of every utterance opposed to the intelligence and good sense of the people, *The Sorrows of Satan* is far from revolutionary, for Corelli did not admire radicalism. The tolerant middle-class worker, represented in this novel by Mavis Clare and her faith in "the dignity of Literature as an art and a profession" (308), is the true redeemer of modern culture.

This last remark reflects Corelli's own belief, and it sounds quixotic, to say the least, when we consider the rivalries and the categorical judgments of the period. Conrad wrote in 1898 that "philistines" are "the sort of people who read Marie Corelli and Hall Caine" and contemptuously excluded both popular novelists from Parnassus: "Neither of these writers belong to literature" (137). Compare this attitude of literary segregationism with Corelli's express desire for "*fraternity* among all these followers of Art—a bond of joyous and sympathetic union" (Corelli-Bentley Correspondence, 6 April 1887). In some moods she almost appears willing to surrender her individual authorship, her identity, and her literary fame to the transcendent claims of art. She wrote earnestly to Bentley, "After all, literature is the edifice, and authors only the working masons—if each one can add a fresh brick or stone to the building, that is something—and the builders should be too intent on the whole architecture to pause for an instant to criticize each other" (6 April 1887).

Corelli wrote this letter in the spring of 1887 when she was finishing *Thelma,* her third novel; she had only appeared in London literary society the year before, after the success of *A Romance of Two Worlds.* Perhaps she was disappointed by the intellectual vanity or the antipopulist feeling she encountered among some of the writers she met at dinners and literary salons. She felt sorry that Eliza Lynn Linton had "sacrificed all the tendernesses of the heart to the power of *intellect*" (Corelli-Bentley Correspondence, 23 February 1887), that Robert Browning was so conceited (Corelli-Bentley Correspondence, 1 January 1887), and although she claimed to like Meredith personally, she disapproved of his opinion of the reading public. There is no question that Corelli could be as stingy about her intellectual property, and as competitive, as any writer of the period—the viciousness of *The Silver Domino* is certainly uncalled for, and Corelli hurt and alienated many people, including George Bentley. We have seen that she was often critical of other authors: Rhoda Broughton's "plots are slight" (Corelli-Bentley Correspondence, 23 November 1886), and Mrs. Humphry Ward's best-seller *Robert Elsmere* has "no plot in it" (Corelli-Bentley Correspondence, 20 April 1888), a "dull book, devoid of incident, and gloomy in the impression it leaves on the mind" (Corelli-Bentley Correspondence, 6 March 1888). She was also fiercely protective of her rights and her deserts. But a sympathetic person could see Corelli as being more or less forced into this position by circumstances. And her literary judgments were based on her own inclinations and literary tastes, which tended toward the voluptuous, the dramatic, the sensational. If these tastes are middle-class, then so be it: for many people *Robert Elsmere is* slow going, and for some readers *Diana of the Crossways* can be difficult to enjoy (Corelli-Bentley Correspondence, 14 May 1886). Despite her opinions about other writers, for Corelli rivalry, superficial evaluations of artistic merit, and arbitrary designations of "genius" are all forms of elitism. They are fundamentally social and political judgments, a residual part of the opposition of the suburban bourgeois and the cosmopolitan aesthete generated by art for art's sake.

Even if there is no place in aestheticism for Corelli's idiom of democratic cooperation in the name of art, the attitude of *service* to art, to something higher, is strikingly similar to, say, Flaubert's claim that it is one's "duty" to pursue art or Wilde's pose as a worshiper of beauty. David Weir has discussed how the aesthete's attitude may be construed as either an elitist rejection of democracy *or* "radical self-reliance and the expression of intense individualism" (93). Corelli's popularity with the middle class and her faith in her own genius, not to mention persecutions from masculine literary cliques, exemplify how the aesthetic pose could cut both ways—even for a writer who is not usually identified with aestheticism. Thus in *The Murder of Delicia* (1896) Delicia Vaughan's novels uplift her readers because she herself embodies virtue: her *moral* superiority (with which Corelli closely identifies) brings her literary fame, compared with the vile band of male critics, reviewers, reporters, and paragraphists who lounge around The Bohemian, a London literary club. These pretenders dismiss Delicia as one of the "female *poseurs* in literature, whose works chiefly appeal to readers up Brixton and Clapham way" (76). In this novel Corelli's scorn is directed at self-promoting fakes who adopt the attitude of the fashionable aesthete in an effort to win approval from gullible publishers and readers. The evocatively named Aubrey Grovelyn is one of these phonies, "a long-haired 'poet' who wrote his own reviews" (98). "This son of the Muses" is "an untidy, dirty-looking man" who sets himself up to be (what else?) "a genius" (98). But, Corelli notes, the public sees he is a humbug and avoids his books "as cautiously as though they had been labeled 'Poison'" (99).

*The Murder of Delicia* is almost entirely without irony. Corelli writes with the bitterness of an outsider, and by 1896 she had had enough of insulting reviewers and sexist critics. If she is partly in sympathy with aesthetic doctrines in her commitment to art and her mythology of artists, her love of spirituality and the imagination, and her critiques of commercialism, she is also in collusion with a consumer society that had become very successful at condensing and marketing ideas. Despite the emergence of distinctions between high and low art at the turn into modernism, these categories were still under revision, and borrowings from aestheticism are ubiquitous in mass fiction, just as aestheticism—and certainly modernism—borrows from middle-class tastes and habits. If Corelli could use Charles Cros and Swinburne, James Joyce could incorporate aspects of *The Sorrows of Satan* into *Ulysses*—indeed, the Joyce scholar R. B. Kershner has claimed that Corelli's novel had a "horrible fascination" for Joyce. As artists, writes Kershner, "Corelli and Joyce stand at the start of our century, . . . busy writing and acting out the myth of themselves" ("Joyce and Popular Literature" 54, 57).

Corelli's participation in the literary trends of the 1890s supports the idea of decadence as an *aesthetic* category that falls *socially* between romantic bohemia and avant-garde belle epoque: "Sometimes the decadent may pursue a bohemian life-style, but he always imagines himself a cultural aristocrat, while being, at base, thoroughly bourgeoisie" (Weir xv). Corelli was the beckoning siren of the bourgeoisie, and she was able to construe the aesthete's antibourgeois pose into a thwarted longing for bourgeois simplicity. Suburbia and Victorian mass-commodity fiction shared the contempt of the cultural elite, and yet, as Holbrook Jackson wrote in 1913, eventually "even poets fell before the seductions of suburban life. . . . Bohemians cut their locks, shed their soft collars and fell back upon Suburbia" (116). Esmé Amarinth, the aesthetic hero of Robert Hichens's satire *The Green Carnation* (1894), utters a lament that is the epitaph to aestheticism's elitist pretensions: "I have been an aesthete. I have lain upon hearth-rugs and eaten passion-flowers. I have clothed myself in breeches of white samite, and offered my friends yellow jonquils instead of afternoon tea. But when aestheticism became popular in Bayswater—a part of London built for the delectation of the needy-rich—I felt that it was absurd no longer, and I turned to other things" (196).

By the middle of the decade shocking books and notorious ideas had become assimilated into the suburban world of convenience and decency. A critic of the new fiction writing in the *Westminster Gazette* in 1895 could assert that the once scandalous "yellow-back" novels had been left behind "in a kind of stranded respectability, for the consolation of those households which the emancipated youth calls 'suburban'" (Spender 82). Appropriately enough, the first planned garden suburb, Bedford Park, was built in the 1870s as a kind of artists' colony and satirized as the "Aesthetic Elysium" (Lambourne 86–87). Even Symons admitted that "the desire to 'bewilder the middle classes' is itself middle-class" (*Symbolist Movement* 4). As it became more and more difficult to bewilder the bourgeoisie, the aesthete eventually gave way to the high modernist, who achieved intellectual segregation not by trying to be shocking but by trying to be difficult.

Ironically, Corelli's novels sometimes bewildered *both* the middle class and the intellectuals—they certainly bewildered Bentley, who often tried to rein in her imagination. One has only to read her long and passionate letters about *Ardath,* a book Bentley apparently thought too esoteric to meet public approval, to appreciate her unshakable faith in her own imaginative powers. In fact, Corelli intuitively knew the public much better than her publisher did. Whereas Bentley was appalled by the violence, lust, and immorality she describes with such melodramatic energy, she insisted to him that readers would accept her work because it is "drawn from *actual life*" (March 1887), that "people crave and *thirst* for the very discussions in my book, which *you* desire to curtail" (13 March 1889), that an artist cannot "paint a lurid subject in soft colours" (8 September 1890). She expressed her regret to Bentley that the hero of *Wormwood* "talks of the Creator in a way that shocks you" (8 September 1890), and she was hurt when he called *Vendetta* "hideous and repulsive" and deplored the "ugly peeps into vice" of *Thelma* (March 1887). Possibly Bentley's reactions were due as much to his refined tastes as to a concern for Mrs. Grundy. Corelli was probably right when she suspected that Bentley did not like her as a writer (Corelli-Bentley Correspondence, March 1887); her books would not appeal to the urbane Victorian man of letters. Still, in her heated response to his criticism of *Thelma* as "repulsive," Corelli implicitly demonstrates that critical acclaim *is* attached to social status. Not only is the bohemian artist a romantic myth, but no artist would choose to live like a bohemian:

(16 March
1887)

*You speak of "repulsiveness"—; look at the success of Rider Haggard!*
*He literally wades, not in society, but blood and savagery of the most*
*unreal and inhuman kind—his books sell by thousands, and he has*
*gone comfortably off to Egypt on the proceeds, which I wish I could do!*
*Zola, again—he gives the best dinners in Paris,—"Ouida" lives like*
*a princess in her Villa at Fiesole,—compare me with these successful*
*writers, and can you say I am "terribly coarse." . . . If I had offered*
*you such an improbable story with all its sickening details as, "King*
*Solomon's Mines"—I am quite certain you would have objected to it.*
*Or "She" . . . Take even George Sand's famous "Indiana" which*
*made her name—I would not dare to offer you a novel grounded on*
*such lines. And yet I can frankly say there are no limits to my imagina-*
*tion,—to let my pen run riot would be my joy, and I believe the result*
*would be worthy of perusal.*

H. Rider Haggard, Zola, George Sand, and Ouida are a motley assort-
ment to group together, writers who worked in genres ranging from
fantastic tales of adventure to scientific naturalism to silver-fork romance,
but they were all living pretty well, going on vacations, giving nice dinners. Considering her family's perpetual financial embarrassments, it is
surely ironic that the first sentence of *The Sorrows of Satan* is "Do you
know what it is to be poor?" Who wants to suffer for art, after all? Despite
her claim that she would continue to write even if she were "a Rothschild," Corelli appears to long for membership in this elite group and
knew that economic success would help get her there.

Furthermore, Corelli was quite right to berate her publisher for his
prudish fear of going too far when the public was buying up Zola and
*King Solomon's Mines.* It is important to bear in mind that she did not
wish to shock or offend her readers, and she was certainly not alienated
from them. Letting her pen "run riot" does not mean violating middle-
class standards of decency, but having the liberty to honor the truth
of her imaginative vision. All accusations of profiteering (Conrad's, for
example, when he claimed she was "puffed in the press"), or of compro-
mising her artistic standards to appease either a publisher or an audience,
are false. Corelli was the late-Victorian incarnation of artistic integrity.
Like a true aesthete, she would rather surrender her vocation than be false
to her vision: "For to alter my work is to alter myself—to become a

servant of the public taste, instead of the *expressor* of instinctive thought; I *cannot* do this for fame or money. What is to be done? . . . Write on, or cease writing? it is a question that must be seriously considered, as I am not content to be like others, but wholly different" (Corelli–Bentley Correspondence, 13 March 1889). On 14 March 1889 she again insisted to Bentley, "I have not pandered to any passing popular taste for 'sensationals' and 'adventures'—I have imitated no one, but have striven after the highest ideals and the most original treatment—moreover I have tried to speak truths that are not often expressed."

There are so many letters written in this tone of urgent sincerity or pleading acceptance that I find it impossible to suspect Corelli's honesty. Such assertions are made repeatedly in her correspondence with Bentley, interspersed evenly and without apparent inconsistency with business and money matters, requests for advertisements, literary gossip, and expressions of gratitude. Brian Masters calls this writer's pride: "She did not pause to construct a pretence of self-confidence; she was hurt in her most tender part, that frail pride which any writer must try to protect, pride in his work" (73). But why *should* she "construct a pretence" of confidence if she believed in her gifts? These letters are extraordinarily bold, fearlessly self-assured. Again and again she reassured Bentley that *Ardath,* to take just one example, would not fail; again and again she insisted on her imaginative integrity, "my brain teems with ideas, but what are ideas, if I may not work them out according to my nature" (14 March 1889). I agree that Corelli had a writer's pride, even a writer's egomania, but she was not entirely blinded by vanity. She wrote with full knowledge of the implications of her publisher's judgments as both a man of letters and a businessman: "You *know* that even if I had written *trash* the public would still demand it, knowing my name,—but I have *not* written trash, and I will trust the public to bear me up in this, as it has done in all I have as yet produced" (14 March 1889). In this same letter she insisted that her novel, *Ardath,* was different and even superior as a work of art to those of her contemporaries: "I have fulfilled my own intention in the conception of 'Ardath' and cannot re-fashion the living creature of my thought, because I instinctively feel it is as I would have it be and I know it is distinctly marked out and separate from the other novels of the day which teem from the press, fall, and are forgotten. Measured by the standard of good literature, I know that it has worth."

Corelli recognized that the categories of "trash" and "good literature" were contested territory in the Victorian literary world, and we should, I think, take her intentions seriously. She was not coldly churning out melodramas or trendy pseudophilosophical romances that would sell well on the book market. When she asked Bentley "Do you notice what immense eagerness there is at the present day to read everything connected with religion and psychology?" (20 April 1888), she was not trying to capitalize on a trend. She insisted repeatedly on the authenticity of her vision and always refused to alter her plots or her tone in order to appease Bentley's delicate tastes.

The only hint of derision for "the people" appears in her very first letters from 1885 and early 1886, one of which I have already cited, when she was no doubt trying to impress her new publisher with her credentials—her *class* credentials, which apparently constituted her claim to legitimacy as a bona fide literary person. On 9 February 1886 Corelli wrote: "I am glad this month will see the book [*A Romance of Two Worlds*] out. I hardly think politics will interfere with the novel-readers, unless the 'mob' smash the Circulating Libraries! What fearful times these are in England just now!" This is an inadvertently penetrating observation, amazingly innocent when we recall the panic-stricken rhetoric of *Blackwood's,* which explicitly linked bad novels with social anarchy, or Gladstone's opposite impression, that good novels will uplift and educate the newly formed middle class. For such commentators the question was not whether politics would interfere with novel readers but whether novel readers would interfere with politics, that is, with British social order. Corelli's reversal of the equation suggests how tricky it is to assign responsibility exclusively to politics, books, or readers for the unpredictable hankerings of "the masses." Her naive, half-amused worry that socialists and anarchists would take to smashing Mudie's windows conjures two constituencies: readers and activists. That she could in a single breath allude to the volatile political climate and the appearance of *A Romance of Two Worlds*—a novel as far removed as possible from social realism—is wonderfully typical of fin-de-siècle sensibility. Terry Eagleton has characterized the last two decades of the century as "an astonishing amalgam of spiritual and material ferment: the boisterous emergence of new political forces . . . but also a veritable transformation of subjectivity" ("Flight" 11). In juxtaposing cultural situations—Aubrey Beardsley and the Second International, aestheticism and anarchism, decadence and the dock strike—Eagleton suggests that one characteristic of fin-de-siècle culture was a capacity to accommodate contradictory ideas, even to encourage them. Experiments in art and personal style, in mysticism and spiritualism, were not incompatible with creating a rational social system, reorganizing industry, and accommodating the rampant consumerism of a generation that had more money, more education, and more leisure than any previous generation in English social history. Materialism and spiritualism, politics and subjectivity, are sides of the same coin, according to Eagleton. Why should the extravagance of Corelli's prose, her Satan and her spiritualism and her crossed subjectivities, be incompatible with a pragmatic populism and class commentary? She wrote for the people and at the same time worshiped at the altar of art. And though it irked her critics, Corelli was nothing if not sincere. But her brand of aestheticism is fissured by the combating interests of the people and those who want to save the people from their own bad taste—fissured, in effect, by changing social and cultural assumptions and arrangements in late-Victorian and early-modern Britain.

Corelli's popular appeal may have caused her eviction from the towers of high art in the 1890s and after, but by reading her novels in the context of the many strands of aestheticism that were being woven into the literary and commercial markets of the period—including new fiction and New Women novels—we can begin to reexamine the shifts in emphasis, the teasing dialogues, the adaptations and contrivances that make up a continuum between the consummately aesthetic and the utterly bourgeois. In chapter 3 I will continue to play out the cultural contradictions Corelli incorporates by examining how the New Woman further complicated the literary marketplace and the political scene. Corelli's apparent antifeminism is worth examining, for surely it has something to do with her continued exclusion from most anthologies and book-length studies of New Women or "daughters of decadence." Her novels both embody and resist the search for a particularly feminine aesthetic in the decades before the twentieth century.

# III

## The Ardor of the Pen

*The Muses are women; so are the Fates.*

Marie Corelli, "The Advance of Woman" (1905)

THROUGHOUT HER LITERARY career Corelli was inspired by and preoccupied with women. Her novels, letters, and essays differently attest to her passionate concern with the cluster of attributes and fallibilities that constituted the feminine in her lifetime: purity and evil, social injustice and spiritual equality, the vices of vanity, pride, and idleness that compromise women's potential for genius, perfect love, and moral power.

Most of Corelli's novels focus on women, and they *all* contain some social commentary about gender equality or proud assertions about woman's special nature. Corelli's anger at social injustice is often combined with a transparent desire to romanticize women, to redefine the feminine by evoking women's physical beauty and spiritual and intellectual independence. Although she was essentially a romantic who called herself "old-fashioned" and not in the vanguard of feminism's first wave, Corelli did not disengage herself from the most imperative social movement of her age. In public addresses and magazine articles she spoke almost as much about women as she did about literature. During World War I she defended British women from journalistic attacks on their political indifference and frivolity, calling them "magnificent!—a glory and honour to their sex" ("Time of Our Lives"). She admired American women, even going so far as to suggest in a speech to the American Ladies Club that "not President Taft, but Mrs. Taft, is the ruler of the greatest republic in the world" ("Speech"). And in 1901 she made a feisty speech to an audience of literary men (she said she felt like "Daniel in the lion's den"), after which young Winston Churchill offered his congratulations, remarking that she had "almost disarmed his opposition to Woman's Suffrage" (Vyver 161).

Churchill's remark is ironic, because Corelli was vocal in her challenge to suffragists, writing in *Harper's Bazaar* in 1907, for example, that she was "*not* a 'suffragette'" ("Man's War" 426), and in the *Idler* in 1893, "I am not a 'strong-minded' woman, with egotistical ideas of a 'mission'" ("My First Book" 246–47). She was repelled by the militants of the twentieth century "who brandish umbrellas and scream for 'Woman's Suffrage' so violently that they have to be taken forcibly in hand by the police," and we have seen how she detested the New Woman of the 1890s ("Man's War" 427). Yet Corelli believed passionately in the intellectual equality of women, supported women's economic independence as an indispensable right, and loudly opposed sexism in the literary establishment. She believed that woman's "mystic power to persuade, enthrall, and subjugate man" was enormous and that once men freed them from sexual tyranny, women would morally rejuvenate the world through their influence ("Man's War" 427). As she boldly insisted in a speech to literary men at London's Whitefriars Club, "Sovran Woman is Queen of the whole world round, and Sovran Man knows it. He pretends he doesn't—but he does!" ("Whitefriars"). She consistently framed her faith in women's talents in terms of social progress and the greater good: women have proven themselves in the arts, she declares in "The Advance of Woman," and now must seek to become lawyers, doctors, and school inspectors but, significantly, not politicians. Corelli's contradictory views are revealed in a long and formidable list of her "dislikes" that was printed in the *Ladies Realm*. Alongside "the woman who cannot consecrate her life purely and faithfully to one great love-passion" and "women bicyclists and he-females generally," she lists "cynics and pessimists," "lack of enthusiasm for a great cause," "sneerers at faith and aspiration," and "the last and greatest dislike of all—moral cowardice" (quoted in Carr 74–75). Her idealism extended to female power and was constantly linked to assertions of women's moral and social responsibilities *as women*.

What can Corelli's apparently contradictory views about the progress of the women's movement tell us about changing social attitudes during the thirty years or so before British women over the age of twenty-one achieved the vote in 1928? Is it fair to view her appropriations of feminism as a legitimate strand of a political movement, or is she hopelessly outmoded, unreclaimable for modern feminist theories? And where should a literary historian look to find the most honest, the most useful articulations of a mood that surely many women who enjoyed Corelli's novels understood? To her polemical antisuffrage essays, her unpublished correspondence, her speeches, her fiction? Or to biography and the extraordinary courage she showed as a woman who was denigrated for almost all of the personal and professional choices she made in her life?

Throughout my readings in Corelli's oeuvre, I have been impressed by the way articulations of feminist resistance are almost always in relation to her situation as a writer. In this section I want to explore her efforts to negotiate a feminine aesthetic against the radically politicized debates about gender and literary merit at the turn of the century. Corelli's feminism is often located in the realm of art, a fluid and ambiguous territory. The extravagances of romance suit her moral imperative, for there her anger at male privilege *and* her desires for female fulfillment can receive their fullest, uncensored expression. Furthermore, her vision of sexual equality is tied to her reliance on displays of descriptive volubility and linguistic license. Her indulgent portrayals of heterosexual desire are always combined with assertions of the ethereal, unsensual nature of true equality and the highest forms of platonic love.

Many of her novels are about the pursuit of perfect love and the discovery of an erotic and psychic soul mate, even if the journey extends over centuries and into unearthly realms. Love is much more than the sexual union of man and woman for Corelli, and in her books uppercase "Love" always means a spiritual journey toward transcendence that is emphatically tied to the paradoxical achievements of female self-discovery and self-erasure. There is a utopian spirit in her romances, but Corelli's books do not belong to the category of utopian feminist fiction, as described, for example, by Ann Ardis in *New Women, New Novels* or by Elaine Showalter in *Sexual Anarchy.* Her mystical utopia is very different from that of the New Woman or, later, the twentieth-century feminist, whose pragmatic dissections of social and sexual relations undermine romantic bliss. Her dreams of sexual equality are located not in politics and praxis but in spirituality, *culture,* especially her faith in the emotional power of literature, and a gendered aesthetic that involves typical "feminine" attributes, such as outward grace and inward purity, gentleness, and beauty. The New Woman's pragmatism combined with her association with the realist school of sexually explicit fiction provokes an antithetical stance in Corelli.

Corelli's emotional defenses of women's special nature and unique contributions to art and literature resemble cultural feminism: feminist writings that can be identified by "their denigration of masculinity rather than male roles or practices, by their valorization of female traits, and by their commitment to preserve rather than diminish gender differences" (Alcoff 437). Celebrating a female counterculture—insisting that women need not wear "mannish" clothing or smoke cigars to enter the male world—promotes an alternative women's culture, full of "superior virtues and values, to be credited and learned from rather than despised" (Alcoff 439).

This position has led some feminist theorists to contemplate a feminine aesthetic, a disputable notion that suggests a fundamental, natural "female" essence or culture, perhaps conforming to the more positive characteristics associated with femininity, such as nurturing, love, and cooperation. There are pros and cons to this approach to female writing and creativity: *écriture féminine* can be liberatory, celebrating an inherent power in women's imaginations and sexuality, but it can also reduce women to quasimystical biological entities, de-emphasizing their social and political circumstances.

I have strong reservations about the essentialist and transhistorical tendencies in the concept of a feminine aesthetic, but the idea of female *difference* can provide a useful angle from which to approach Corelli's involvement in the contest for cultural authority at the turn of the century. Any reading of the aesthetic is potentially conflicting, fundamentally ambivalent, and these ambiguities are multiplied when we also consider inflections of gender. If there is a strategic advantage in the concept of feminine difference in that it endorses women's writing as a descriptive category, there is also the disadvantage of evoking negative constructions of femininity, which can be read as either oppressive or liberatory (or both). For example, Silvia Bovenschen has argued that the supposed dominance of "gentleness" in the feminine repertoire is inherently ambivalent: on the one hand, it is an emblem of female subjugation and passivity, but on the other hand, it "contains utopian moments and lends us an idea of human behaviour beyond oppression, competition, and compulsory achievement" (35).

In my view, Corelli made a serious effort to mediate the ambivalence inherent in constructions of the feminine at the end of the century, to work out the connections among literature, feminine nature and emerging feminist politics, and the broader realm of social practice. In reading Linda Alcoff's essay on cultural feminism and poststructuralism, I was struck by some similarities between these postmodern strands of feminism and Corelli's rough maneuvers toward a consistent view of women. If Corelli embraces a kind of cultural feminism, celebrating women's unique power, she also exhibits a strain of antiessentialism in that she does not believe this power stems from biology. Her ideologically reflexive invocations of motherhood and female beauty often coexist with contrary examples of drudgery and unfulfilled lives. The heterosexual romance is never completely overturned, but virginity is always valorized and spinsterhood or female independence passionately defended.

However unlikely, it is possible to interpret Corelli as an effective "resister of logocentrism" (Alcoff 441). In her various uses of *feminine writing* as a descriptive term and in her novels, she dodges all dominant gender ideologies at the turn of the century. On 1 January 1887 she proudly declared to George Bentley, "I have resolved that no two books of mine shall be in the least alike, so that neither the critics nor the public shall know what to expect from me," paradoxically combining "feminine" evasiveness with an assertive personal voice. Corelli did, in fact, use a variety of images, genres, and voices in an effort to reconcile her ideal faith in female difference with her personal experience as a woman in Victorian and Edwardian society. This conflict between an idealized hope and real-life discrimination accounts, I think, for the occasionally strident, insistent, or enraged tone in her fiction when the subject is women. Despite her romantic view of feminine superiority, she was constantly reminded of her social inferiority in her daily life and in her business dealings. Showalter has written that fantasies of a cultural "wild zone" for women will always come up against historical reality: "there can be no writing . . . totally outside of the dominant structure; no publication is fully independent from the economic and political pressures of the male-dominated society" ("Feminist Criticism" 31). Corelli surely experienced this; if she was a romantic, she was also a hardheaded business-woman. Her efforts to formulate a feminine aesthetic were continually influenced by her real-world experiences in a patriarchal literary market.

Instead of resolving the ambiguities inherent in the attempt to formulate an aesthetic of feminine difference, I hope to heighten the contradictions Corelli presented to her Victorian critics and continues to present to modern feminist theorists. Even if she did not succeed in asserting a feminine aesthetic, she was right, intuitively, to see that a utopian ideal could be usefully envisioned for women in the realm of art and that even a flawed and partial vision could act as a counterweight to some of the more dominant tendencies in Victorian patriarchy. In the first part of this chapter I will discuss Corelli's efforts to assert a feminine aesthetic in the literary world of the fin de siècle and before World War I. Her essays and letters supply fascinating evidence of how difficult it was to write against the grain of realism during this period, especially for a woman. Lyn Pykett has argued that "by foregrounding the figure of the woman writer, [New Women] novels foreground the problems of their own production" (177). A great many Corelli novels contain passages about women artists or writers or include them as characters; the subject of female genius and the claim for complete equality with men in the arts and in literature were central preoccupations during her entire career. But in her unusual novella *My Wonderful Wife* the woman artist is presented differently from the heroic and brilliant women writers and artists in *The Sorrows of Satan, The Murder of Delicia,* and *The Master Christian* (in which a woman painter, Angela Sovrani, is literally stabbed in the back by her less-gifted lover, who is jealous of female success). Still, Corelli's repeated portrayals of women in the arts in these and other novels (such as *A Romance of Two Worlds, The Soul of Lilith,* and *Innocent: Her Fancy and His Fact*) and her insistence on female creativity reveal a writer who desired both critical acceptance among her peers and a secure resting place for her feminist leanings.

Janet Galligani Casey has argued that Corelli's "conflicting views of womanhood make her a notable transitional figure among the 'literary feminists'—a curious link between George Eliot and Virginia Woolf" (164). The link is curious indeed, but I agree with Casey. Without trying to claim Corelli for contemporary feminism, I do think she had an inchoate feminist philosophy and that her novels demonstrate the various ways she worked it out over some twenty years. Toward the end of this chapter I will look at how female biology figured in feminine writing and feminist politics for Corelli and how she revised the figures of the virgin and the femme fatale in one of her later novels, *The Young Diana: An Experiment of the Future* (1918). This novel may be read as a study in self-alienation and the social value of unmarried women. But these judgments inevitably intersect with the aesthetic—and political—value of female-authored texts.

### The Uses of the Aesthetic

" 'Equality of the sexes' is one of the advanced feminine war cries," Corelli wrote in 1918, "when everyone with a grain of common sense knows there is and can be no such equality. Nature's law forbids. Nature insists on contrasts" ("Woman's Vote"). This passionate belief in sexual difference and the law of nature is weighed against Corelli's equally strong faith in the transforming powers of literature, "the greatest power for good or evil in the world" (*Free Opinions* 325). In several public addresses (some of them later collected in *Free Opinions* [1905]) Corelli makes very large claims for "Literature" as "the *idealisation* of human thought into *ideal* language," asserting that "all art, all poetry, all music" represent a "spiritual attempt to break open the close walls of our earthly prison house and let a glimpse of God's light through" (*Free Opinions* 307). Literature is the supreme calling, "the greatest, the highest, and the noblest that is open to aspiring ambition" (*Free Opinions* 326). The woman who holds the pen has the power "strongly, boldly, and faithfully" to move toward human happiness and the achievement of "great ends" (*Free Opinions* 330). Her potential power in the realm of art—power to influence, to draw out sympathy for human suffering, to "command more millions of human beings than any monarch's rule"—far outweighs gaining the dubious right to cast a ballot (*Free Opinions* 327).

Corelli's assertion of the transcendent power of the aesthetic is not an unfamiliar reaction to the encroachments of politics on the literary. Her insistence on the centrality of the imagination and her almost religious devotion to "Literature" belong to a conservative tradition that claims the aesthetic for its own purposes. As Terry Eagleton explains in *The Ideology of the Aesthetic,* "From Burke and Coleridge to Matthew

Arnold and T. S. Eliot, the aesthetic in Britain is effectively captured by the political right. The autonomy of culture, society as expressive or organized totality, the intuitive dogmatism of the imagination, the priority of local affections and unarguable allegiances, the intimidatory majesty of the sublime, the incontrovertible character of the 'immediate' experience, history as a spontaneous growth impervious to rational analysis: these are some of the forms in which the aesthetic becomes a weapon in the hands of political reaction" (60). Eagleton's list of absolutes describes Corelli's beliefs and motives perfectly. Her faith in the "majesty of the sublime" and the "intuitive dogmatism of the imagination" is expressed in many statements about "the dignity of Literature" and the magical powers of the imagination, "the first element in artistic greatness" (*Free Opinions* 309).

The use of the aesthetic as a conservative platform intersects with Corelli's mid-Victorian views on woman's sphere, but it is less clear that the latter is also evidence of "political reaction." In chapter 2 I described how Corelli's commitment to art was influenced by her family background and social class. In the same way, she was forced to politicize her aesthetic because she was a woman, and her status as "literary producer" was bound to be affected by extraliterary factors, such as "the debates concerning mass and high culture, the social position of the arts institution, the stage of the development of the women's movement and the place of women in society" (Watts 89). Far from reactionary, women may gain real social power when they are allowed to contribute to literature and art, and many Victorian feminists believed that women's literary success was clear evidence of their intellectual equality. Women's writing *can* wield definite social influence.[1]

The question is what kind of influence should women strive to attain? For Corelli the answer is typically Victorian: moral influence. Woman's beauty, purity, and innate selflessness lay special moral claims on her when she enters the realm of the aesthetic, for the imaginative is a place for "beauty and harmony . . . poetry and prophecy" (*Free Opinions* 320–21). Women writers should be committed to an ideal: beautifying life, morally and spiritually. Corelli scolds New Women writers and "erotomaniacs" who, "for the purpose of *degrading* and *debasing* human thought to the low level of coarse 'realism' and 'materialism,' [use] . . . 'slang' diction, and what may be termed an ignorant brutality of 'style'" and therefore are a shame to the profession of humane letters ("A Little Talk"). Corelli's concern with aesthetic matters here—diction, style, subject matter—suggests that she is sensitive to formal considerations. But form and diction should be used in the service of the ideal: "What is called Realism, or Materialism is the decadence and death of Art—for Art's mission is to lift the aspirations of Man upward—not to drag them downward" ("A Little Talk"). Thus Ouida is Corelli's favorite woman writer because she is "a *romancer*" who writes against an age of "Prose and Positivism" ("Word about 'Ouida'" 370–71). Furthermore, as a woman, Ouida has a natural tendency to write with emotion, fervor, and occasionally excessive passion: "Her faults are those of reckless impulse and hurry in writing; being a woman, she has all that warm and often mistaken *ardour of the pen* which a man, unless he be young, very gifted, and very enthusiastic, generally lacks" (369). Ouida's "pure, fluent, eloquent English" and her "perceptive delicacy" are admirable feminine attributes for Corelli (366, 367); she praises "the 'Ouida' eloquence. There is no living author who has the same rush, fire and beauty of language" (370). Although Corelli recognizes Ouida's exaggerations and occasional moral lapses, she forgives these flaws as evidence of genuine passion: "It is the reckless expression of impulse, and, rash as it may be, it is more commendable than the cold-blooded casuistry of Mrs. Mona Caird, who has recently made what seems like a deliberate and dispassionate magazine appeal for universal polygamy!" (370).

The reference to Mona Caird's essays on marriage, which first appeared in the *Westminster Review* in 1888, underscores Corelli's distaste for factual rhetoric and coolly argumentative discourse. It is acceptable to Corelli if an author makes occasional errors in syntax or logic as long as the writing is hot: "This gift of *inspiration* which cannot be bought, or sold, or taught, 'Ouida' possesses, not in a small, but in a very large and overflowing degree" (370). For a woman writer inspiration is better than argumentation. The New Woman writer has shifted attention away from the true and the beautiful, and her "ardour" is misdirected and constrained. Even her "mannish" appearance is an affront to Corelli's aesthetic faith, since feminine beauty is itself a means to moral reform. In this sense, what Corelli chiefly objects to in the New Woman is her unloveliness, and this extends to the sordid realism of New Woman fiction. The cold-bloodedness of Caird is unfavorably compared with the "warm" and fiery prose of Ouida, Caird's intellectual "casuistry" is held against the spontaneous inspiration of the *romancer.* For Corelli the less disciplined and, implicitly, more erotic language of romance was mysteriously attached to true feminine expression.

Corelli's valorization of the true feminine is instrumental in her reaction to suffragists and New Women, for the politics and poses of female reformers are dangerous precisely because *these* women are romanticizing masculinity. It is not so much the New Woman's politics that Corelli objects to, for she believes in women's equality and when she sees sexism she names it. But she views the New Woman's apparent betrayal of feminine culture as a misguided allegiance with men rather than a commitment to women. For Corelli sexual equality must not erase sexual difference, for women possess special gifts that she fears are disappearing into the dominant sphere of the masculine. In a letter written in 1889 declining an invitation to contribute to a new magazine called *Woman,* Corelli expressed her doubts about the direction the women's movement was taking: "Again, though I wish to admire 'progressive womanhood'—the 'progress' is assuming disastrously masculine forms which I shall never consent to approve or uphold, my theory being that woman is never seen to better advantage than when in her own naturally ordained sphere of action and influence" (Corelli-Bentley Correspondence, 6 December 1889). Corelli's repulsion of "masculine forms" on the political front was pretty staunch, and it was partly based on her suspicion that masculine culture—including the results of science, technology, and industrial capitalism—trampled on distinctly feminine features. She even says she would not want to see women in Parliament because the sex "pre-eminent for grace and beauty" would be degraded by having to participate in "'scenes' of heated and undignified disputations" (*Free Opinions* 202). In "The Advance of Woman" Corelli writes: "In claiming and securing her intellectual equality with Man, she should ever bear in mind that such a position is only to be held by always maintaining and preserving as great an Unlikeness to him as possible in her life and surroundings. Let her imitate him in nothing but independence and individuality. Let her eschew his fashions in dress, his talk, and his manners. A woman who wears 'mannish' clothes, smokes cigars, rattles out slang, gambles at cards, and drinks brandy and soda on the slightest provocation, is lost altogether, both as woman and man, and becomes sexless" (*Free Opinions* 203).

This is a clear statement of Corelli's limited concession to feminism: equality is asserted on the level of intellectual and economic independence, but the feminist's masculine attitude makes her sexually neuter—and neutralizes her power, for a woman cannot combat patriarchal oppression if she longs to be a patriarch herself. But neutrality is exactly what is most valued in the male literary establishment. In "The Feminine Note in Fiction" (1904) William Courtney claimed, "It is the neutrality of the artistic mind which the female novelist seems to find it difficult to realize" (quoted in Ardis 54). As Ardis has explained, Courtney ensured the marginality of New Woman fiction by "feminizing" this literature: "'femaleness' . . . is a synonym for aesthetic second-rateness" (54). Thus Corelli's heroic rejection of masculine style is complicated by the cultural authority of the masculine and the practical value of male approval for a woman writer. Her skepticism of supposedly male-identified New Women inevitably conflicts with the cultural prestige of so-called masculine writing. Although she defended her feminine aesthetic by repeatedly asserting the value of romance over realism and by criticizing the prejudices of male critics, Corelli appreciated that in literature to be "manly" is not without its advantages. But she also realized why this is so: it is often a matter not of aesthetic value at all but of prejudice, politics, and power.

### "You Write with a Man's Pen!"

Pykett has explained that the "gendered discourse on fiction" at the turn of the century "was part of a broadly based nineteenth-century crisis of gender definition" and that arguments about fiction were "a site of struggle between differently structured oppositions of masculinity and femininity, and between contending versions of the feminine" (23–24). Pykett and other critics, including Showalter, Ardis, Sally Ledger, and Rita Kranidis, have described in rich detail how the periodical "fiction wars" repeatedly and emotionally stressed categorical views of gender: "feminine" writing was realistic, explicit, obsessively self-occupied, emotional, and commercial, whereas "masculine" writing was objective, disciplined, suggestive, and artistic. Naturalism, new fiction, and the revival of boys' adventure tales at the fin de siècle have been cited as attempts to "masculinise," according to Pykett (36), or "de-feminise," according to Ledger (179), the literary market—or as Showalter has put it, "to reclaim the kingdom of the English novel for male writers, male readers, and men's stories" (*Sexual Anarchy* 79).

This campaign to capture the aesthetic flag for manliness was maddeningly transparent to Corelli. "If 'Rudyard Kipling' were to suddenly turn out the *nom de plume* of a *woman,* you would soon see the wind blow in a different quarter!" she grumbled to Bentley (7 February 1892). Obviously, Corelli's frustration derives from the fact that significance and value are attached to "masculine" writing. But she has a crucial insight: there may be no intrinsically "feminine" or "masculine" writing at all—change the nom de plume and expectations of worth will change as well. In a Corellian outburst affirming her awareness that aesthetic values are everywhere mediated by social values, Irene Vassilius, the woman novelist in *The Soul of Lilith* (1892), exclaims, "George Eliot and Georges [*sic*] Sand took men's names in order to shelter themselves a little from the pitiless storm that assails literary work known to emanate from a woman's brain; but let a man write the veriest trash that was ever printed, he will still be accredited by his own sex with something better than ever the cleverest woman could compass" (205). Despite her romantic view of women's superiority, Corelli saw—and resented—how interpretations of style and subject matter could be manipulated to suit ideological demands that were based on the sex of the writer. What happens if one reverses these values or, better yet, simply ignores them? She is bitterly sarcastic, for example, in her discussion of Ouida's language: "There is no faltering feminine weakness in these expressions; they are as pointed, as ruthless, as witty, as any sayings of Rochefoucauld. A Man might have written them—ye gods! think or it—the Nobler Creature might have penned such lines and smiled complacently at his own cleverness afterwards" ("Word about 'Ouida'" 368). If this contradicts her defense of Ouida's special feminine "ardour of the pen," it is because Corelli was caught in the cross fire of debates about gender and aesthetic value. She took her best shot by promiscuously dispersing the meaning of *masculine* and *feminine* among literary practitioners of all stripes. Corelli effectively deconstructed her culture's gendered assumptions about writing, even while she desired to preserve the idea of woman's "Unlikeness" to men in valorizing feminine difference.

There is a liability in the attempt to shift the political ground or to reclaim negative epithets for one's own political purposes: a tendency to emotional overstatement. In a vituperative section of *The Silver Domino* (the whole book is vituperative) Corelli dons the mask of a literary critic in her discussion of writers who fall into ruts or "grooves." Her deconstruction of gendered criticism is scathing. She says William Black's novels are so full of "'feminine twaddle,' that one has to look back to the title-page in order to convince one's self that it is really one of the 'virile' sex who is telling the story" (138); she calls Marion Crawford "our best man-novelist," thereby turning the tables on segregated judgments of "lady novelists"; and although Ouida tends to tell the same old stories, Corelli praises her fiction's "gorgeousness of colour and picturesqueness of description. . . . 'Ouida' holds a pen such as many a man has good secret reason to envy" (154). Under the cloak of anonymity, the author of *The Silver Domino* cunningly includes "Marie Corelli" in the discussion: "it may be truly said that she has written no two books alike, either in plot or style," yet "her very name is, to the men of the press, what a red rag is to a bull" (157–58). Corelli was well aware of partisanship in the book business, and, for better or worse, she took it personally. These narrow-minded and defensive examples do not show Corelli at her most generous and exhibit the strain she felt in trying to preserve her amour propre. *The Silver Domino* may be the angriest, and perhaps the cruelest, public attack on the literary system of the 1890s, and it was written by a woman who was in the thick of it.

I cite these brief excerpts to emphasize Corelli's growing impatience with the critics' gendered categories of writing when clearly none of the authors they reviewed quite fit the mold assigned to them according to sex. Corelli suffered ideological contortions to gain cultural legitimacy as a woman writer. In a private letter to Bentley, she said, "I feel that it is impossible for a woman-writer ever to receive justice from *men* critics, more particularly if she chance to show masculine power. If any man had written 'Wormwood' there would have been a grand shouting over it both in the French and English press. . . . Well may I strive to be 'masculine' in style! I must also be masculine in endurance, for if I were weak-spirited I might sit down idly and weep" (15 November 1890). Here

Corelli inadvertently draws attention to the various meanings assigned to the masculine in her culture: the term is pejorative (to her) when it is applied to literary style but not necessarily so when applied to human life, and I will return to her creative dismantling of masculinity later in this chapter. For now it is enough to note that Corelli had learned that to have a "masculine" style was a *practical* asset only if the writer was a man, and yet it was a trait that carried such symbolic importance that she did not wish to relinquish the label when it was applied to herself. Further-more, the contentious atmosphere of the book world, the pervasive anxi-eties about gender and cultural control, and the fear of being edged out by realist competitors forestalled her efforts to claim solidarity with other literary women. On 8 September 1890, after the publication of *Worm-wood,* she wrote to Bentley:

> *And here we come to your allusion to my "sister authors"! Do I not know them? Have they not hurt me, while I was yet weak enough to be hurt? Have they not taken my hand and kissed my lips, and then gone away to write abuse of me afterwards? Yes, indeed— over and over again, and I have never paid them back in their own coin—I could not do so. I have never had a moment's jealousy of any other living writer, male or female. The principal thing my "sisters" grudge me is the "man's pen" that one amiable critic allowed I possessed; I do not write in a "ladylike" or effeminate way, and for that they hate me.*

What is to be done? She was proud of the critic's praise of her "man's pen" because she wished to identify with the top of the literary hierarchy, yet this alienated her from "sister authors" who had conformed to cul-tural expectations of "ladylike" prose in women. But in fact there was no consensus among reviewers about the gendered qualities of Corelli's writing. She boasted to Bentley that the Prince of Wales admired her books for the "fearless courage" of her opinions: "He said, 'There is no namby-pamby nonsense about you—you write with a man's pen, and I should think you would fight your enemies like a man!' These words delighted me, for to be 'namby-pamby' would be a *horror* to me" (15 September 1892). But plenty of critics slighted her novels for being *very* namby-pamby and effeminate, and they used typical sexist epithets: "the hysterical vapourings of a mind without balance" ("Miss Marie Co-relli"), "feminine redundancy of adjectives" (quoted in Masters 102), "extravagant flights of fancy" ("New Novels" 583), "the littleness of the woman thrust in every chapter" (Stead 453). Henry Harland, writing in the *Yellow Book,* said her novels were "gushing" and compared her style to a "formless, unclipped white Poodle, with pink eyes" (quoted in McDonald 118).

Corelli found these press reviews sheer obfuscation of the issues at stake, and in an essay published in *Free Opinions Freely Expressed on Certain Phases of Modern Social Life and Conduct* she wittily demonstrates how meaning is creatively revised by critics to suit their own agendas. The word *strong,* she says, used to mean "a powerful style, a vigorous grip, a brilliant way of telling a captivating and noble story," but now it has acquired the connotation of "unclean" (273). Corelli claims that the average person who reads literary reviews needs to understand this shift in meaning. Likewise, she detests the positive connotations reviewers attach to "virile" writing:

(275)
> *"Virile" is from the Latin* virilis, *a male—virility is the state and characteristic of the adult male. Applied to certain books, however, . . . it will be found by the discerning public to mean coarse—rough—with a literary "style" obtained by sprinkling several pages of prose with the lowest tavern-oaths, together with the name of God, pronounced "Gawd." Anything written in this fashion is at once pronounced "virile" and commands wide admiration . . . particularly if it be a story in which women are depicted at the lowest kickable depth of drabism to which men can drag them, while men are represented as the suffering victims of their wickedness.*

This passage suggests that literary judgments can be reduced to a matter of interested semantic ploys. There is nothing to prevent a woman from taking an approbatory (or declamatory) expression and revising it according to her own aesthetic or political values. Why should *virility* mean good writing? Corelli simply decodes the word from a female perspective: "'Virility' . . . means . . . men's proper scorn for the sex of their mothers, and an egotistical delight in themselves, united to a barbarous rejoicing in bad language and abandoned morals. It does not mean this in decent every-day life, of course; *but it does in books*" (emphasis added) (*Free Opinions* 275–76). Importantly, in everyday social life virility and strength are not necessarily pejorative—Corelli even says, "I cannot abide the 'flabby-minded' of my sex, who show no fight" (Corelli-Bentley Correspondence, 5 September 1892). But virility in books is another thing: it is an *unacceptable aesthetic*.

In the same essay Corelli admiringly quotes an M.A. who asserts, "Art, . . . if it be genuine and sincere, tends ever to the lofty and the beautiful. There is no rule of art more important than the sense of modesty" (*Free Opinions* 274). That Corelli's own books were occasionally considered immodest and coarse astonished her. She accepted the burden of artistic womanhood—to beautify, inspire, and change a world she felt was corrupt, materialistic, and godless. If her unshakable faith in her moral message and her confidence in her own talent blinded her to the possible immodesty of her style, this is arguably a feature of many political writers. Writing in 1901 about the enormous success of *The Master Christian,* Arnold Bennett conceded that "Miss Corelli has the not-ignoble passions of the reformer" (89). Bennett was right to assert that Corelli believed her books approached the sublime, that they raised people's thoughts to higher levels: "I hope my last chapter may help to induce women to become as much as they can like *Angels!*" she wrote to Bentley about *Ardath* in 1889. Corelli felt that it was part of her duty both as a woman and as a writer to carry out her moral mission. William Gladstone's opinion must surely have inspired her: "An earnest woman-thinker . . . is more likely to gain a quick and sure insight into the problems of her time than a man,—first, because she is by nature sympathetic, secondly, because she has such an amazing instinct, thirdly, because if virtuous at all, she is certain to be *sublimely unselfish*" (Corelli–Bentley Correspondence, 5 June 1889). The aesthetic was for her not a value-free arena but a cherished cultural space that was deeply concerned with changing the lives of real people. Corelli's social-problem novels attack the big vices of her time: *The Master Christian* is about (among other things) corruption within the Roman Catholic Church; *Temporal Power: A Study in Supremacy* is an attack on the corruption of Edward VII's government; *Wormwood,* as we know, goes after corrupt Parisians; *Holy Orders: The Tragedy of a Quiet Life* blasts the corruption in the trade of intoxicating liquors; and at least a half dozen novels lash out at the corruption of the marriage market. All of these more or less social-problem novels still must be classified as romances, and Corelli's womanly sublimity is in full force.

But Corelli also wrote in ordinary workaday prose, and a few critics noticed the variations in her style. In 1906 J. M. Stuart-Young, writing in the *Westminster Review,* stated, "There is nothing you can't find in her pages, from the most flowery periods of Lytton to the commonest journalese" (682). And in 1914 Horace Samuel observed, "At one moment her weighty nouns, guarded not infrequently by a triple score of epithets, possess the pomp and luxuriance of the true Asiatic style, at another the brisk horsiness of her diction has all the spontaneous force of English as it is actually spoken" (131). Corelli's style, says Samuel, is sometimes "reminiscent of the mellifluous cadences of *Dorian Gray.* Anon she will indulge in a vein of frank but militant simplicity that bears a greater resemblance to the style of Mr. Robert Blatchford, the celebrated atheist" (132).

This stylistic blend of masculine militancy and feminine mellifluousness is apparent in passages in Corelli's novella *My Wonderful Wife* (ironically subtitled "A Study in Smoke"), which was originally published in 1889 and included in her collection of shorter works, *Cameos,* in 1895. *My Wonderful Wife* is a humorous send-up of New Women and the marriage question, and it definitely belongs to New Woman fiction, although I have never seen it anthologized as such. In this satiric attack on "manly" women, Corelli plays with gender and gendered styles, first by using a male narrator and second by inserting discussions that duplicate current debates about masculine and feminine roles. It is a clever story that reveals Corelli's contradictions on several levels: she exposes male vanity and defends traditional gender roles and at the same time engages in a sustained argument against New Women and a polemic for women's equality. The story is narrated by William Hatwell-Tribkin, "an old-fashioned sort of fellow" who marries Honoria Maggs, a progressive woman who smokes cigarettes, shoots partridges, writes sporting novels, and eventually becomes a well-known "platform woman" giving lectures on such topics as "the Advisability of Men's Apparel for Women" (186, 267). At first the narrator is pleased to have wedded "a thoroughly practical, capable, healthy female, utterly devoid of romance . . . because I had been lately reading in the magazines and newspapers that romance of any kind was unwholesome, and I did not want an unwholesome wife" (181). This, for Corelli, is the ironic voice of sanity in an unsentimental age. But the narrator's growing bewilderment at his wife's manner and opinions carries the suggestion that even for Corelli his notions of feminine conduct are passé. He describes himself as "a soft-hearted booby," often looks like a fool, fears he will be taken for a lunatic, and is always intellectually bested by his wife's practical wit and brilliant critiques of the double standard, which literally unman him (270). When he tells her, "You don't deserve to be a mother!" Honoria replies, "You're right, Willie; that's one for you! I don't deserve to be and I didn't want to be. . . . Would you like to take baby out for once?" (213). Willie beats a hasty retreat, banging the street door to release his rage: "I went out with a violence that I freely admit was femininely pettish and unworthy of a man" (213). Later he deals with his mother-in-law by "surveying her with a proper manly scorn," and when he gets in rows with his wife, her self-possession causes him to blush, fume, and throw fits of mild hysterics (243). Corelli's satire is half directed at the old-fashioned male's befuddlement when women do not recognize his social superiority and masculine prerogative.

Nevertheless, a reader of *My Wonderful Wife* would undoubtedly take the story, as a whole, as a critique of sexual "topsy-turvydom" and a satire on the New Woman (232). But Honoria is not wickedly perverse in her mannish behavior. She is a comical example of the modern woman who has genuine brilliance and beauty and a real, if myopic, belief in her cause. In this story Corelli incidentally shows that she thoroughly understands the feminist platform of the 1890s, however much she disagrees with it. The feminist diatribes against marriage as tyranny, love as the feminine opiate, and women's fashions as intolerably restricting are delivered with a degree of warmth. Thus when Honoria is laughed at by her audience, she counters in the true progressive style: "All great ideas have been first laughed at ever since the world began. . . . But nevertheless [dress reform] will take root—it *is* taking root—and it will win its way in spite of all opposition" (281). When his wife asks him bluntly whether he considers women inferior or superior to men (because he cannot concede equality), Willie gives a trite mid-Victorian speech about her physical inferiority and her moral superiority: "woman is therefore . . . both in one—a complex and beautiful problem, a delicious riddle which the best men never wish to have completely guessed; they prefer to leave something behind the veil—something mysterious and forever sanctified" (223). Corelli was very attached to the myth of the feminine mystique, but she nevertheless supplies an acid feminist retort to the romantic male view: "That sounds all very nice and pretty . . . but to speak bluntly, it won't wash! Don't talk of your sex, my dear boy, as though they were all romantic knights-errant of the olden time, because they're not! They're nasty fellows, most of them . . . and as for their admiration of all those womanly qualities. . . . they'll run after a ballet dancer much more readily than they'll say a civil word to a lady" (223–24).

Here again, Corelli inserts her opinions about female superiority even as she ostensibly derides feminist reforms. Although Corelli's views appear closer to those of the old-fashioned husband, Honoria's feminist speeches carry surprising conviction. When William makes a bitterly sarcastic reference to his wife's "tender maternal care" for their young son, she lashes out: "You want me—*me*—to be a docile, thank-you-for-nothing-humble-servant-yours-faithfully sort of woman, dragging about the house with a child pulling at her skirts and worrying her all day long; you want to play the male tyrant and oppressor, don't you? but you *won't!* not with *me,* at any rate! You've got a free woman in me, I tell you, not a sixteenth-century slave! My constitution is as good as yours; my brain is several degrees better; I'm capable of making a brilliant career for myself in any profession I choose to follow, and you are and always will be a mere useful nonentity" (259–60). Honoria's energetic resistance is much more rousing and persuasive than the feeble clichés offered by her wimpy husband in reply. Even her lecture on dress reform, a movement Corelli abhorred, contains more sense than satire.

Dress reform is one thing, but Honoria is also a novelist. If Corelli only obliquely sympathizes with her character's social resistance, she is unequivocal in her opinions about literature. The mannish, cigar-smoking Honoria Maggs represents female *and* artistic irresponsibility, for when a woman uses the pen she takes on a serious moral and intellectual burden. Honoria has not the feminine literary qualities of virtue, unselfishness, and instinct invoked by Gladstone. Her husband describes her book in terms that clearly violate a feminine aesthetic: "She wrote a novel—yes, and published it too; but it was not rubbish, you understand. By rubbish, I mean it was not full of silly sentiments, like Byron's verses or Shakespeare's plays; it had no idyllic-sublime stuff in it. It was a sporting novel, full of slap-dash vigour and stable slang; a really jolly, go-ahead, over-hill-and-dale, cross country sort of book, with just a thread of a plot in it . . . in short, the kind of reading that doesn't bother a fellow's brain" (181). The masculine devaluation of "silly sentiments" and "idyllic-sublime stuff" as "rubbish" is consistent with mainstream Victorian critics. But the narrator has already established his sentimentality against his wife's pragmatism (she cannot understand Shakespeare and thinks the classics are "old bores" [201]). Later the narrator defends his idealism, and surely this represents Corelli's view:

> *I am a great believer in woman's literary capability. I think that,*
> *given a woman with keen intellect, close observation and large*
> *sympathies, she ought to be able to produce greater masterpieces of*
> *literature than a man. But there is no necessity for her to part*
> *with her womanly gentleness because she writes. No, for it is just*
> *the subtle charm of her finer sex that should give the superiority*     (203)
> *to her work—not the stripping herself of all those delicate and*
> *sensitive qualities bestowed on her by Nature, and the striving to*
> *ape that masculine roughness which is precisely what we want*
> *eliminated from all high ideals of art.*

*My Wonderful Wife* is a provocative text to study against Corelli's notions of feminine writing, for it is written almost on the pattern of New Woman fiction, with a male narrator, lengthy dialogues on social questions, a feminist protagonist, and a failed marriage. It is also highly topical: Honoria reads *Truth* and back numbers of the *Daily Telegraph's* correspondence on the topic "Is Marriage a Failure?" and there is even an allusion to Oscar Wilde. Corelli's rhetorical flourishes appear only occasionally, usually in speeches given by both characters as they urge their points of view. If any of her work is written with a "man's pen," it is *My Wonderful Wife*. What, then, is the difference between the positive connotations of Corelli's "man's pen" and the New Woman's aping of "masculine roughness"?

If, as Pykett claims, gendered discourse on fiction was a political struggle for "contending versions of the feminine" (23–24), Corelli implies that the masculine is likewise diverse and can be appropriated differently by women writers. Her interference in the gender and fiction debates is unusual in that she inadvertently dislodges the assumptions behind *both* masculine and feminine attributes. Critical opinion was divided about whether Corelli wrote with a man's pen or with womanly delicacy. But regardless of these interpretations, it seems clear that she self-consciously tried to articulate a specifically feminine aesthetic in opposition to both patriarchal literary values *and* the New Woman novel and that this was tied to her belief in the sanctity of literature and the moral influence of women. Unfortunately, she had to defend her faith in both within the context of an extremely divided and competitive literary market.

### Literary Sisterhood

The Victorian publishing world was insensitive to Corelli's professed love of her fellow authors and her idealistic view of literature. The cultural stakes were high, and Corelli was forced into an attitude of unwomanly aggression. The "Authoress," she wrote, must learn to take part in the "rough-and-tumble" of professional life: "she cannot too quickly learn the truth that when once she enters the literary arena, where men are already fisticuffing and elbowing each other remorselessly, she will be met chiefly with 'kicks and no ha'pence.' She must fight like the rest, unless she prefers to lie down and be walked over" ("The Happy Life" 74). Corelli's scrappy temperament served her well when it came to her masculine enemies, but the competition inherent in a patriarchal and highly stratified literary market can thwart the impulse for female solidarity. As we have seen, Corelli was not afraid to complain to Bentley about her "sister authors" or write publicly about what she saw as literary women's jealous backbiting. In the essay on Ouida she wrote, "*Women* reviewers are comparatively few, and when they do take to the reviewing line of business, it is very frequently after they have failed as novelists. Now, to expect feminine non-success to applaud feminine triumph would surely be like asking women to become full-fledged angels at once, without giving them time to grow their wings!" (363). Angelic sisterhood is a long way off; I could cite many more examples of Corelli's antagonism toward the "remorseless literary female" (*Silver Domino* 144). There is even a humorous episode in *Thelma* where two "masculine-looking" "lady-authoresses" end up sitting apart from each other with their backs turned for an entire evening (300). Sisterhood with other women writers is problematic, to say the least, but this made Corelli all the more appreciative of sympathy and concord. When she received one kind review of *The Soul of Lilith* in the *Literary World* and later learned that the critic was a woman—"a literary woman, too, fighting a hard fight herself"—she expressed her gratitude to and respect for a potential rival who, instead of "slating" her, wrote generously and justly ("My First Book" 243).

As these examples suggest, there are problems in constituting "women" as a distinct literary group in the 1890s. What are the possibilities of finding common ground among women writers at this historical period? Can there be a feminine aesthetic (or a feminist movement) if there are broad differences, even hostilities, between women? And after all, what *is* the difference in and among women's writing?

It is well beyond the scope of this chapter to enter into the complicated discussion of women's language or to draw connections with French theorists of the feminine with the sophistication their theories deserve. But the various approaches offered by Hélène Cixous and Julia Kristeva, for instance, do provide interesting perspectives on Corelli's urge toward a feminine aesthetic, that is, an aesthetic of difference. In her book on Victorian sensation fiction and New Woman writing Pykett concludes that *écriture féminine,* the concept of a feminine mode of writing, can offer an important "difference of view" when we keep in mind the genres and the sociohistorical conditions under which women write. French feminist theory has been influential in raising the issue of how gender operates "on and in writing" and in deconstructing privileged masculine terms and values (Pykett 205). By foregrounding differences, *écriture féminine* shifts the value from "masculine" intellectualism and circumspection—Corelli's "virility"—to "feminine" "abundance, generosity, openness, and multiplicity" (Pykett 208). Cixous's spontaneous prose and Kristeva's theory of the hysteric who speaks as an outsider and whose strengths come from her "repetitive, spasmodic separations from the dominating discourse" are helpful analogues to Corelli's love of excess, impulse, and warmth (Jones 358).

Corelli's equation of "ardour" and "rush" with women's writing approximates Cixous's claim for the "infinite richness" of women's constitutions: "women's imaginary is inexhaustible, like music, painting, writing: their stream of phantasms is incredible" (334). Recall Corelli's letter to Bentley cited in chapter 2, where she insists, "there are no limits to my imagination,—to let my pen run riot would be my joy" (16 March 1887). Riotousness is precisely what Victorian masculine literary culture disliked in women, of course, as in Alfred Austin's criticism in 1869 of "the feminine element . . . unrestrainedly rioting in any and every area of life in which an indiscriminating imagination chooses to place it" (quoted in Pykett 25).

It would appear that a counteraesthetic of *jouissance* could be an evocative and positive way to read Corelli's novels. In writing against the grain of neutrality and restraint, she can voice her resistance to patriarchal norms. Such an analysis would make sense to me if Corelli purposely celebrated the feminine as "plural, spontaneous, chaotic" and feminine writing as fluid and diffuse (Felski, *Beyond* 37). But as we have seen, she was not consistent in her practice either as a writer or as a critic. Furthermore, unlike the French theorists, Corelli de-emphasizes the metaphorical powers of the female body, especially of maternity and of female sexuality; the "good mother's milk," the "white ink," the woman who "nourishes," and the "body—shot through with streams of song" (Cixous 339)—and even the "utopian" or "religious" moment of female reproduction do not apply to Corelli's oeuvre (Kristeva 206). The excessiveness and fluidity of her "feminine" prose come up against the moral elevation of chastity and sexual postponement for women: "a chaste women is an embodied defiance and reproach to man," says El-Rami in *The Soul of Lilith* (205), just as the scientist in *The Young Diana* states that "girls and women who have not been touched by man" have a strong "life-principle [because] it has not been tampered with" (165). If a feminine aesthetic promotes uninhibited release, Corelli seems to have imagined women's political power in sexual containment, not in sexual indulgence.

### *"The Mother of the World"*

Brian Masters has observed that Corelli's voluptuous depictions of women amount to a "full-blown celebration of the female" (277–78). It is true that her lush and erotic portraits of female beauty, which appear in almost every novel, indulge fantasies of released sexual desire, but the same scenes also dwell on the woman as aloof and unobtainable. For Corelli, as for many Victorian women, virginity symbolically evoked both vulnerability and power. Her uneasy treatment of women's biological functions and her valorization of chastity may be linked with the social-purity campaigns of the 1880s. Christabel Pankhurst, for example, confidently declared, "There can be no mating between the spiritually developed woman of this new day and men who in thought and conduct with regard to sex matters are their inferiors" (quoted in Showalter, *Anarchy* 22). Female celibacy seems incompatible with Corelli's emphasis on heterosexual love. Rita Felski has argued that this is one of several contradictions that articulate "an inchoate dissatisfaction with the ideal of heterosexual romance that [her novels] simultaneously seek to evoke" (*Gender of Modernity* 131). I agree and would add that her dissatisfaction is graphically linked to women's biological destiny, for Corelli repeatedly describes the tragedy of female careers that are explicitly tied to female biology. The fantasy of rejuvenation is omnipresent in her romances (and she did adjust her own age by ten years). There is nothing of the Victorian genealogical imperative in her novels. If the traditional female narrative ends with marriage and children, Corelli is determined to rewrite that story, even if it takes her into the realms of science, outer space, and elixirs of eternal youth.

In this context it is worthwhile to examine Corelli's plots, and I would like specifically to look at her view of maternity as either woman's most sublime social and personal achievement or her physical degradation and personal erasure. Like many New Women writers, Corelli reconstructs an "essentialist ideology of sexual difference in which woman, as a more highly evolved form, was held to be more civilised . . . and [paradoxically] also closely associated with nature" (Pykett 156). Pykett argues that some New Women writers "resolved this contradiction by both spiritualising and moralising maternity and womanhood" (156). In her fiction Corelli neither spiritualizes nor moralizes maternity, although there is occasional rhetoric about woman as the "Mother of the World." For example, in "Accursed Eve" she writes passionately, "What higher thing does [Woman] seek? Mother of Christianity itself, she stands before us, a figure symbolic of all good, her Holy Child in her arms, her sweet, musing, prayerful face bending over it in gravely tender devotion. From her soft breast humanity springs renewed,—she represents the youth, the hope, the love of all mankind" (*Free Opinions* 175). Corelli's theory of electric Christianity also sought to incorporate an idea of the Virgin Mary: she is a *"special message to women,"* who are the "mothers of the human race." In *A Romance of Two Worlds* she writes, "Mary's life teaches women that the virtues they need are—obedience, purity, meekness, patience, long-suffering, modesty, self-denial, and endurance. She loved to hold a secondary position; she placed herself in willing subjection" (247).

Corelli's struggle to insert women into the Christian narrative clearly leads to overstatement. Given that she did not love to hold a secondary position in anything, these assertions strike me as incongruous, perhaps even untrue to her own experiences. It is the *rhetoric* of glorified motherhood, but the ideas expressed are rarely, if ever, dramatized in Corelli's plots, where marriage and motherhood seldom lead to the heroine's fulfillment. It is instructive to place these hymns to motherhood beside a dialogue in *The Young Diana* between the scientist, Dimitrius, and the heroine, Diana May:

> "No—*you have been brave, docile, patient, obedient. All four things rare qualities in a woman!— or so men say! You would have made a good wife, only your husband would have crushed you!"*
>
> *She smiled.*
>
> *"I quite agree. But what crowds of women have been so 'crushed' since the world began!"*
>
> *"They have been useful as the mothers of the race,"* said *Dimitrius.*
>
> *"The mothers of what race?"* she asked.
>
> *"The human race, of course!"*
>
> *"Yes, but which section of it?"* she persisted with a cold little laugh.

(274)

When she thinks of the women who were sacrificed for civilizations that have long since perished, this unusual heroine concludes that reproduction is "waste—wanton, wicked waste" (274). This sentiment may be a sign of the times: the same novel includes references to the problem of overpopulation and to the "useless holocaust" of the World War (208). But if we look back, the bitterness about waste and disappointment was there as early as 1892: El-Rami, for instance, in *The Soul of Lilith* thinks bringing children into the world is "a wild waste of love and affliction [*sic*]" (182). In 1907 Corelli complained that men value women only for their reproductive functions: "Whatever she does—save and only the bearing of children—is distinctly wrong. Whenever she elects to be something more than a gentle cow with its calves, she is 'unsexed.' . . .

For, says he grandiloquently, she has no 'brain' for any higher development" ("Man's War" 426). Clearly Corelli had doubts about the glorified iconography of motherhood and saw how it could be used against intelligent, ambitious modern women.

Corelli was thirty-seven when she wrote *The Soul of Lilith,* a novel about a twelve-year-old Egyptian girl who is kept alive through injections for six years by the magus El-Rami, who wants to possess her soul. When he falls in love with her radiantly virginal body, however, she disintegrates into a pile of dust before his eyes, and he ends up in an insane asylum. The description of the integrity of the female in both body and soul is paradigmatic. For thirty years Corelli romanticized woman's nature and particular knowledge by focusing on the physical woman as untouchable and intact. The eternal feminine is, in the best of all worlds, eternally young and pure. Even the overwrought view of woman as "Mother of the World" evokes spiritual maternity, not physical reproduction. Cixous's "more body, hence more writing" does not apply to Corelli (343); excess of female flesh is always mocked, and her heroines are consistently chaste, slim, spiritualized. We have seen that she sought to represent herself in just this way in frontispieces to her novels and poetry. Corelli believed that beauty empowers women and that often enough marriage and motherhood spoil women's beauty, draining them of their energy and leading to their utter absorption in domestic cares. Marriage threatens to drag women down to the level of the sensual animal. A long speech in her first novel of 1886 about women who are "nothing but lumps of lymph and fatty matter—women with less instinct than the dumb beasts, and with more brutality" (*Romance* 86)—receives full dramatization in 1918 in *The Young Diana,* where after years of marriage the heroine's mother has "sunk into a flabby condition of resigned nonentity," "corpulent and unwieldy,—her original self was swallowed up in a sort of featherbed of adipose tissue" (11). Another fat wife in this book is portrayed as a "smug, self-satisfied constitution of oozing oil" (210). Similarly, the irresponsible mother in *Boy: A Sketch* (1900) becomes "a loose, floppy sort of figure," "a devil encased in fat" (14, 177); later in that novel, a male character makes an eloquent if superfluous speech about men's abhorrence of fat women. The tone of absolute disgust is unmistakable.

In *The Soul of Lilith* there is a more direct connection between motherhood and female degradation that is close to Corelli's own distaste for the typical feminine career (it is only one of several passages throughout her work). The speaker is the mystic El-Rami, who addresses the unmarried novelist Irene Vassilius, "a slight fair woman" (157):

(209)

> *The life of the average woman is purely animal; in her girlhood she is made to look attractive, and her days pass in the consideration of dress, appearance, manner, and conversation; when she has secured her mate, her next business is to bear him children. The children reared, and sent out into the world, she settles down into old age, wrinkled, fat, toothless, and, frequently, quarrelsome; the whole of her existence is not a grade higher than that of a leopardess or other forest creature, and sometimes not so exciting. When a woman rises above all this, she is voted by the men "unwomanly."*

El-Rami earlier has admitted that although he despises the majority of women, he profoundly pities those who are mothers: "The miserable dignity and pathos of maternity is, in my opinion, grotesquely painful" (182). Designed from birth to be docile and decorative, told that her supreme function is bearing children, a woman sacrifices the best part of herself to the next generation, who often enough are ungrateful.

Corelli seems to admire the suggestions of power inherent in an iconography of the "Mother of the World," but she cannot endorse motherhood as feminine destiny. In *Boy,* for example, she dismisses "the mere figure-head of femininity, just capable of wearing a gown and having a baby" (191). The good virgin in that novel is predictably jilted by her rich fiancé, but unpredictably she gets an education and becomes a nurse in the Boer War. Corelli harps on her belief that women need to rise above the level of sensual existence.

Two of her biographers have asserted that Corelli's apparent squeamishness about sexuality is a symptom of female neurosis (Masters 234–42; Bullock 28–34). I would like to suggest that her partial resistance to the myth of motherhood and her alternations between rapture and repugnance for the female body are a potentially significant aspect of her politics and her aesthetic, especially if we consider her novels in the light of the female quest plot or as stories of female becoming. Felski has described Corelli's spiritual romances in this way, calling the heroine of *A Romance of Two Worlds,* for example, "a bold seeker after knowledge" (*Gender of Modernity* 135). The many female out-of-body experiences in

Corelli's novels underscore her discomfort with the way a woman's body determines the place she occupies in the world. Judith Kegan Gardiner has explained that "a woman's sense of her gender, her sexuality, and her body may assume a different, perhaps more prominent, shape in her conception of her self than these factors would for a man. Women are encouraged to judge their inner selves through their external physical appearance and to equate the two" (190). Women writers interpret this alienation between outer and inner selves in various ways. It may even be difficult for a woman writer, especially one of Corelli's generation, to verbalize this alienation without recourse to dominant masculine myths about femininity, which split women into goddesses and devils, virgins and whores. According to Nina Auerbach, Victorian patriarchs "disposed of their women by making myths of them," but exploring those myths— or fabricating one's own, as Corelli does repeatedly—is evidence of a growing belief in feminine strength, a movement toward subjective authority (111). Again, I want to locate the *meanings* of subjective authority for Corelli in the aesthetic, because feminism at this period was a contest for cultural images as much as for political reforms. The femme fatale and the chaste maiden, the angry feminist and the patient Griselda, the woman of genius and the lady of leisure are revolving images in Corelli's creative repertoire of the feminine.

### The Young Diana

In *The Young Diana,* published when Corelli was sixty-three, these feminine types are literally merged in one heroine, Diana May. The novel offers refracted images of women. The heroine, for example, is at times narrow spinster and rosy maiden, long-suffering jilted lover and vengeful beauty, student of science and society vixen. She is also split into the "old" and "young" Diana, a dissection that allows Corelli to explore a woman's possibilities for mature fulfillment given her culture's discrimination against older women. Furthermore, this novel is generically split between a sentimental story about a lonely woman who is "obsessed by the Duty fetish" and a quasifeminist science-fiction fantasy about finding the elixir of life (47).

Diana May, an intelligent fortyish spinster, fakes her own death by drowning in order to flee her selfish parents after she overhears them discussing her as "*in the way*": "Unmarried women of a certain age always

are, you know. . . . To be a spinster over thirty seems . . . a kind of illness,"
says her father, a lewd and vain man who fears his daughter's company
makes him look old (50–51). She makes her way to London and stays
with a suffragette friend, Sophy Lansing, the only person who knows that
Diana is not really dead (her parents make a show of grief that the women
find both hilarious and repulsive). Without a job or any family ties in
England, Diana decides to reply to a curious advertisement for a "Cou-
rageous and Determined Woman of mature years [with] a fair knowledge of modern science" to assist in important and difficult scientific
work in Geneva (34). Dr. Feodor Dimitrius lives in an elegant chateau
with his aged mother and a mute Negro servant. He approves of Diana's
application and proceeds gradually to involve her in dangerous experiments intended to restore her youth and beauty. Although an urbane
and kindly man, as a scientist he sees Diana only as a subject for study:
"for my purposes, you are not a woman—you are simply an electric bat-
tery" (206). Their relationship becomes a battle of wills, although Diana
keeps her promise and obeys Dimitrius's orders even when he warns her
that she may die. The experiment is a success, however: Diana grows
younger and more beautiful every day. When her two-year contract has
expired, she leaves the chateau and returns to London, but Sophy does
not recognize the "young" Diana, and her parents think she is a crazed
stranger. Diana's remarkable youth and beauty make her a society celebrity: "photographers, cinema-producers, dressmakers, tailors, jewellers
besieged her" (348). Her physical attractions, however, become weapons
of female vengeance: she psychologically manipulates her father, who is
"afflicted by the disease of senile amorousness for all women," and tor-
tures the lover who jilted her twenty years ago, a lascivious married man
who is now fifty (356). Importantly, Diana does not try to pass as anyone
other than herself; her schemes for justice rely on the cultural value
placed on youth and sexuality, something she has recovered but the men
who have scorned her have not. She is suddenly summoned to Paris by
the news that a kind and elderly scientist who had proposed to her in
Geneva has died and left her an enormous fortune. The novel ends with
an epilogue in which Diana explains to her "master," Dimitrius, that he
no longer has any claim on her, for she is "a new creature, no longer of
mortal clay, but of an ethereal matter which has never walked on earth
before" (378). The narrator tells us that Diana still lives in Paris, alone "in

a strange world of unknown experience to which she seems to belong. She is happy, because she has forgotten all that would have made her otherwise" (380).

There is a lot going on in this peculiar story. First, there is the obvious theme of the discarded spinster, jilted in her youth, now "angular and flat-chested" and disastrously "clever," who has no social worth once her sexual attractions have gone (14). Corelli lashes out with a vengeance at the devaluation of unmarried older women. Diana's superfluity intersects with treatments of women's opportunities for employment and social usefulness after the war. The suffragette Sophy Lansing represents the voice of progressive womanhood. "What a life for you, patient Grizel!" she writes to Diana. "You are really clever and could do so much. This is Woman's Day, and you are a woman of exceptional ability" (29). Even her father says, "we ought to have trained her to do something useful. Nursing, or doctoring, or dressmaking, or typewriting" (52).

Corelli's feminist voice comes closest to the surface, however, when she describes Diana's transformation from an angular nobody to a femme fatale. In certain ways *The Young Diana* is like Fay Weldon's *The Life and Loves of a She-Devil* (1984) but without Weldon's wry humor and feminist wit; both novels are protests against society's constructions and idealizations of woman, and both involve biological manipulations of a female subject. "To-day our surgeons can graft new flesh on old and succeed in their design —why should not fresh cells of life be formed through Nature's own germinating processes to take the place of those that perish?" asks the daring scientist, Dimitrius (240). In a sense, the 1890s prototype of male mastery à la Svengali and Dracula has given way to the geneticist and the plastic surgeon.

Of course, Corelli's novel is not a fantasy of reconstructive surgery, but the issue of woman as a repairable construct takes precedence over all other themes. The heroine moves through stages of alienation, from her society, from her body—and from Corelli's fictional world. At the beginning of the novel Diana seems another of Corelli's old-fashioned Victorian heroines, the single woman who accepts her solitude and brings smiles and goodwill to all who know her, a version of the generous "old maid" Letitia in *Boy* or the self-sacrificing Mary Dean in *The Treasure of Heaven* (1906): Diana "bore her lot with exemplary cheerfulness,—she neither grizzled nor complained, nor showed herself envious of youth or youthful loveliness. A comforting ideal of 'duty' took possession of her mind, and she devoted herself to the tenderest care of her fat mother and irritable father" (14). There is a hint that underneath this feminine subservience lies the rebellious virago. When Diana arrives in London after her supposed death, she makes long and angry speeches to Sophy about her desire for revenge "on all and everything that has set me apart and alone as I am!" (94). Sophy is amazed that the "always gentle, patient, and adaptable" Diana can sound like a tragedy queen (94). Corelli has remodeled a feminine ideal with a feminist's resistance. After twenty years of submission and domestic slavery, Diana wants freedom and power.

Importantly, she wants sexual power over men, not a typewriting job or the vote. Part of *The Young Diana* is a fantasy of female sexual domination, and Corelli seems to imagine that this is a legitimate route to equality. But another part of this novel is a fantasy of female autonomy. I have alluded to Corelli's spiritual-quest tales, stories of becoming and of female identity that are linked to a desire to resolve the socialized division of women's inner and outer selves. After the "old" Diana is rejuvenated, the difference between her outer beauty and her inner experience is painfully manifest. She tells Dimitrius, "I am not really young . . . I know myself. Deep in my brain the marks of lonely years and griefs are imprinted. . . . So it happens that beneath the covering of youth which your science gives me, and under the mark of this outward loveliness, I, the same Diana, live with a world's experience, as one in a prison" (276). Like Frankenstein's monster, the "young" Diana resists her creator's will, and her female becoming takes an unexpected trajectory. Denied authentic love, she feels herself *"hardening,"* she has no sentiments, she "is no longer capable of loving, but she knew she could hate!" (247, 283). With glittering eyes, Diana tells Dimitrius that when she looks at her face in the mirror "it seems to me the face of somebody else! I don't feel in myself that I possess it! . . . *it is not human!*" (260). Men, women, and Victorian ideology are complicit in the creation of the beautiful female monster.

*The Young Diana* seems to have little in common with the homosexual subtext of *The Picture of Dorian Gray* (1891), but there is a passage that employs the same metaphor of the picture as the self: "My own interior self admires my outward appearance without any closer connection than that felt by anyone looking at a picture," Diana admits. "I live *within* the picture—and no one seeing the picture could think it was I!" (280).

Although outwardly the picture of feminine perfection, Diana is no longer a "woman"; she has been (re)constructed as a physical ideal but paradoxically has no place in the biological order. She has a secret life. Dimitrius says, "The magnetism of sex is the thing that 'pulls'—but you—you, my subject, have *no* sex! The 'love' which is purely physical,—the mating which has for its object the breeding of children, is not for you any more than it would be for an angel" (252). Although Diana's life is presented as an escape from degrading sexual urges, Corelli's fantasy of eternal youth is sadly barren, without the charms of athletic exuberance, intellectual curiosity, or fresh and vibrant feelings. The heroine has been made into the "young" Diana, but as she says, "I'm growing young looks with old experience!—rather a dangerous combination of forces" (248). As she becomes physically younger and thereby acquires more social and sexual power, she suffers an identity crisis that bears relation to the task of contemporary feminists to reconceptualize woman. Carol Watts has described the body in discourse as a "'locus of cultural interpretations' which have been socially preestablished, *and* a 'field of interpretative possibilities' in which possible roles and identities proliferate" (85). Culturally Corelli's heroine is already spoken for, but psychologically she is still in the process of discovering an identity that transcends her own bodily imprisonment *and* cultural readings of her body, both old and young. But her proliferating identities paradoxically erase her individuality. As a spinster, Diana was socially invisible; as a wife, she would have lost her individuality: Dimitrius tells his mother, "you have sacrificed your own identity—the thing that Miss Diana calls her 'significance.' You lost that willingly when you married—all women lose it when they marry" (171). As a young beauty, she is alienated from her own face, her prettiness seems to belong to others, and her "master" claims her as his property. The only escape to personal autonomy, what Diana calls triumphantly "a Self independent of all save its own elements," is the destruction of the entire construct woman (379). Science fiction enables Corelli to dissolve woman into "an ethereal matter," further underscoring her own sense of being trapped as much by her corporality (and her mortality) as by the roles assigned to woman at various stages of her physical maturity. In the epilogue Dimitrius tells Diana, "so far as you are a woman, your circumstances are little changed," for she is still as alone in the world as she was when she came to Geneva years ago

(376). Diana says, "You say, and you say rightly, that 'so far as I am a woman'—my circumstances are not changed from what they were when I first came to you in Geneva. . . . But only 'so far as I am a woman.' Now—how do you know I am a woman at all?" (378).

### An Open Secret

I have said that Diana's proliferating identities paradoxically erase her identity as an individual woman. This may be a useful way to approach Corelli's negotiations of gender difference. Poststructuralism has evoked the evasiveness of woman as a signifying category. Linda Alcoff explains, "For Derrida, women have always been defined as a subjugated difference within a binary opposition. . . . The only way to break out of this structure, and in fact to subvert the structure itself, is to assert total difference, to be that which cannot be pinned down or subjugated within a dichotomous hierarchy" (441). It is tempting to read Corelli's instability and evasiveness as negative resistance. In 1890, for instance, she wrote triumphantly to Bentley, "my puzzled critics will consider me a sort of literary *chameleon!*" (10 August 1890). But her chameleon strategy had the liability of endangering her commitment to feminine writing, and in *The Young Diana* she suggests that the fantasy of female autonomy can be fulfilled only by sacrificing her status as a woman, a negative strategy that holds small liberatory potential for the woman reader of 1918 (or of 1999). The subtitle to *The Young Diana* is "An Experiment of the Future"; according to Masters, Corelli conscientiously wished this novel to be about the coming preeminence of women. She wrote an unpublished letter to the editor of the *Observer* in self-justification: "My book is a practical and passionate effort to save *Woman* alive! beautiful and exquisite Woman!—the mother of all Man!" (Masters 271). Her moral earnestness is everywhere apparent, but ultimately the novel seems depressing and far from a proclamation of feminine ascendancy.

We have seen how Corelli was unable to resolve the contradictions implicit in the idea of difference: assertions of essential feminine traits bump up against deconstructions of gendered terms and values. Gender, politics, and writing constituted a solemn trinity at the turn of the century. But there also existed a certain playfulness in transposing strict gender categories. It is surely ironic that Joseph Conrad would call Hall

Caine "a kind of male Marie Corelli," given how much she tried to differentiate her novels from those of her biggest competitor (137). The remark gathers resonance when we consider that Caine's sexuality, like Corelli's, was undecided: Philip Hoare reveals that Caine carried on an affair with a male doctor who was a suspect for the Jack the Ripper murders (67). Hoare also states unproblematically that Corelli was "probably a lesbian" (90).

In 1898 Wilde could joke, "the public like an open secret. Half of the success of Marie Corelli is due to the no doubt unfounded rumour that she is a woman" (*Letters,* 8 January 1898). Wilde's remark is not kind, but his own experience with open secrets lends it authority. Alan Sinfield offers the open secret as a paradigm for homosexuality, citing D. A. Miller's claim that the function of the secret "is not to conceal knowledge, so much as to conceal the knowledge of the knowledge" (8). The open secret "helps to constitute the public/private boundary—the binary structure that seems to demarcate our subjectivities—and thus facilitates the policing of that boundary" (Sinfield 8). Victorian literary critics may have been the border police of gender identity. But Corelli's popularity with readers partly may have relied on her uneven management of open secrets and the broader cultural obsessions about women, men, sexuality, and aesthetics.

"Is there a feminine aesthetic?" asks Silvia Bovenschen. "There is, thank heaven, no premeditated strategy which can predict what happens when female sensuality is freed. . . . Art should become feminised, and women's participation . . . would do it a lot of good" (49–50). Corelli had no premeditated strategy, but she shared the self-consciousness of modernist women writers such as Virginia Woolf, Dorothy Richardson, and Djuna Barnes who *were* strategically concerned about avoiding masculine literary habits. In the following chapter I will examine Corelli's uses of subjectivity in the context of modernist strictures against self-expression, focusing on two texts: her unpublished correspondence with Arthur Severn and the imaginative version of their relationship that was published by Bertha Vyver the year after Corelli's death. Feminist theorists have argued that an aesthetics of impersonality may be handled differently by women writers. I want to take off from this suggestion and in the process think also about the role Corelli's religious beliefs, her metaphysics, played in her utopian vision of sexual equality.

# IV

## The Weltanschauung
## of Marie Corelli

*She grappled with magnificent themes with all the
reckless energy and* désinvolture *of her temperament,
but I doubt if she could have written a work of fiction
founded on the stream of consciousness, for her stream
of consciousness was like a series of geysers continuously exploding.*

E. F. Benson,
*Final Edition*
(1940)

SEVERAL RECENT FEMINIST approaches to literary modernism and the
melodramatic mode, in particular Ann Cvetkovich's *Mixed Feelings,* Rita
Felski's *The Gender of Modernity,* and Suzanne Clark's *Sentimental Modernism,* have opened up new approaches to the way we read Victorian sensation fiction and early-twentieth-century mass fiction.[1] Although the
subjects of their books differ, these critics examine the subversive potential of what Cvetkovich terms "the literature of affect." Whereas
Cvetkovich's focus is on Victorian sensation fiction and mass culture,
Felski and Clark study the modernist's notion of impersonality and emotional distance, seeking either to construct an alternative aesthetic for
women writers or to deconstruct modernist detachment by placing ca-
nonical texts alongside sentimental or melodramatic works by women.

I have found Felski's formulation of the "popular sublime"—an ad-
aptation of Barbara Claire Freeman's "feminine sublime" in the context
of modernist discourse—especially relevant to my study of Marie Corelli. Following Peter Brooks's arguments in *The Melodramatic Imagination,*
Felski argues that "the aspiration to the transcendent, exalted, and ineffable [is] a central impetus of modern mass culture" but that the sublime
has been identified historically as a masculine form belonging to the

avant-garde rather than to the mass market: "The search for the ideal, eagerly endorsed by critics when expressed in difficult works of modern high art or organic forms of preindustrial folk culture, is redefined as nothing more than falseness, self-deception, and banal escapism when manifested in popular, mass-produced texts" (119). The search for the sublime, or for transcendence, is also bound up with the idea of imper-sonality, an "accepted precondition for the practice of art," which, as Carol Watts has explained, "also involved, within one particular modern-ist ideology, a hidden cultural agenda: a 'dehumanizing' voyage out away from the soilure of the everyday social world, away from the political and historical demands of embodied life, into the autonomous realm of art" (91).

Taken together, these interpretations raise problems for a writer such as Corelli: popular women writers who ignored the modernist stric-tures against self-expression and longed for the ineffable and the ideal still had to confront the "soilure" of their experience with twentieth-century materialism and with gender politics in the real world. This leaves open the question of whether popular novels by women were able effectively to address women's social and political condition, and this is especially pertinent when women employ genres that have been seen as escapist and politically uninvolved, such as the heterosexual romance or the confes-sional love story.

In this chapter I want to introduce Corelli in the conversations about women, modernism, and subjectivity begun by Felski in her chap-ter on Corelli in *The Gender of Modernity* and by R. B. Kershner, who has argued that Corelli's characteristic blend of the sexual and the spiritual, her use of myth and allusions within a present-day narrative, her attitude of persecuted artist and her high moral claims for art make her a "Mod-ernist hybrid" ("Modernism's Mirror" 79). The work of these scholars has made me think through the connections in Corelli's later novels, chiefly those published after the start of World War I, among subjective or expressive writing, ethical and political consciousness, and the search for spiritual transcendence, which, according to Felski, characterizes mo-dernity. Although the modernist zeitgeist seems describable in terms of skepticism, impersonality, transcendence, and artistic aloofness, all of these factors or impulses are rendered complex when the writer is a woman. In the first part of this chapter I explore the notion of Corelli's metaphysics against her interest in women's social equality, and then move the discussion to female subjectivity and confessional writing by closely studying two documents, a private ten-year correspondence with the painter Arthur Severn and its public reconstruction, published after Corelli's death.

*Open Confession* is an unrestrained statement of disillusioned love, a self-defined "'record' of a perished passion" (162). This text is also the record of both a moral crisis and a feminist transvaluation of the ideology of romantic love and surrender, what Adrienne Rich called, in 1973, "the central temptation of the female condition" (96). If we accept Rich's formulation of love as a "temptation" to capitulate to an ideology of heterosexual romance, the loss of love can provoke a corresponding temptation to capitulate to bitterness, cynicism, and despair. *Open Confession* is Corelli's last admission of faith in her ideals of love and equality, a document that describes the process of comprehending the world from the feminine (or feminist) point of view. The absolution that results from a confession of emotional vulnerability and disappointed desire is akin to the consciousness-raising essential to feminist politics: the self-forgiveness and understanding that come when a woman realizes her problems are not private but communal.

### The Soul That Has Found Itself

Corelli's popular success was in part due to her understanding that almost every thinking person in the last two decades of the nineteenth century was occupied with religious questions. For Corelli scientific skepticism needed to be reconciled with spiritual longings. She claimed that this was precisely the point of *A Romance of Two Worlds:* "to *try* and attach *scientific* possibility to the perfect doctrines of the New Testament, in order to appeal to those whose minds refused to accept anything but that which could be presented to them as a *possible* scientific fact" (Corelli–Bentley Correspondence, 15 November 1886). Two years later, she wrote to George Bentley, "Do you notice what an *immense* eagerness there is at the present day to read everything connected with religion and psychology," acknowledging that Mrs. Humphry Ward's *Robert Elsmere* was making a "hit" for this very reason (20 April 1888). Corelli's astuteness was not a matter of marketing. She seems to have possessed a profound

responsiveness to the intellectual and emotional currents of her day. In
1889 she wrote to Bentley:

> *I don't suppose there is any question more burning at the present*
> *hour than that of faith or non-faith in the Divine Supernatural.*
> *Neither love, nor war, nor adventure stir a society of people into*
> *such eager attention as the discussion of this vaster subject. Wher-*
> *ever I go, whoever I meet, it is the same thing . . . always the*
> *same anxious, almost feverish interest. Politics and Parnell are*     (27 March
> *nowhere, directly you touch ever so distantly on the religious*       1889)
> *phase of things—and the most practical business people are to the*
> *full as eager as the most romantic. The fact is, the times are*
> *evil—and there is an instinctive sense in everyone that some-*
> *thing is wrong, something that will have to be set right, probably*
> *at a frightful cost of trouble and sorrow.*

The cultural mood of confusion and degeneration demanded a
counterassertion of order and optimism, and Corelli was able to supply
her audiences with an original and reassuring philosophy. Importantly,
gender equality enters into Corelli's notion of the universal order. In *The
Soul of Lilith* a mysterious monk from Cyprus articulates a worldview that
makes sexual equality a cosmic mandate: "There are Two Governing
Forces in the Universe. . . . One, the masculine, is Love, the other, the
feminine, is Beauty. These two, reigning together, are GOD; just as man
and wife are One. From Love and Beauty proceed Law and Order. . . .
[W]hen God made Man in His Own Image, it was as Male and Female"
(136). These statements approximate Corelli's worldview, which was essentially dualistic (according to the monk, there are even male and female
atmospheres). But there is no reason why even such a strange belief as
that articulated in this quotation should relegate Corelli to the level of an
eccentric crank. Her creative blend of science, paganism, the Hebrew
God, and quasitheosophical mysticism appealed particularly to female
readers (and maybe to some modernists) because it offered a version of
God that differed from that of the Christian patriarchs. For Corelli "in
His Own Image" means in the image of both female and male; it means
an androgynous god, the harmony of whose creation depends on the
reflected complementarity of her/his dual nature. There are repeated
statements to this effect in all of her mystical romances. As the philosopher

and mystic in *The Life Everlasting: A Reality of Romance* (1911) declares, "For surely you know there is no single thing in the Universe. The very microbes of disease and health go in pairs . . . all things are dual" (244).

Given this picture of the universe, the central female quest in Corelli's supernatural romances—*A Romance of Two Worlds, Ardath, Ziska: The Problem of a Wicked Soul* (1897), *The Soul of Lilith,* and *The Life Everlasting*—is twofold: spiritual union with a masculine counterpart through death or some other means of mystical recognition and female self-discovery. The heroine must overcome several obstacles, such as hostile public opinion, self-doubt, or material temptations, in order to reach the goal of sexual and spiritual equilibrium. There is usually a risk of failure or death but never within the mystical enactment of male-female completion. Conventional marriage and sexual passion are insignificant in comparison with the sublime achievements of spiritual union. Felski has pointed out the emotional ambivalence in Corelli's representations of gender, explaining that she often oscillates between expressing "anger, frustration, and resentment toward the male sex" and yearning "for oceanic dissolution of the self in an ecstatic merging of souls" (*Modernity* 130). It is possible, though, to see this merging as a fantasy not of female erasure but of human completion. There is never a "dissolution of the self"; rather, Corelli's heroines assert their power as sexual equals and as desiring subjects. Repeatedly she insists that what the world understands as love is mere sensual passion, which pales in significance when male and female souls, in the words of Elizabeth Barrett Browning, "stand up erect and strong" as equals before a higher power. It is primarily women who make these psychic journeys in Corelli's fiction, often in overt resistance to social convention.

The politics of all of this, however, is ambiguous: the pursuit of the ideal gestures toward unresolvable social tensions, but it also evokes the eternal verities of sexual otherness. In this context it is helpful to study the language of Corelli's "utopian gesturing" (Felski, *Modernity* 143). The underlying assumption in these spiritual quests is that the social situation of sexual inequality is a human error attributable to masculine egotism that should and will be rectified in the hereafter. Corelli's rhetoric is one of fairness and egalitarianism. In *The Soul of Lilith* Irene Vassilius calmly says, "I am not what is termed 'strong-minded,' I simply seek justice" (204). The electric religion in *A Romance of Two Worlds* contains utopian visions not of sexual dominance but of a balance of powers. The Chaldean priest, Heliobas, explains to the female narrator: "Now, you will not be dominated—you will be simply *equalized;* that is, you will find the exact counterpart of your own soul dwelling also in human form. . . . There is no union so lovely as such an one—no harmony so exquisite" (316). The same theme is taken up in *The Life Everlasting:* "We—my Beloved and I—can only prove the truth of the Soul's absolute command over all spiritual, material, and elemental forces by our One life and the way we live it" (437). For Corelli sex warfare is a perversion of this higher power, this fabulous energy that can command so much of the material world. She continually reminds her readers that to mistake marriage and reproduction for this exalted view of love is to miss her spiritual message altogether. Even in a novel such as *Ziska,* where the femme fatale reclaims her soul mate by murdering him as he has murdered her, the rhetoric is of justice. At the end of this extraordinary novel, Ziska lures the reincarnated Araxes to an Egyptian tomb, where she is transformed into an angelic spirit before claiming his life as her own. A voice is heard out of the heavy gloom of the sarcophagus: "Peace! The old gods are best, and the law is made perfect. A life demands a life. Love's debts must be paid by Love! The woman's soul forgives; the man's repents" (302).

Is there a social message about sexual inequality in these esoteric stories, or does peace from sex antagonism exist only in the ineffable beyond? I agree with Felski that Corelli's novels cannot be read simply as subversive or ideologically resistant texts; although they describe heroines who reach unattainable heights of mystical knowledge and ecstasy, most of her romances do not "translate into any external challenge to the subordinate social positioning of women" (136). Nevertheless, a woman writer's desire for spiritual transcendence may well be tied to her desire for political, social, and personal autonomy, the transcendence of restrictive gender roles, even if that aim is not explicitly dramatized or asserted polemically in her work. Diana Basham, in *The Trial of Woman,* has studied how the Victorian occult revival was repeatedly linked with the woman question (Basham never mentions Corelli, which is surprising, given the nature of her romances). Furthermore, the notion of the triumphant human will may carry a different meaning for women. Although one could argue that Corelli's novels exhibit a neodeterminism based on her belief in the unique destiny of each soul, she was vigorously opposed to the philosophical positivism fashionable in the 1880s and 1890s, and she made every effort to resist the skepticism of the twentieth century. She wrote frequently and passionately about the power of the human will.

*The Life Everlasting* is probably the best dramatization of her creed; it follows the same lines as her other spiritual-quest stories, but the plot is pared down, unencumbered by mad scientists or society dinners. The story is told by a nameless female narrator who willingly undergoes a spiritual ordeal at a mysterious, secluded monastery in order to be re-united with a masculine spirit from her previous incarnations. Although this sounds like a spiritualized romance plot, the narrator's quest is ulti-mately for self-knowledge and perfect freedom. She explains that the chief point of the guru Aselzion's instruction "was the test of the Brain and Soul against 'influences'—the opposing influences of others"—which are the chief hindrance to spiritual progress, and throughout she resists the pow-erful attractions of her soul mate, Santoris (436). "Did he assume to mas-ter *me?*" she wonders. "No! I would not yield to that! If yielding were necessary, it must be my own free will that gave in, not his compelling influence!" (238). Corelli underscores the importance of the individual will in a thirty-page prologue to this novel:

(21)

> *To multitudes of people this expression "the Soul" has become overfam-iliar by constant repetition, and conveys little more than the suggestion of a myth, or the hint of an Imaginary Existence. Now there is nothing in the whole Universe so real as the Vital Germ of the actual Form and Being of the living, radiant Creature within each one of us,—the crea-ture who, impressed and guided by our Free Will, works out its own delight or doom. The WILL of each man or woman is like the compass of a ship,—where it points the ship goes. . . . God leaves the WILL of man at perfect liberty. His Divine Love neither constrains nor com-pels. We must Ourselves learn the ways of Right and Wrong, and hav-ing learned, we must choose. We must injure Ourselves. God will not injure us. We invite our own miseries. God does not send them. The evils and sorrows that afflict mankind are of mankind's own making.*

Although this formulation does not account for accidents of birth and political circumstances, it is an important assertion for a woman writing in 1911. Linda Alcoff has explained that "the place of the free-willed

subject who can transcend nature's mandate" has been historically re-
served for men (435). But Corelli insists that women possess moral agency
and that spiritual and intellectual transcendence is women's task as much
as it is men's. If these claims seem no more than superstition or boiled-
down metaphysics, far removed from feminist politics, I want to suggest
that for Corelli the realm of the spiritual *was* the realm of equality. Her
way of understanding the world was fundamentally religious and her instinct was affirmative, yet she lived long enough to feel a sense of alienation, loss, and regret for the Victorian past. Her impulses are not all that
different from some of the major modernists of the period, but she was
not an intellectual and had no scholastic training. Furthermore, to dismiss metaphysics as obfuscation, "an exercise in mystification" (Alcoff
448), is to dismiss any "attempt to reason through ontological issues that
cannot be decided empirically, including Derrida's analysis of language,
Foucault's conception of power, and all of the post-structuralist critiques
of humanist theories of the subject" (449). Alcoff asserts that "the problem of conceptualizing 'woman' is . . . a metaphysical problem" in that it
is a question that cannot be determined through empirical means alone
(449). Corelli's metaphysical fantasies of reincarnation, romantic soul
mates, and female spiritual transcendence may be closely linked with
her rudimentary efforts to answer the ontological question "What is a
woman?"

### Feminist Consciousness

One answer to this question suggested by Corelli's quest romances is that
woman is an identity in process. I would like to add another layer to this
discussion by evoking feminist phenomenology. In an essay published in
1975 Sandra Lee Bartky contends that marxist scholars have not paid sufficient attention to the "anguished consciousness, the inner uncertainty
and confusion which characterizes human subjectivity in periods of social
change" (398). Corelli lived through a time of radical questioning about
women's roles and women's nature. Bartky argues that when a woman
"becomes" a feminist she recognizes the contradictions of social reality
and internally negates them in behalf of a transforming project for the
future. For Bartky feminist consciousness is "an anguished consciousness" characterized by an apprehension of injustice and the knowledge

that what *is* is not what *ought to be*. Bartky ties feminist consciousness to the existentialist project of transcendence, the trajectory of negation and transformation. Feminist consciousness is living part of one's life in "the sort of ambiguous ethical situation which existentialist writers have been most adept at describing" and includes "double ontological shock": "first, the realization that what is really happening is quite different from what appears to be happening, and second, the frequent inability to tell what is really happening at all" (402). Though this awareness is difficult to live with, feminist consciousness is shaped by existential self-determination: it embraces a "joyous consciousness of one's own power," hope in the possibility of change, and a new identification with women.

It is feasible to look at Corelli's output over thirty years and trace this kind of unfolding knowledge—that the world is not as it should be, that women's lives are unfairly circumscribed, that contradictions between her experiences and her ideals seem frustratingly unresolvable. I see Corelli's last published book, *Open Confession,* as the result of expanding consciousness, moral growth, and emergent feminist understanding. But it is vital to bear in mind that by 1924 her novels were going out of fashion, and despite having a certain amount of literary prestige, a Corelli novel belonged firmly to modern mass culture. Andreas Huyssen has cataloged mass culture at the turn into modernism as "serialized feuilleton novels, popular and family magazines, the stuff of lending libraries, fictional bestsellers and the like," arguing also that high modernism insistently inscribes mass culture as feminine (55). Huyssen persuasively argues for the destabilizing potential of such popular texts, but his delineation of mass culture as "the stuff" of Mudie's, as best-sellers and "the like," dismisses the possibility that there may be a certain amount of linguistic and psychic difficulty in giving expression to emotions, dreamworlds, and fantasies. Fredric Jameson, in describing the dilemma confronted by an attempt to coordinate marxist and Freudian criticism, strikes a chord that sounds like a feminist slogan when he notes "the difficulty of proving mediations between social phenomena and what must be called private, rather than merely individual, acts." Jameson continues: "Anyone who has ever tried to recount a dream to someone else is in a position to measure the immense gap, the qualitative incommensurability, between the vivid memory of the dream and the dull, impoverished words which are all we can find to convey it: yet this incommensurability, between the particular and the universal, between the *vécu* and language itself, is one in which we dwell all our lives, and it is from it that all works of literature and culture necessarily emerge" (338–39).

The metaphor of recounting a dream is particularly appropriate for a discourse of love, which, according to Roland Barthes, has no systematic idiom (*Lover's Discourse* 210–13), and it is the love story, with its dramatic appeal to emotional and sexual fulfillment, that chiefly occupies the popular genres Huyssen identifies as feminine and mass literature. As I have explained, recent critics have shown that this literature should not be overlooked when discussing some aspects of the modernist sensibility: ironic detachment, emotional inhibition, and a mood of alienation or lost idealism. Since the love story dwells on the expression of feeling, this genre may be paradigmatic of the need Jameson describes to make sense of the world through language, especially for women, for whom the gap between the particular and the universal may be intimately tied to politics and self-determination. Women are also the chief consumers of sentimental love stories in a literary culture that privileges intellectuality, formalism, and restraint. If "romance is a primary category of the female imagination" (Snitow 160), this may have as much to do with the emotional and linguistic license of the genre as with the details of the generic heterosexual love story.

*Expression of Personality*

Feminist critics have analyzed the consequences for literature of the prejudices against women's self-expression, but self-suppression and silence also have emotional and psychological repercussions for the individual woman (whether she is a writer or not). In *The Second Sex* Simone de Beauvoir argues:

> *Living marginally to the masculine world, she sees it not in its universal form but from her special point of view . . . she protests against [reality], with words. She seeks through nature for the image of her soul, she abandons herself to reveries, she wishes to attain her* being—*but she is doomed to frustration; she can recover it only in the region of the imaginary. To prevent an inner life that has no* useful *purpose from sinking into nothingness, to assert herself against conditions which she bears rebelliously, to create a world other than that in which she fails to attain her being, she must resort to* self-expression. (783)

Although extremely interested in *being,* early literary modernists wanted little to do with self-expression. T. S. Eliot's famous dictum in "Tradition and the Individual Talent" (1919)—"poetry is not a turning loose of emotion, but an escape from emotion; it is not the expression of personality, but an escape from personality"—defined the aesthetic values of much early-twentieth-century writing. Alex Zwerdling has explained that "fiction was to follow the same rules, and women writers voiced this belief as regularly as men" (247). Zwerdling cites Katherine Mansfield, who in 1927 wrote, "I think there is a very profound distinction between any kind of *confession* and creative work" (247). Virginia Woolf was unusually anxious to avoid the stigma of personal writing, or sentimentality. "The word 'sentimental' sticks in my gizzard," she wrote in 1925 (79). These aesthetic standards contributed to the devaluation of popular fiction and especially works by Victorian writers born a generation earlier than the high modernists who had not adjusted to the new mood of restraint.

Corelli was the queen of self-expression. In 1886 she meekly asked readers of *A Romance of Two Worlds,* "In these days of haste and scramble, when there is no time for faith, is there time for sentiment?" (333–34). Her affirmative reply resounded for the next thirty years. If her sentimental novels aggravate the tensions between high art and popular culture, as well as between masculine taste and feminine trash, they also struggle against an incommensurability that is tied to an ontological assertion: the validity of an inner life that is meaningful, of her *being* over her nothingness, of her dreamworld over reality. Not surprisingly, her overwrought, obsessive narratives forcibly represent extreme emotional or psychological states: they are defiantly melodramatic.

*Open Confession* is a peculiar form of melodrama, however, and I will later discuss its generic complexity as a confessional woman's novel. Corelli's determination to recount publicly the pangs of love is potentially transgressive, since such sentimentality can evoke repressed, uncontained feeling. Why does a writer in 1906 call her "a social menace" and urge that her books be "banned from the public libraries as insidious and harmful to public morality" (Stuart-Young 692)? In 1914 another writer claimed, "The sexual problem clutches Marie Corelli hotly in its drastic grip" (Samuel 126). In *A Lover's Discourse* Barthes offers an intriguing theory about the obscenity of love for modern subjects:

*Discredited by modern opinion, love's sentimentality must be as-*
*sumed by the amorous subject as a powerful transgression which*
*leaves him alone and exposed; by a reversal of values, then, it is*
*this sentimentality which today constitutes love's obscenity.* . . .
*The moral tax levied by society on all transgressions affects pas-*
*sion still more than sex today. Everyone will understand that X*
*has "huge problems" with his sexuality; but no one will be inter-*
*ested in those Y may have with his sentimentality:* love is ob-
scene precisely in that it puts the sentimental in place of
the sexual. *(emphasis added)*

(175, 178)

This acute observation sheds light on some of the more violent reactions
to Corelli's romances. Unable to deal with her sentimentality problem,
which is the real source of discomfort, critics readily discuss her sexual
neurosis: well before Corelli's death, Freudian converts and amateur psy-
choanalysts were suggesting publicly that she was a sexual neurotic and
that her preoccupation with romantic love was morbid. There is certainly
no sex in *Open Confession*—in fact, the narrator cherishes her love the
more for its being free from the taint of carnal desire. Indeed, if Corelli is
an "erotic degenerate" (as one writer called her), it is because of her
emotionalism, not her eroticism. The sentimental, rather than the sexual,
is what is indecent.

If expressing feeling is indecent, *Open Confession* is surely a dirty
book, for it is a confession less of sexual transgression than of emotional
crisis. The book disciplines and formalizes the psychological struggle for
personal, sexual dignity that is revealed in Corelli's private letters to
Severn. The text is a testimonial, in the sense Shoshana Felman uses the
word: "Because trauma cannot simply be remembered, it cannot simply
be 'confessed': it must be testified to, in a struggle shared between a
speaker and a listener to recover something the speaking subject is not—
and cannot be—in possession of. In so far as any feminine existence is
in fact a traumatized existence, feminine autobiography *cannot be* a confession. It can only be a testimony to survival" (16). What survives in
Corelli's book is both feminine self-love and the ideal of love as a spiritual
possibility and a cosmic force. It is both a celebration of love and a ter-
rorist attack on love's distortions in the modern world, especially for
women.

In her novel *Innocent* (1914) Corelli claims, "One of the advantages or disadvantages of the way in which we live in these modern days is that we are ceasing to feel. . . . We are beginning not to understand emotion except as a phase of bad manners . . . and to express sorrow, pity, tenderness, affection, or any sort of 'sentiment' whatever is to expose oneself to derision and contempt from the 'normal' modernist who cultivates cynicism as a fine art" (327–28). In opposing herself to the "normal" modernist and evoking the sovereignty of feeling—that is, *feeling for others*—Corelli seeks to defend the most cherished illusions of the Victorian period from the revelations of Freudian psychoanalysis and the miseries of World War I. The return to feeling and to *expressing* feeling, the appeal to the power to dream, is for Corelli a moral and political commitment, as well as a very personal need.

### "Studio-Boy"

This discussion of literary self-expression is haunted by other records that are even more passionate and spontaneous than *Open Confession:* Corelli's unpublished correspondence. The library at the University of Detroit Mercy owns boxes and boxes of letters and notes, more than ten years of Corelli's almost-daily correspondence, overwhelming testimony to her volubility in both words and feelings. *Open Confession* is undoubtedly based on her disappointed love for the painter Arthur Severn. Severn testified for John Ruskin in the Whistler trial in 1878, and by the end of the century he had respectable credentials as a watercolorist but no great success.[2] Corelli met Severn and his wife, Joan, in the summer of 1906, when she was fifty-one. By all accounts she was utterly smitten with both of them, and they were perfectly charmed by her. The Severns' personal attractiveness and their congenial and easygoing domesticity were combined with some irresistible literary and artistic associations: Arthur was the youngest son of the painter Joseph Severn, who was an intimate friend of John Keats's, while Joan Agnew Severn was Ruskin's cousin. When away from their home in London, the family lived at Brantwood, Ruskin's picturesque house in the Lake District; Corelli met the Severns when she asked to see Ruskin's home during a vacation with Vyver in Cumbria.

Corelli's affection for the couple was irrepressible. "Crystallization,"

Stendhal's wonderful word from his novel *De l'amour* (Love, 1822), was inevitable to someone of Corelli's romantic nature, and she particularly crystallized Severn, who at sixty-four was still dashing and flirtatious and, like Corelli, an artist, someone who knew the struggles of creativity and the delights of imaginative expression. His special interest was light, landscape, and studies of nature, and he was attracted by the subtle as well as the spectacular: sunsets gentle and fiery, seas tranquil and stormy. To Corelli's imagination he was a reincarnation of J. M. W. Turner, and in her epistolary lexicon he became "King Arthur" and "Beloved Pendragon" (shortened to "Pen"), "Carissimo Benissimo Pendragonissimo," and, very often, "Maestro." Over the course of their long friendship, Severn enjoyed many long visits at Corelli's home in Stratford-upon-Avon, without his wife, to work: he could row in Corelli's gondola, catch the light on the river Avon, absorb the beauties of the English countryside. Severn occupied a music room with his paint and canvases while Corelli worshipfully (at least at first) cleaned the brushes, filled his pipe, and tried to restrain her joy. She signed her ardent letters "Studio-Boy."

Corelli was on terms of intimate friendship with the Severn family for more than ten years, until the strain of her attachment, her possessiveness, and her unsatisfied need for both affection and respect from Severn caused the relationship to break down. The hundreds and hundreds of letters she wrote attest to the strength of her feelings for Severn and his family and to the strength of her self-respect. It is a remarkable correspondence, full of overstated affection, nagging concerns, professional support, pleas for respect, and, finally, reproach and disillusionment. The climax comes in a letter dated 1 August 1917: "I can only *deeply* regret *that I ever saw Brantwood or its inhabitants*—it's the last of my 'illusions' as to the worthiness of the associates and descendants of really *great* men." Four months earlier she had asked Severn to return all of her letters: "As for my letters, I believe you to be sufficiently *at heart* a gentleman *to return them as I ask you to do* without reference to a 'lawyer'! Though *he* would tell you that no real *man* would refuse to return a woman's private letters if she asked him to do so in exchange for his own" (3 April 1917). Despite her appeal to his chivalric courtesy, Severn did not comply with her request, and she apparently destroyed the letters he wrote to her. So outside of a few fragments of Severn's letters that Corelli attached to her own, or comments from him scribbled on her letters, the correspondence is monologic: it is Corelli's insistent voice we hear, like overhearing one-half of a heated telephone conversation.

Given this one-sidedness, it is a remarkably interdependent (some would say codependent) and self-referential correspondence to read through today, with a private vocabulary of slang and baby talk and perpetual allusions to and quotations from previous letters. The correspondence taken as a whole thus constitutes another " 'record' of a perished passion."

Brian Masters published some of these letters for the first time in his 1978 biography, and his is the only sustained reading of the correspondence that has been published. His biography is informative and detailed, but his interpretation of Corelli's relationship with Severn begs for feminist revision. He writes: "Women who have husbands or lovers are not fundamentally unhappy, although they may have moments of discontent. They are still able to achieve the satisfaction of giving and receiving love. . . . [Corelli] was without the normal satisfactions of the human condition, and had to find substitutes to replace them, of ever deeper intensity—pride, ambition, subjection, humiliation, submissiveness, cannibalism, all succeeding each other in a helter-skelter of illogical emotional chaos" (238–39). This view of Corelli's abnormality is condescending in the extreme; Masters simply cannot take her emotional life seriously. He also occasionally mixes passages from *Open Confession* with the letters, but the two documents are not identical. Whereas *Open Confession* is an imaginative reconstruction, the letters are evidential. For example, one letter recounts the trajectory of their relationship, using past letters and other writing as emotional evidence: "I never think of time or age in matters of friendship or love, for these sentiments, if *true,* are the elixir of eternal youth—or they mean *nothing!*—and the passing of years does not count. It was in *1906* that you and Joan paid your first visit here [to Mason Croft] and wrote in my 'Guest Book'—'After one of the happiest visits in our lives!' So this chronicles the fact that our acquaintance, if not our friendship, is one of *nine years!* . . . How changed is the 'tone' of your letters now!! It's a *long,* long, long time since you wrote me any kind words like these!" (3 June 1915). Here Corelli uses Severn's letter to chronicle a change in their relationship. And yet, as Ellen Moers has put it, the letter is the central form in the literature of love precisely because "letters . . . stand or fall not by the test of truth to fact, but by the test of truth to love" (149). Which document passes the test of truth? Not only is the ordinary lexicon of correspondence differently coded in the published text, but the emotions are filtered through an elaborate mythology. Whereas the speaker in *Open Confession* proclaims, " 'I love you!' . . . is the beginning and the end of the alphabet of my life" (52), in all of the letters I have read, never does Corelli say the words "I love you." Instead she says, "Be fair to me—let your own heart speak for me! I who have loved your *work* at least as much as anyone—perhaps *more than most* . . . for I think of you in a way you could not possibly 'resent' but would rather appreciate if you knew *all*" (18 February 1915). Only in art can she tell all the truth that must be suppressed in the letters, inadvertently following those modernists for whom the imaginative, poetic reach toward truth is more important than objective tests of factual truth or error.

The letters I have cited are examples of many from 1915 that expose Corelli's unhappiness. But there are many, many earlier letters expressing delight and even rapture. For example, she wrote on 15 April 1910, following Severn's departure after a long visit: "Oh Pen! I am in the Studio!—seated in *your* chair and writing at *your* little table! . . . The silent evidences of your presence are everywhere—the chair behind the palm,—the painter's table,—the easel . . . I really can almost *see* you in that chair behind the palm!" Severn dismissed these letters as foolish "sentiment" or female "twaddle." His dislike of Corelli's expressiveness made her concerned about how much she *could* express and what for propriety's sake she had to withhold. When Severn complained about her handwriting, she replied, "That it was not 'clear' expressed emotion,—that it was spluttery declared strongly repressed grief!" (29 December 1908). In 1910 Corelli was reading the love letters of Elizabeth Barrett and Robert Browning, some of which had been published in 1899. She thought the Browning love story was "an ideal, all too rare" (Corelli-Severn Correspondence, 16 April 1910), and she quoted several lines from one of Elizabeth Barrett's sonnets. When Severn replied rather coolly that one of the lines was obscure and "far fetched," Corelli wrote: "But . . . she wanted to express something which she found beyond expression. She should not have tried. In great love as in great grief one very quickly passes the boundary of mere speech—and, I think, all very true and deep emotion is wordless. But I suppose she wanted to *tell* him what she felt, when it might have been better to let him *guess*" (18 April 1910). A few months later she wrote, "I never flatter—I can only speak what I feel—and very often I cannot even do that when the feeling is very deep" (23 August 1910). All of these letters are poignant examples of Barthes's insight in *A Lover's Discourse:* "But for the lover the letter has no tactical value: it is purely *expressive*" (158).

Corelli wrote letters or notes to Severn once or twice a day for more than ten years. I can certainly understand how this steady stream of passion may have been embarrassing to a man who had been happily married for more than forty years. But my point in dwelling on the correspondence is that I find in it an implicit comprehension of the contradiction between Corelli's assumption of intellectual and social equality with Severn, based on her hard-earned fame, her age, her professional commitment, and her financial success, and the social reality of gender roles, which consigned her to a position of subservience or inferiority. In the fictional *Open Confession* this understanding is psychologically accessible because it is formalized—it is *analyzed*—but in the letters it is only bewilderingly perceived and contested. For every letter gaily signed "Studio-Boy," for every claim of affection, servitude, and longing, there is a counterassertion of feminine self-respect. Sometimes it is revealed subtly or flirtatiously: "'Poor pen!'—Yes—and 'Poor studio-boy!'—to be told she has yet to learn to look at pictures in a good light!" (12 April 1910). But Corelli could also be sarcastic: "Me going to be a mild jellyfish of a woman, flopping whichsoever way the waves turn me. Would you like that?" (26 March 1915). Her emotional vacillations attest to how hard it was for her to rein in her feelings while at the same time insisting, like one of her heroines, on the validity of her point of view. Masters sees her as obsessed, absurd, a nuisance. But given her idealization of love, her emotional temperament, and her fame as a novelist, Corelli is also amazingly subdued. She rarely reminds Severn that she is a writer, and yet she published six books between 1906 and 1918, while also giving lectures in large and prestigious forums. Even Masters concedes Severn's tendency to make light of Corelli's literary pretensions. Indeed, Severn seems insensitive to the demands of writing and the pride she takes in her work, and on at least one occasion she wrote bitterly, "You have *never* 'shown joy' at any success of mine" (20 October 1915).

The psychological breakthroughs come when Corelli links her personal resentment, hurt feelings, and Severn's "bullying" with sexist stereotypes and power structures. The idiosyncratic personal relationship is seen as part of an institutionalized view of women as inferior. It is no wonder that Corelli, an independent woman in her mid-fifties, resented Severn's half-teasing project to "mould" her or to make her a "pet" ("I have worked too hard and suffered too much for that sort of thing," she wrote). When she comprehends that her reality is not the same as his, she can abjure his put-downs as narrow-minded sexism: "but then what are *'women'*? Their 'feelings' are 'all twaddle'! and no one knows the fact better than you, who have so often asserted it!" (4 February 1915). On 12 September 1915 she wrote: "It's a thousand pities you seem to think all women can be treated like blocks of wood! Some phlegmatic fools of the under-bred British matron type (such as you call the back-bone of England) may thrive on that sort of 'knock-me-down, batter and blow' system but women who are *brain-workers* and *bread-winners* and owe nothing to heritage or other support are made of keener and finer material." A month earlier (this is during the war, of course) she had written, "Why were you not born a German? Your notions of women are far more *'Hun-like'* than English. 'I *rather* like a woman to *see to my tea and tobacco*, and to be agreeable in the evening *when I have had my game at billiards*. Poor crushed worms as we are!' I think the 'poor crushed worm' would be the *fool of a woman* who accompanied you on such an understanding!"

Although the letters are monologic, there is a dialogic relationship between the private voice of the letters and the public one in *Open Confession*, even though both voices are feminine. The rapport between these two very different records raises questions about women's writing, genre, and subjective self-knowledge. I would like briefly to return to Moers's idea of letters as a "test of truth to love," for there is no doubt that "To a Man from a Woman," the subtitle of *Open Confession*, is more distant and less intimate than "To Pen from Studio-Boy" would have been. The letters are informal and spontaneous rather than orderly and aesthetic; they are reciprocal rather than isolated; there are hundreds and hundreds of them and only one compressed volume of fiction. Letters also serve to establish a history of relationship. What the amorous subject engages in with an epistolary form, even if combative, is "a *relation,* not a correspondence" (Barthes, *Lover's Discourse* 158).

But the problem with letters is that there are blanks between them: "Like a bad concert hall, affective space contains dead spots where the sound fails to circulate" (Barthes, *Lover's Discourse* 167). Many letters from Corelli begin with the sad words "No letter from you today," and just as often she angrily threatens to stop writing altogether. On the other hand, fictionalized letters, or fiction that imitates a direct address, can sustain feeling, and as a self-contained artifact, a representation, it can do so without "dead spots," in one uninterrupted utterance, and at a high emotional pitch.

The novel also illustrates Barthes's idea that the loneliness of the amorous subject is a "philosophical" solitude, a confrontation with the meaning of one's life that occurs in identification with the other (*Lover's Discourse* 210). What I hope to suggest, and what I think is revealed in the letters, is that this solitude is constituted not only in existential longing and the contradictory and anguished feelings that accompany psychological change but in a woman's ambiguous moral position in early-modern society.

### Confession of Faith

Bertha Vyver supervised the serial publication of *Open Confession: To a Man from a Woman* in the *Daily Express* in late 1924 and its appearance in volume form in 1925. It is a fictional reconstruction of romantic turbulence and an unrestrained statement of disillusioned love. As a "'record' of a perished passion," it is an extraordinary book. A sustained monologue spoken by an unnamed woman to the man who has betrayed her, *Open Confession* is divided into twenty sections. The first ten describe the intensity of their love and celebrate its mystery; the last ten, which are slightly longer, deal with the woman's pain, anger, and self-accusation when her imagined love is destroyed. I cannot think of another literary work—high or low—by a writer of Corelli's generation that describes so determinedly the experience of love in the form of a fictional confession. As a testimonial, it is closer to what Felman calls a *"screen confession,"* in the Freudian sense of "screen memories": emotions are condensed, rewritten, transvalued (158). But this does not make them less real, since even a fictional confession is addressed to someone. The test of truth to love is, for Corelli, to test an ideal that is bound to a faith in spiritual transcendence, with connection to life. Disenchantment, loss of the other, and psychological emptiness bring the speaker of *Open Confession* into painful confrontation with the modern condition: the position of being *without relationship*. The sentimental document that confesses love's follies contains an equally serious confession of lost faith, in the tradition of religious confession, which seeks to acknowledge sin through self-castigation. The speaker even says, "I could scourge myself after the fashion of the medieval nuns in the way of repentance for what was a positive crime against my better reason, and an outrageous wrong done to my higher self!" (114). Corelli's romantic disillusionment brings the temptation of cynicism and so morally endangers her. As I have already suggested, this is a genuine threat to her "higher self," that is, her human potentiality and her dignity as a woman. It is this personal threat that is so rawly revealed in the private correspondence. *Open Confession* is worth studying alone for its self-mythologizing strategies and its unusual manipulation of both the confessional mode and the romance. But it also participates in some of the major worries of modernity—with love as the catalyst—and is a striking account of a woman's moral crisis at the end of the Victorian era.

Although the confessional form is often "less concerned with making an explicit political point than in 'telling all,'" there may also be a covert social critique. As Felski has explained, "The strength of the confession as a genre lies in its ability to communicate the conflicting and contradictory aspects of subjectivity, the strength of desire, the tensions between ideological convictions and personal feelings. It can be said to expose the psychological mechanisms by which women 'collude' in their own oppression, but it also reveals the realm of personal relations as fraught with ambivalence and anxiety, intimately interwoven with patterns of domination and subordination, desire and rejection, which cannot be easily transcended" (*Beyond* 116). In reading *Open Confession* in the context of Corelli's life and her status as a popular novelist, I want to explore the tension and ambivalence Felski describes. Corelli's book raises significant questions about gender, sentimentality, modernist literary culture, and philosophical anxiety. The layers of contradiction in *Open Confession* make it a compelling text. There is an element of collusion in Corelli's deeply personal feelings of loss and resentment in that, to a large extent, she reaffirms her culture's myth of romantic love as woman's whole existence. Yet this conservatism paradoxically evokes resistance, since high culture devalues sentimental writing that seeks to express this mythology directly. Protofeminist resistance and philosophical and moral concerns adhere to the modernist allowance of emotional expression only when it is protected by irony or masks.

### Confession of Doubt

The crisis described in *Open Confession* is at odds with the pose of confidence and optimism that Corelli projected to her public. With all her contradictions and her feminist compromises, Corelli, more than anything, I believe, wanted to restore women's confidence, independence, and sexual self-esteem and invest women's lives with dignity. Accordingly, the most significant disclosures in *Open Confession* are those that admit a desire for self-renunciation: "I lose myself in your arms and forget that I have any separate identity; I am glad to feel myself as nothing in your all. . . . Why should women seek to be equals with men when their very existence depends on their ability to be lost like melted jewels in the wine of life! Individuality? Liberty? These two war cries are screamed by women who not only have never loved, but who have never been loved. What woman desires 'individuality' with her lover's kiss upon her lips? Or seeks 'liberty' when his arms are round her and his heart beats against her own?" (49–50). The woman's willing absorption cannot be seen merely as sexual weakness, however. It is linked with a mystical union— "the mystic output of the soul"—and this brings her into contact with her "higher self." When love evaporates, the speaker in *Open Confession* does not just have to give up sexual love. She must either renounce the idea of transcendence or discover her "higher self" in some different moral and ontological paradigm.

This apparently sentimental scenario is as serious as the preoccupations of the next generation of English writers, those born in the 1880s, and represents an authentic reaction to the intellectual advances of modern European civilization. Corelli knows all about the modern ethos of disillusionment; even the titles of books published just before and after the war evoke the oppositions of materialism and romance, cynicism and idealism: *Innocent: Her Fancy and His Fact* (1914), *Love and the Philosopher: A Study in Sentiment* (1923). In *The Secret Power* (1921) a character describes the coming generation as "disillusioned," even putting the word in quotation marks (16). *Open Confession* is unlike these other books, though; the satiric quotation marks disappear, and the *feeling* of disillusionment is powerfully displayed. The speaker has seen through what she calls "the lovely lies" of poets and philosophers and the "deep sea of masculine egoism." Some passages are so despairing that I have to agree with Masters that it is a wonder Corelli managed to retain her faith at all.

There is a real concern in all these books about the erosion of spiritual values that accompanies lost faith in the redemptive powers of love. In *Erotic Faith* Robert Polhemus describes "an emotional conviction, ultimately religious in nature, that meaning, value, hope, and even transcendence can be found through love. . . . Men and women in the hold of erotic faith feel that love can redeem personal life and offer a reason for being" (1). Polhemus traces the belief in the redemptive powers of romantic love in novels from 1800 to the 1930s; this suggests to me that Corelli's feelings are part of a fabric of belief that has been shared by many people. *Open Confession* is a desperate effort to defend this belief, especially after the Great War. Two examples out of hundreds from the Severn correspondence bear out this connection. In a letter written in 1915, Corelli bursts out, "it is *Man* alone who makes *War,* and invents the fiendish means there with to murder his brother-man. It is his incurable Egotism and greed that make a hell of a beautiful world which might so easily be a paradise" (9 November 1915). A year later, more resigned to unhappiness, she wrote, "one is not really sorry for the loss of a child or a person one has never known! I can honestly say I am not sorry!— the dear little soul is out of all sorrow and (as I believe) in a happier world. I think one may be far more sorry for the living than the dead" (29 November 1916). The frustration of disappointed love at middle age leads to a confrontation with meaninglessness and the fact that the world of Victorian certitude has once and for all vanished.[3]

Ardent feeling accompanied by disappointment and anger is the rhythm of the later letters, and it is also the consistent feature of *Open Confession.* Corelli's text is structured in ambivalence: "*If* I love you" is the question with which the speaker begins and to which she perpetually returns: "*If* I love you" means whether I love you and also whether I understand what it is to love at all. The speaker is in a position of uncertainty and vulnerability, but she is also intent on discovering the flux of her emotions and is aware of a potential for self-delusion. Doubt haunts the text, but it is not the kind of doubt that suggests possessiveness or insecurity. She does not ask "Do you love me?" Her concerns are both experiential and abstract: "I could rend myself piecemeal to find out this mystic problem, 'if I love you,'—yes, or no? But the question evades answer" (8). The task the speaker sets before herself, this violent rending of herself, is undertaken in order to understand what is happening internally, without reference to the other. "For if I,—I, who am writing this record, love you, it is indeed nothing to you, and should be nothing," she says. "You have actually no more to do with my emotions than the wind or the sea" (7). That this inward journey is potentially threatening is also apparent, since the speaker fears that the mysteries of her own heart will be too terrifying to articulate: "I can never get close enough to my own self to force from it its intimate interior confession. I am not certain that I would do so if I could" (8).

Open Confession thus begins with conflicted subjectivity: the speaker declares a disciplined assertion of self but is equivocal in her desire for total self-knowledge. The tone throughout is pensive. The speaker bears out on every page de Beauvoir's statement that "the woman in love knows the most bitter solitude there is" (742), or Barthes's idea that "the lover's discourse is today *of an extreme solitude*" (*Lover's Discourse* 1). This is not because she wishes for an unachieved union with the other: the woman openly values desire over possession, claims she would not "have you bound to me by Law and State and Church," and prefers the "suffering entailed by separation" to the cloying necessity of constant companionship (66, 84). Corelli would have been appalled by D. H. Lawrence's sensuality, and yet the speaker in *Open Confession* articulates the extremities of some Lawrencian lovers: to merge or not to merge? The spiritual idea of love as a manifestation of the divine, an avenue for connection with a transcendent mystery, is troubled by the feeling, familiar in modernist writing, that this connection is unattainable, even delusional—Birkin's heartbreaking insistence in *Women in Love* that "[a]t the very last, one is alone, beyond the influence of love. . . . The root is beyond love, a naked kind of isolation" (137). *Open Confession* does not reconcile these ideas but gives full and defiant expression to their momentousness: "You are to me a mystery that is almost superhuman,—

'how foolish!' exclaims the prosaic would-be wise person of the world,—
or 'how blasphemous!' seeing that nothing is superhuman but God!
Nevertheless to me there is a mystic unreachableness and depth which
even the searching measure of my love can scarcely fathom" (26–27). She
claims that "consciousness of your love gives me a power beyond mere
mortality," and spiritual union with the other causes the material world
to drop away (35). At such moments she "approaches the divine in the
very expansion and creativeness of love,—for God Himself is greatest in
Love and in the creation of Life. The whole secret of the universe seemed
given into our possession,—and nothing that science can teach or that
inspiration can prophesy went beyond the simple fact of love!" (61–62).

If the "whole secret of the universe" is thus imaginatively revealed
to the subject, then love likewise promises an exalted knowledge of loss
and death: [4]

> *What clouds of dark foreboding and depression shadow the land-*
> *scape of life . . . darkness and loneliness that I cannot explain*
> *away,—hours when it seems that even your love is removed from*
> *me, and that I stand alone in a vault of silent cold, estranged,*
> *apart, weary and solitary . . . the feverish restlessness of my spirit*
> *wears me to such a fineness of torture that I can hardly endure the* (59)
> *pain and half wish it would kill me so that I might have peace!*
> *Do you know—can you guess—this corroding mental suffering*
> *which makes me unlike myself? Would you understand it if you*
> *knew?*

For Corelli the answer is "Probably not." Here, as in all of her novels,
and despite the language of transcendent union, Corelli concludes that
men and women are fundamentally different. In *Open Confession* she says,
"I suppose no man living has ever understood the strangely pitiful sensi-
tiveness of a loving woman's heart," and later she asks, "Is it so difficult
for a man to be gentle to a woman?" (42, 72). It is typical of Corelli to
rely on sexual stereotypes: his brutal sexual instinct opposed to her chaste
spirituality. Still, at its best and when experienced to the full, ideal love
can become a vehicle for a spiritual experience, and the lover and the
beloved, operating on a plane outside mere social convention, are mani-
festations of mystical divinity. This intense experience of life must also

embrace death. The revelation is uttered when the speaker acknowledges that "love [has] taken me by the hand and I [am] willing to follow him through all things even unto death" (13).

My point here is that Corelli's faith in ideal love, love that is freely and fully given, is the foundation of her morality, as it no doubt was for many of her readers and as it remains for many people today.

### A Waste Land

Although there are plenty of recriminations from the woman scorned, the last ten parts of *Open Confession* describe a serious intellectual crisis: when her lover betrays her, the speaker is "thrust back into the blackness of doubt" (147). She must somehow reconstruct an acceptable idea of the world in the face of skepticism. That her idealism has been radically undermined by modern discourses of science, history, and psychology is clear to anyone who has read Corelli's fiction: "All our scientists are busy telling us of our utter worthlessness and the uselessness of our best efforts,—the excavators of tombs and buried cities exhibit the remains of long past civilisations, proving the futility of all their attainment and progress" (184); "Teachers and preachers are assuring the world that there is no God,—no moral force of Right or Wrong, and that what we call the Beautiful and the True is only the particular view we elect to take. So it is, and so let it be!" (120); "Grant that we are here simply to propagate and continue our race, again the 'Why?' blazons itself on the blank unresponsive darkness. The unanswerable question has become more pathetic in recent years since the Great War, because of the dictatorial utterances of certain scientists who aver there is no God and no after life" (152). She even speculates at some length on the rise in the suicide rate and relates the story of a woman who killed herself for "such a trivial cause" as her husband's desertion (172).

The scorn rather than sympathy for a desperate woman in this last example indicates that science and war are not entirely to blame for her despair. It is the loss of erotic faith and the collapse of her idol that have emptied the universe of all meaning or purpose. If ideal love is a fraud, everything is a fraud: "Now I have learned that it was no more than one of those many delightful cheats . . . we are cheated from the first to the

last" (105). The world is now a "waste," "cruel," and the mystery of love
that she pondered in the first half of the book has expanded into the
"impenetrable mystery—the 'why' of such waste of material!" (183).[5]

Given Corelli's emotional and moral investments in her ideal, it is
not surprising to find that lost love brings feelings of self-hatred and
moral desperation. Many feminists have pointed out that the myth of
love equaling happiness is the opiate of women, that romantic love is the
pivot of women's oppression. Feminists since Mary Wollstonecraft have
given out that love for women is misery and self-sacrifice—witness
pop-psychology books directed to help "women who love too much."
De Beauvoir calls love "the curse that lies heavily upon woman confined
in the feminine universe" and refers to the "innumerable martyrs to love"
who "bear witness against the injustice of a fate that offers a sterile hell as
ultimate salvation" (743). Rather a harsh view, I think, and one that
sounds more like the romantic Corelli than the philosopher de Beauvoir.
Still, such testimony lends weight and authenticity to Corelli's feelings
and shows that it is not merely indulgent raving when she evokes "the
unselfishness and life-sacrifice of women for whom love—even a despised love—sufficed!" (111).

These metaphors of warning, martyrdom, and salvation suggest a
symbolic dimension that a woman faces as she accepts this new and painful consciousness, this "fate" that brings her into a confrontation with
her humanity. The essential insight of Corelli's fictional confession is that
in this critical and awful experience of love the speaker finds not only her
womanhood but her *being,* a place of suffering but also of personal
growth and renewed relationship with the world. At the very end of *Open
Confession* we learn that the speaker is aware of another audience for
her emotional disclosures: "But—what thousand, aye, what millions of
women could tell the same little tale of woe as mine! It is a common
story—and yet I have set it down so that other silly souls like mine may
read themselves in my hand-mirror and see that there is nothing mo-
mentous in a man's deceit of any credulous feminine creature who loves
him" (182–83).

The revelation in the second half of the book, after her love has been
betrayed, may be in the claim, "I now know what millions of my fellow-
women have to endure" (176). This altered consciousness, the awareness

of a new relationship that springs from suffering and apparent isolation, is related to the speaker's existential anxieties. Faced with a world of shattered hopes, self-determination is an act of heroism.

As in Bartky's analysis of feminist consciousness, the speaker in *Open Confession* sees herself as a victim, and she is wary, defensive, and angry. She is also in a moral predicament, by turns self-castigating, a fool to have believed "the all-mastering lie of love itself," and self-righteously "enshrined in self-respect" (113, 116). She is at once critical of "the 'social order of things' . . . devised by men to suit their own convenience and liberty of action" and devoted to women's "true sphere . . . [for] a woman deprived of love is starved of the very essence of her life" (159, 159–60). She is proud of her independence yet feels she has had to surrender all the pleasures of intimacy and relationship:

> *Nature teaches [men] that women are their breeding ground; they are created for this alone. When they break away and make a "try" for independence and the usage of their brains on a higher level, men resent their action, and still more keenly resent any triumph they may win. . . . Moreover I absolutely agree with the masculine view. It is useless to thwart Nature or seek to invent barricades against her action.*
(164–65) > *Women are never really happy in the possession of fame—they would rather clasp a little child to their bosoms than a wreath of laurels. The child may grow up to be a curse to the mother who bore it,—nevertheless she can seldom forget the first little cry, the first feeble caressing movement of its tiny hand. I, like most women, would have welcomed maternity as a blessing had it been my lot,—though not unless the deepest and most lasting love had brought the benediction.*

I have discussed Corelli's highly qualified views of the "Mother of the World" in chapter 3, but this passage from *Open Confession* is worth examining. Two of Corelli's biographers, Masters and George Bullock, can only conclude that here she reveals her unhappiness at having "failed" to marry and have children. Bullock says, "There, with surprising frankness, she spoke from her fundamental self. She wanted marriage and all its encumbrances. With feminine perversity her longing increased as the possibility of achieving the state became more remote" (200). Bullock ignores what follows in this passage, which, given the ideology of motherhood as fulfillment, is in some ways even more surprisingly frank and perverse: "I am more than thankful that I never married, and that I never shall marry. Deeper thankfulness I have that no children of mine will endure the buffetings of fate and fortune in this cruel world" (183).

If Corelli began to connect the personal with the universal in her letters to a man to whom she was deeply attached, in *Open Confession* she more fully articulated an awareness of perceived social contradictions— including contradictory ideologies of marriage and maternity. Thus the speaker says that to "train" a woman for marriage and her role as man's complement, "she must be drawn by Love"; she points out that love is the center of poetry, the pivot of art, the very keynote of religion; she explains how, like all young girls, she had dreams of love and marriage, for this was the well-known formula for personal fulfillment (160). But the policing of feminine desire and especially of feminine expression by social and literary conventions has constricted her full participation in human experience. The social commandment is not so much "thou shalt not love" as "thou shalt not express"—a stricture Corelli understood both in the circumscribed relationship with Severn and in the disgust of reviewers who mocked her sentimental effusions. The repressive discipline of gender roles combined with elite literary tastes imposes a psychological price: "This is often a strain on a woman's nerves—she longs to speak, yet she knows she must not—she would give all, but feels that she must refrain—and for ever and ever the iron fetters of convention lie coldly round her heart" (*Open Confession* 69).

There are many emotional moments in *Open Confession,* resignations to loneliness, fears that she has lost "all that makes life worth living" (170). Yet because she is aware that her culture has defined femininity as complaisance, dependence, and self-sacrifice, the speaker decides on principle to eschew stereotypical feminine virtues. Thus there are repeated assertions of female strength, self-sufficiency, and integrity: "I move through the world independently, owing nothing to any man"; "I do not propose weeping outside the shut door of a worthless love . . . I am free of bondage—and I shall never wear fetters again. Not for any man shall I forget my liberty of soul"; "there are more things for me to do than to wait, hand and foot, on the moods of a man" (155, 102–3, 106). These theatrical assertions work to confirm the Corellian faith in expressiveness, but such stony resolve cannot possibly satisfy an emotional person. Must a woman's duty to herself always win out over her feelings for others?

It was never Corelli's intention to overthrow the existing social order. She wished her books to revitalize people and restore hope, and she used the mythology of love because it was what she knew and because she felt that sympathetic feeling was lacking in her society. "The people,—the Peoples—are turning their backs on all Idealism," she laments (*Open Confession* 137). For women who write fiction rather than theory or philosophy, romantic love may furnish a paradigm for metaphysical meditations and for self-understanding. More grieved than recondite, *Open Confession* ends with an affirmation of the "mystery" and the sense of necessary suffering but adds the claim of a political identity: "Strange mystery!—strange chance! Cruel destiny! How shall we bear it best, we women? We may set our souls toward ambition—we may win the laurels of fame if we make a good fight for it—but what worth are such laurels? They bring no real joy—no real peace of mind. But then neither does love bring joy or peace of mind—rather the contrary. Yet one thing remains true—that the pain and bitterness of love is sweeter than all other sweet things,—and that its suffering moves the soul to a keener delight than happiness!" (160–61).

This idea is somewhat differently articulated in modernist writing, but such moments of exhilarated or distressed apprehension are characteristic of the modernist sensibility and should not be dismissed as mere emotionalism. In *Open Confession,* and in the letters as well, it is love that has the capacity to bring this consciousness into being, and from this may be patterned existential becoming: it is both a political reorientation—"we women"—and a moral and psychological liberation. For the speaker in *Open Confession* reality has to be confronted, but the ideal must still be given to exist. She concludes, "I am . . . a Worker and a Weaver of Dreams. One of the dreams was Love—and though rudely awakened, I still have the power to dream again" (190). By apparently asserting that a woman's illusions must be held on to for dear life, Corelli's book unexpectedly describes the opposite: the importance of discarding false consciousness in order to claim identity with women and so reimagine women's shared "fate" in the ideal hope of human connection and individual liberation.

Leonard Woolf called *Open Confession* "a lyrical ecstasy of bathos," and Masters says it is Corelli's "relentless scratching at her own nerves" (Masters 263–64). The book's rhetorical excesses are melodramatic, but as Brooks has argued, melodrama is precisely a "sense-making enterprise," a psychic drama of ethical and emotional conceptualization in a postsacred era (xvii). Furthermore, the reflections in the book must be apprehended in the context of paradigmatic shifts in the modern world *and* in the discourse of love: this is no longer the eighteenth-century sensibility of Johann Wolfgang von Goethe or Stendhal or of romanticism's young male lover. Corelli's allusions to Albert Einstein, microbes, distant planets, motorcars, New Women, the wireless, "the amazing cruelty of the late war," and "the irresistible march of science" make her faith in love all the more meaningful (173).

This book also raises questions about genre. According to Maureen Honey, a woman's "true confession" story in the 1920s would have implied a painful tale of sexual transgression followed by guilt and self-debasement, ultimately leading to the confessor's realization of her misdeeds and the resolution to lead a decent life (306–7). Even in a secular package the word *confession* has religious connotations, as in a disclosure of deviance or religious doubt that restores the subject to orthodoxy; confession may operate as a form of social control. And there is a self-disciplinary impulse in Corelli's book, since the experience of love and disillusionment is a moral crucible.

But, according to Felski, in the development of bourgeois society, "confession comes increasingly to symbolize a private assertion of *freedom* which may challenge rather than simply conform to existing social norms" (emphasis added) (*Beyond* 104). Similarly, Leigh Gilmore has argued that "the confession's persistence in self-representation" lends cultural authority to the author (108). Such a confession is especially important for women, since in the tradition of romantic love women have been deprived of subjectivity, understood primarily as objects of masculine desire.

Although I feel *Open Confession* is too stylized to be a "posthumous journal," as Masters claims, there is no doubt that the emotional core of the book comes from private experience (245). *Open Confession,* like Molly Bloom's "yes," is a dramatic gesture toward the future and toward human love in an age of advancing technology, emotional isolation, and cynicism; the experience of lost love imaginatively projects the speaker into modernity, and modernity cannot be detached from a transvaluation of romantic ideology nor from the religious (and melodramatic) impulses from which that ideology comes. As Brooks has argued, "Romanticism is the genesis of the modern, of the sensibility within which we are still living. . . . [M]odern art has typically felt itself to be constructed on, and over, the void, postulating meanings and symbolic systems which have no certain justification because they are backed by no theology and no universally accepted social code" (21). Even though this means a confrontation with skepticism, it also demands a terrifying freedom to determine one's life. The unconstrained expression in popular literature helps a writer such as Corelli to do this, for, once she bravely confesses her disillusionment, she is able to brace herself for the future: "Paradoxical as it may seem, life is sweeter than it was before,—I am conscious of such a wonderful freedom" (*Open Confession* 115).

### The Spirit of Modernity

Perhaps it seems incongruous to discuss Corelli as a modernist, but some of her contemporaries did. Horace Samuel's *Modernities,* published in 1914, is a collection of ten chapters on individuals he feels characterize the "spirit of modernity" since the French Revolution, "a spirit of energy, of fearlessness in analysis, whose sole *raison d'être* and whose sole ideal is actual life itself" (2). I have borrowed the title for this chapter from Samuel's "The *Weltanschauung* of Miss Marie Corelli" precisely because of the apparent incongruity of its assumption that a popular woman novelist would have a weltanschauung of any sophistication to discuss. Samuel's chapter on Corelli is placed rather oddly among chapters on Stendhal, Heinrich Heine, Benjamin Disraeli, Friedrich Nietzsche, August Strindberg, Frank Wedekind, Arthur Schnitzler, Émile Verhaeren, and the futurists. Samuel's treatment of Corelli is condescending, despite his proposal to examine her works "with the maximum of seriousness at our command" (116). But if we use his standards, Corelli qualifies as a representative modern: she possesses fearlessness and a genuine, a passionate, concern with "life itself."

When Corelli wrote in 1886 "We live in an age of universal inquiry, *ergo* of universal scepticism," she spoke to her contemporaries' deepest concerns (*Romance* 1). According to Samuel's analysis, the key to her psychology and worldview is "the religious instinct," a susceptibility that easily tilts into the occult (117). This sensibility belongs to both the Victorian and modern eras. William Butler Yeats published *A Vision* the year after Corelli's death,[6] and at least two books were written in her name in the 1930s by people who communicated with her spirit: *Paulus Antonius, A Tale of Ancient Rome,* subtitled "By Marie Corelli—in Spirit. Through the Hand of M. Elfram"; and *The Voice of Marie Corelli: Fragments from "The Immortal Garden" through the Hand of Dorothy Agnes.*[7] Corelli insisted that "the mere fact of *the existence of a desire* clearly indicates an *equally existing capacity* for the *gratification* of that desire. Why all this discontent with the present—why all this universal complaint and despair and world-weariness, if there be *no hereafter?*" (*Romance* 334). Interest in Corelli today comes primarily from people who feel exactly this way, who are attracted to her esoteric blend of Christianity and mysticism and especially to her unshakable confidence in the immortality of the soul. I have received E-mail messages from complete strangers who are drawn to Corelli's New Age spiritualism. And it is telling that the only available reprints of her twenty-six novels are from Kessinger Publishing, a firm that exclusively publishes "mystical and freemasonry books" and "classics of spiritual literature."

Masters claims, "The post-war era regarded [Corelli] as a fossil. . . . With her messianic fervor, Marie stubbornly refused to change; while the world went forward, she stayed transfixed in the nineteenth century, gazing bewildered at the vortex of events and fashions which made her an anachronism" (273–74). I cannot agree. Despite her feelings of emotional displacement in the modern age, Corelli did move with the times: for all her moral concern over "the Wilde cult" in 1918 (Hoare 90), she seems to have obtained tickets to Richard Strauss's *Salome* in 1910, a performance that was considered fairly avant-garde;[8] she bought a motorcar (a Daimler) as early as 1910; she was fascinated with the possibilities represented by the telephone and radio. Furthermore, several of her novels forecast scientific discoveries. For example, in *The Secret Power* there is a spaceship that uses light rays and a scientist who claims to hold the power to end war because he possesses a substance that could annihilate whole countries through "a holocaust of microbes" (132); William Stuart Scott claims that *The Life Everlasting* prophesied "the hydrogen bomb, and the application of atomic power to transport" (55). In 1911 Corelli was at the opening ceremony for the first Railophone service, a system of radio communication to and from moving trains (Scott 233). She seems to have had faith in scientific progress: sound waves, light rays, microbes, electricity, radium—all are treated in her novels, not only after the war but from the very beginning of her career, without apparently jeopardizing her religious beliefs. She readily moved on from the Victorian age of steam to the modern age of electricity; if you take seriously her creed of electric religion, she was even ahead of her time. Far from being the enemy of religious faith, science provided Corelli with more metaphors for divinity. At the start of the new century she has a Roman Catholic bishop in *The Master Christian* say, "The toy called the biograph, which reflects pictures for us in a dazzling and moving continuity, . . . is merely a hint to us that every scene of every life is reflected in a ceaseless moving panorama *Somewhere* in the Universe, for the beholding of *Someone*. . . . The wireless telegraphy is a stupendous warning of the truth that 'from God no secrets are hid.' . . . Science is, or should be, the Church!— science is Truth, and Truth is God!" (105).

Granted, the reconciliation here between metaphysics and mathematics is rather forced, and Masters is right to say that Corelli did not change her religious beliefs. *The Life Everlasting* only reiterates the creed from *A Romance of Two Worlds* of twenty-five years earlier, except Corelli substitutes radium for electricity, noting that by 1911 "'radio-activity' is perhaps the better, because the truer term to employ" (*Life Everlasting* 19). Still, the rhetoric of doubt was familiar to her, and evocations of nothingness and unbelief show up consistently. It is no exaggeration to say that almost all of her novels dramatize the temptations of atheism. Corelli always evokes a brave new world, while at the same time warning of its imminent destruction. She strove to assert what Richard Ellmann has called "an affirmative capability" but not all of the time and not without a streak of Schopenhauerian pessimism (*Identity of Yeats* 238).

It is certainly not true that the postwar era heeded her not. In August 1919 the *Philadelphia Public Ledger* included Corelli alongside four other writers (Gilbert Parker, Edward Oppenheim, Ernest Hornung, and W. B. Maxwell) in an oversized magazine piece, including illustrations, titled "What's Next in Literature? Opinions of Leading English Novelists." The authors were asked to respond to three questions facing the future of literature: "What sort of reading should be prepared at this time for the world masses?"; "Are wartime stories the proper sort of literature to be presented in the magazines . . . or through books?"; and "Whether it is not important for serious writers to bestir themselves before the neighborhood picture theatres have entirely captured the time and interest of the average public?" Corelli, in the words of the reporter, "sharply rebukes the tendency of the times in her caustic answers." She predicts that the "world masses" will be ill served by commercialism and blames the press; that the war stories that will be written in the future will be for the most part dashed off on typewriters to make a few dollars and will likewise be involved in commercial exploitation; and that the restlessness of modern people, who are "forever 'on the go,'" has compounded the unavoidable fact that so-called educated "people *do not read*" and that the movie theater suits a public that "is being thrust back by a greedy commerce" into ignorance (Carroll 1). I do not know if I would call this cynicism, exactly, but it suggests that, given the commercialization of art and the rapid pace of modern life, there is nowhere to go but up—into the heavens (in a spaceship, perhaps), embracing the dream of perfect love and beauty and freedom.

It is probably not surprising that Corelli continued to write books until the end of her life; she published her last novel when she was sixty-eight, less than a year before her death. By that time her contemporaries with a taste for romance were picking up books by Elinor Glyn and Ethel M. Dell instead of by Corelli. In the next chapter I will look at Corelli's cultural afterlife and her place in literature. When she died at Stratford-upon-Avon in 1924, newspaper headlines exclaimed, "Who Was Miss Marie Corelli?" The question has been embedded throughout this book. Instruments more diverse than photographs, newspaper scoops, and letters, and categories of knowledge less determined than fact and fiction—not to mention self-reflexive and historically informed biographies and criticism by new scholars—are still needed if we want meaningful answers.

# V

## Who Was Marie Corelli?

*You do well not to care for fame. Modern Fame is too often a crown of thorns and brings all the vulgarity of the world upon you. I sometimes wish I had never written a line.*

Alfred, Lord Tennyson, letter to Marie Corelli (July 1890)

*The good that this little lady has done will not be forgotten in this generation, and the work of her wonderful creative brain, enjoyed by countless thousands, has made her name a household word in many lands.*

Edith Stanley, obituary in the *Stratford-upon-Avon Herald* (28 April 1924)

THIS CHAPTER IS about cultural readings of Marie Corelli in the decades after the Victorian age, during the interwar years, and up until about 1955. My interrogative title echoes sections in biographies of Corelli by Eileen Bigland and Brian Masters, but unlike a biographer, I am not interested in uncovering the facts or arguing from incomplete evidence about her life. I want to look chiefly at how later generations understood the Victorian phenomenon called Marie Corelli and how her identity and reputation were construed in various public forums; my sources will range from obituaries to biographies and memoirs, letters, and literary reviews.

When Corelli died on 21 April 1924, one week short of her sixty-ninth birthday, *A Romance of Two Worlds* was in its thirty-eighth edition, *Barabbas* in its fifty-fourth, *Thelma* in its fifty-sixth, and *The Sorrows of Satan* in its sixtieth (Scott 251). More than 140 obituaries and articles from April and May 1924 are pasted in a large leather-bound scrapbook, which belonged perhaps to Corelli's housemaid, Augusta Ellen Long, or to Bertha Vyver, the woman Corelli lived with for almost forty years. The scrapbook is now part of the Corelli archives at the Shakespeare Birthplace Trust in Stratford-upon-Avon, her home for the last twenty-five years of her life.

Although this scrapbook cannot possibly contain every newspaper column that mentioned Corelli's death, those the compiler included are remarkable for several reasons. First, they reflect the loyalties and antagonisms that Corelli inspired in her lifetime, evidence of a continuing dialectic of personal and public opinions about her fiction, her personality, her opinions, and even her appearance. Second, they provide some insight into the speculative quality of English literature and show how the death of a writer raises questions about literary canonization and the meanings of cultural legacies. Third, the items printed in the English and American press in the days following her death and in various literary reviews display a profound preoccupation with the Corelli "secret," a professional curiosity about the mystery of her huge appeal to thousands of readers. Her unstoppable success, as I have already mentioned in chapter 2, was an irritation to critics and men of letters throughout her career. The theories about her popularity that appeared in the years after her death—in memoirs, biographies, letters to editors, and magazine features—perpetuate the mixture of respect, curiosity, and disdain for both the woman and her books. I find these later appropriations and interpretations both insightful and unimaginative, but they are for the most part only dimly and condescendingly evocative of her bygone celebrity.

The headlines in 1924 also pried into other secrets, particularly those surrounding Corelli's family history and her romantic friendship with Vyver. Indeed, some of the newspaper memoirs or recollections echo or anticipate the biographies of Corelli written between 1901 and 1955 by Kent Carr, T. F. G. Coates and R. S. Warren-Bell, Vyver, George Bullock, Bigland, and William Stuart Scott, whose very subtitles suggest Corelli's multiple identities: "The Writer and the Woman," "The Life and Death of a Best-Seller," "The Woman and the Legend," "The Story of a Friendship." They present to the modern reader various interventions into Corelli's life and celebrity from provocative angles that are at once historically revealing and oddly difficult to locate. At the end of this chapter I will focus on how these versions of Corelli's life specifically

Fig. 13. The Corelli mystique: Marie Corelli at the window of the Elizabethan tower at her home, Mason Croft, in Stratford-upon-Avon. (By courtesy of the Shakespeare Birthplace Trust, Stratford-upon-Avon)

address her feminism or antifeminism, for her "man-hating" and her attitudes about women, femininity, and sexuality are among the most remarked on—and the most evasive—aspects of both her life and her fiction.

Most of the texts discussed in this last chapter, then, were published after Corelli's death. I have tried to keep the discussion unencumbered by secondary works of literary theory, history, and criticism, although certain interpretations will suggest themselves from the approaches I have already taken to Corelli's negotiations of photographic celebrity, aestheticism, New Woman fiction, and modernism. I have kept my own interpretations of the obituaries to a minimum, and although the scrapbook nature of this chapter may be taxing, I am deliberately excessive in my examples because I want to sketch out as broadly as possible the reactions in the press to Corelli's death and her reputation. In fact, I want to overdo it, since the clippings in the Stratford scrapbook, although their inclusion may have been selective in order to protect her image, do display the range of media reactions Corelli provoked in the next two generations of readers, reviewers, and biographers.

Many of the death notices written between Easter Monday, 21 April 1924, and the funeral on the following Saturday, 26 April, are predictably eulogistic. The *Evening Standard* declared, "In the passing of Miss Marie Corelli a great figure in the fiction of the last thirty years is lost, to the regret of many friends and a world-wide public." A columnist in the *Daily Mail* recorded that "Marie Corelli exercised a greater personal influence than any other novelist of her day," even suggesting that she had a quasireligious function: "Some of her admirers would write to her as though she were their Mother Confessor." The women's magazine *Queen* similarly emphasized her feminine wisdom or power: "And the power to be the mouthpiece and consolation of the millions has never been given to any woman in a greater degree." Periodicals as diverse as *Christian World* and *Horse and Hounds* noted her death, as well as the *Occult Review, British Australasian,* the *New York Evening Post* and the *New York Herald,* and several French papers, including *Journal des Débats* and *Libre Parole.* J. Sadler Reece, in the *Methodist Recorder,* was reverent and mournful: "She was a good woman; she had vision; she had purity; she had intensity; she had power." Reece compared Corelli with two rather different writers, Charlotte Brontë and Olive Schreiner, insisting they were all "children of the wind and flame, [who] served God and their generation with clean hearts." Indeed, many notices remarked on Corelli's role as moralist to her own generation and often admitted that, whatever her faults, she was not coarse or indecent. The *Bristol Times* said she "wrote healthily" and the *Sheffield Independent* that she was "never unclean," the *Stratford-upon-Avon Herald* praised her avoidance of "the morbid colouring of the darker passions" that other novelists indulge, and the *Daily Graphic's* headline heralded her (somewhat ironically) as the "Puritan of the Pen."

But other notices were derisive and superior. At least a third of the clippings in Stratford emphasized that before she died Corelli wished the hour of her death to be given by "God's Time" rather than by the new Summer Time (the Summer Time Act advanced Greenwich mean time by one hour; it was passed in 1916 but not made permanent until 1925, and many people were opposed to it [Scott 100]). This detail, sometimes given in headlines or large typeface, could be read as a sign of Corelli's quaintness, naïveté, or stupidity, depending on the overall tone of the article. There were also many comments on her personality and appearance. The *Star* wrote, "A strange, difficult, and rather stormy person disappears from the world with Marie Corelli"; the same paper stated that she was extraordinarily sensitive about her "short plump person." But even her appearance was contested, and different people remembered Corelli differently. Given the vindictiveness of some male critics when she was alive, and her manipulations of her public image, it is interesting to find many articles offering testimony to her physical warmth and attractiveness. T. P. O'Connor, M.P., described Corelli as "a little bit of Dresden china," a compliment that was often cited during her life. In a lengthy personal memoir in the *Daily Telegraph* of 22 April 1924, O'Connor wrote: "If you had expected to meet a tall, lank lady, with spectacles and blue stockings, you had a pleasant surprise when you met her in the 'eighties and 'nineties. She had a small, well-proportioned figure, abundant clusters of fair hair, rosy cheeks, lightish blue eyes, and very small and dainty features." O'Connor's "surprise," of course, is tied to stereotypes of women writers during the last two decades of the century and is based on the cliché of the intellectual woman's grotesqueness that Corelli knew so well. O'Connor's slant is typical. In fact, almost all of the 1924 notices that deal with Corelli's appearance are interested in reconciling her loud advocacy of women's brainpower with her exaggerated pose of prettiness and demure femininity. Thus the *Manchester City News* (in a special piece called "Marie Corelli: Her Ideals of Womanhood by One Who Knew Her") completely endorses the myth Corelli had created of "the blue-eyed, golden-haired girl, with her manuscript novel in her hands," who "sought feverishly for some recognition of her ability and found that the world's attitude, if not actually resistant, was unfriendly to the woman with ambition to use her gift to the utmost capacity." The *Nottingham Guardian* on 28 April recalled her visit to Nottingham to give a lecture on Byron nine years earlier: "Literary ladies are commonly believed not to be engaging persons as a rule and a certain dowdiness of dress is excused and even looked for. . . . Miss Corelli was a radiant figure in pale blue—a vision of middle-aged beauty in full evening dress." Finally, for this will suffice, the *News of the World,* on 24 April, dealt with Corelli's appearance, her feminism, and her anti-feminism all at once: "In appearance Miss Corelli was striking. She had shining golden hair, and she always wore very simple gowns, usually Greek models in various pale colours. . . . Miss Corelli did not marry. . . . Miss Corelli always denied the suggestion that she was a man-hater. In later years her anti-feminist views were considerably modified."

It is amazing how much copy was devoted to describing Corelli's appearance. Several papers reprinted the official photograph; the *New York Evening Post* offered the tidbit that "in her private circle of friends she is famous for her lovely arms and hands which are the admiration of many a sculptor." It seems that the subjective reactions she inspired in her acquaintances, and the fact that the world still had no consistent version of what Corelli looked like, were in themselves good copy: "She has been described by various authorities in her earlier days as a beautiful, fair-haired, sylph-like creature, and as a dumpy and determined little woman," wrote the *Evening News* on the day of her death. "Even her eyes have been classed—and that by admirers—as anything from soulful to saucy."

After her death personal recollections of Corelli must have interested a segment of the public. William Stuart Scott, a clergyman, wrote in a memoir published in 1955, "Two lectures which I delivered at Stratford, in January 1925, 'Marie Corelli—as the world knew her,' and 'Marie Corelli—as I knew her,' drew large audiences, for interest in her as a writer had not entirely evaporated then. Positive evidence of this was the serial publication late in 1924 of her *Open Confession: To a Man from a Woman* in such a widely read journal as the *Daily Express*" (193). In May 1924 a writer for the *Bookman* offered a balance to the composite picture of Corelli that the newspapers had evoked, recalling his (or her) personal impressions: "She could be hasty and furiously outspoken in response; she could be dreadfully vain, difficult, stormy, headstrong, intolerant—all that I see the obituary notices have been saying of her; but that was not the whole of her character—there was a pleasanter, more gracious and more dignified side that I would sooner recall." Clearly the official versions, whether orchestrated by Corelli or by those in the media who took credit for revealing the "true story," had their complements in unofficial personal recollections on impressions of Corelli's style, manner, voice, and temperament that could not be conveyed by fact finders or photographers.

The personal memories and interpretations grew more serious, however, when the matter of Corelli's literary legacy was raised. In an article in the 27 April 1924 *Newcastle Sunday Sun* headlined "Marie Corelli and Her Public: Her Art and Place in Literature," C. Creah-Jerningham wrote, "It may now be asked, therefore, what place will Marie Corelli occupy permanently in the world of fiction?" Almost the exact same question was asked by the *Birmingham Sunday Mercury* in May. There was no consensus, but it is striking that by 1924 no one writing for the press had the courage to predict with confidence that the works of Corelli would endure. Even those who admired her energy and were astonished by her sales felt constrained by high literary values and conceded their judgments to posterity. The *Daily Express* used the headline "Writer and Controversialist," diplomatically asserting, "However difficult it may be to define the precise place in English literature of Marie Corelli, whose death occurred yesterday, it remains the fact that for twenty years she was the most popular woman novelist in this or any other country. 'A new Corelli book' was a tremendous event; an edition would be sold in a day." The *Times,* on the other hand, could confidently dismiss her contributions: "Even the most lenient critics cannot regard Miss Corelli's works as of much literary importance." The *Yorkshire Post* recorded, "Miss Corelli wrote without distinction and without any particularly competent craftsmanship, but she wrote, in Wilde's phrase, 'at the top of her voice.' " This is somewhat misleading, since Oscar Wilde was describing not Corelli but, of all people, Hall Caine ("Decay of Lying" 219).

The question of immortality or ephemerality was tossed about by a great many journalists in 1924, some speaking with certainty that Corelli was already half forgotten and others saying it was too soon to be sure. The whole discussion often sounds like a commentary on a horse race, with critics referring to a good "run" and laying down bets on posterity. My impression is that those who may have liked reading her books were afraid of looking old-fashioned and foolish and so attributed Corelli's fame to the singularly odd tastes of Victorian middle-class readers. The *Review of Reviews* quoted the *London Mercury:* "Miss Corelli, in her heyday, was read by the entire middle-class, who bought in all many hundreds of thousands of her works at six shillings a volume. And if it be conceded that her decline began about fifteen years ago, she had had a run of twenty years." The *Sheffield Independent* agreed with the *Times,* but with a significant concession: "Marie Corelli has left a collection of novels ephemeral in character and fated soon to be in the dust. Yet she ministered to the idleness of tens of thousands." The *Buchan Observer* was unable to make a commitment either way and hedged all bets: "though we shall not here speak of immortality, it is certain that her books have yet a long lease of life to run, and must not be classed as ephemeral."

Other reviews placed her squarely in the Victorian past. The *Daily Sketch* wrote that a new generation found her "old-fashioned" and compared her to "Jules Verne or a very early H. G. Wells." There were generous efforts to acknowledge the historical context of her popularity: "Her death severs another link with the literary world of the 'eighties and 'nineties, which has bequeathed to our own times the popular magazine, the 'best seller,' and the 'shilling shocker,'" said the *Yorkshire Post* on the day after her death. The fact that Corelli represented a time past, that she practically embodied the popular spirit of a generation, gives some reviews an air of poignancy. As H. W. Seaman wrote in the *Daily Mail,* "Marie Corelli belonged to a great company of story-tellers, but the world they wrote about is gone. If the fame of some of them is forgotten it is because they wrote not for all times but for their own times. And times have changed" (quoted in Scott 31).

But with change there is also continuity. A surprising number of the notices and reviews from the 1920s mentioned Ethel M. Dell (1881–1939) as the modern inheritor of Corelli's "kingdom" (*Christian World*). Just as Corelli's contemporaries dubbed her the "Queen of Best-Sellers" in the 1890s, Rebecca West, in 1928, called Dell the undisputed "queen" of "tosh" literature (323). This suggests that by the time of Corelli's death the figure of the popular female novelist was familiar and inevitable and the antagonisms of the literary elite toward a successful romance writer had somewhat abated. Mrs. Henry Wood, Mary Elizabeth Braddon, Ouida, Rhoda Broughton, and other Victorian sensationalists had preceded Corelli, but it was Corelli's willingness to defend her fiction to the male literary establishment that definitively paved the way for other successful women writers in the twentieth century, such as

Elinor Glyn and Barbara Cartland (who, in fact, condensed many of Dell's novels). Thus, even though writers in the periodical press in 1924 questioned whether Corelli would have any lasting impact on English literature, in their pointed references to Dell, they acknowledged implicitly that she already had.

If the verdict on Corelli's literary reputation was postponed, the race for theory had only just begun. By the 1930s, of course, the opposition of popular and highbrow literature was being examined as a subject in its own right. In *Fiction and the Reading Public,* for instance, Q. D. Leavis explained that "suitable readers" of the popular formula were people "who can read a novel in the spirit in which it was written, because at a corresponding stage of development to the author" (64). Leavis writes that best-sellers use an emotional vocabulary that corresponds to feelings evoked by religious language and that "responses can be touched off with a dangerous ease—every self-aware person finds that he has to train himself from adolescence in withstanding them—and there is evidently a vast public that derives great pleasure from reacting this way" (64–65).

Corelli was a model case for theories of the popular, but she also presented peculiar problems for critics after her death. She was a case to crack, a riddle, a puzzle. Perhaps because she dangerously tempted the "self-aware" intellectual into adolescent indulgences, she provoked both reductive criticism and respectful bewilderment. Nearly twenty-five years after Corelli had reached the height of her fame with *The Sorrows of Satan,* the *Morning Post* asked on the day following her death: "Where, then, lay her secret?" Articles and reviews published between 1924 and 1955 represent an entire class of professional appraisers of the popular, each believing that his or her analysis is the key to all interpretations, the solution to the Corelli mystery. Corelli's fame was an invitation to dissect mass culture. Writing in 1925, Osbert Burdett asserted that "romance is the victory of imagination over intelligence, and the result in art of imagination uncontrolled by conscience. The Corellian recipe is here, and the secret of all immediately popular successes" (238). But this is rather glib and very vague. Indeed, what *was* the Corellian secret formula? West believed that true popularity eschews all trace of irony or intellectual superiority: "No one can write a best-seller by taking thought. The slightest touch of insincerity blurs its appeal. The writer who keeps his tongue in his cheek, who knows that he is writing for fools and that, therefore, he had better write like a fool, may make a respectable living out of serials and novelettes; but he will never make the vast, the blaring, half a million success" (320–21).

Critics were still speculating on the matter twenty years later. In 1947 D. L. Hobman, writing in the *New Statesman and Nation,* asked: "Why, at the turn of the century, did Marie Corelli achieve a popularity seldom gained by any novelist before or since? . . . What was the way of escape which she offered to her contemporaries, and which they were so eager to tread?" (93). His theory: she was immensely preoccupied with religion, she dabbled in science, and she had violent prejudices. Hobman astutely concludes that "the answer to the riddle of her immense popularity" was her contradictions: "she managed to let her readers have their cake and eat it" (93).

T. P. O'Connor also had a tripartite theory: "What were the qualities with which Marie Corelli was endowed? The first was an extremely powerful imagination; the second an inventive faculty, occasionally melodramatic, but always fertile and suggestive; and the third was a style rich and prodigal in colour, not always chastened, but everywhere vivid and alert." "Colour" seemed the key to another critic, Douglas Goldring. In a 1920 essay titled "Clever Novels," Goldring expressed his impatience with writers of clever novels—mostly intellectuals suffering from "Freud-fever"—which often contain portraits of clever novelists (171). In comparison he praises "the courage and originality in the choice of material for their stories, and in the wide range of their imagination," of popular writers: "The 'clever novel' gets long notices in the weekly reviews; but Miss Marie Corelli, Mr. Robert Hichens, and Miss Edith [*sic*] M. Dell rake in the shekels. . . . Perhaps the secret of the whole business is *colour.* The 'clever' writers are afraid of colour. Genius is never afraid of it" (180–81).

These accounts seem strictly literary, even akin to New Criticism, but personality and gender bias entered into almost every treatment of the Corelli "secret." The "riddle" of Corelli's success as a novelist was often tied to the worst encroachments of psychoanalytic theory in the 1930s. Writing in the *Daily Express,* James Agate, for example, approached the problem of "who Marie Corelli was" this way: "The answer is that she was a squat, tubby, little woman who pretended to a non-existent ancestry, gave herself out to be ten years younger than she was, wrote a series of novels which for pretentiousness and bosh have never been approached and which, though they were torn to pieces by the critics, took in nine-tenth of the reading public of this country" (quoted in Scott 25). This notion of the public being taken in was especially offensive to some critics—although Horace Thorogood saluted the fact that Corelli "attempted a big job and brought it off" (quoted in Scott 34). The *Times Literary Supplement* seemed amazed that Corelli was able to "'put it over' the public" in her books, as though she had pulled off a major cultural heist (quoted in Scott 27). In fact, it claimed that "to anyone with but a smattering of the psycho-analytic theory the riddle of . . . Marie Corelli is easy." Solution: her books compensate for the loneliness of her childhood and the stigma of her illegitimacy.

There is obviously a superior tone to these reviews. Even Scott bluntly states that Corelli's feminine mystique worked to her advantage, sheltering her from harsher criticism: "She was in every sense a womanly woman. . . . She is about the only forceful woman writer whom no one has dared to endow with a 'masculine mind.' For the reason, I think, no male with a mind like hers could ever have 'got away with it' for nearly a quarter of a century, as she did. Being feminine much, she was forgiven much" (151). In Scott's version Corelli's womanliness gave her an advantage, but only because she was not held up to the same standards as her male competitors in the popular market (such as Caine). It is instructive to observe the way Scott manages to turn the disadvantages she felt because of sexual discrimination into advantages—a strategy used effectively by other critics, as well. Writing in the *Dictionary of National Biography* in 1937, Michael Sadleir asserted, "The tragedy of Marie Corelli was her inability to understand either why she was popular or why she was unpopular" (541). Again, this is a neat way of turning success into failure, and Sadleir is not the only one to reduce Corelli's life to tragedy: Bullock wrote that her "real tragedy" was that of most idealists (265), but Agate was undecided, saying her life "was either a comedy or a tragedy, or both" (quoted in Scott 25). Sadleir's version demonstrates how the incapacity of educated literary men to account for Corelli's popularity was turned on the writer herself, that is, she did not know what she was doing. This is an ideological tactic, familiar from the beginning of the nineteenth century, to describe women writers, not just romance writers, as being without craft or method, simply emotional geysers. It is the opinion of Desmond MacCarthy, for example: "whatever she wrote gushed unchecked and uncensored straight from the burning centre of her desires at the moment. This was the secret of her appeal" (quoted in Scott 33). H. W. Seaman likewise said her "real secret" was that she believed every word she wrote (quoted in Scott 31). Neither critic examines the potential difficulty of writing with sincerity and vigor or the phenomenon of such earnestness finding an enormous audience. I have already cited West's idea that "no one can write a best-seller by taking thought," meaning that irony and sneering are fatal to popularity. In fact, West wrote with insight and sensitivity that "some wild lust for beauty in [Corelli] made her take a wild inventory of the world's contents and try to do what it could with them" (321–22). Or, in the words of the *Yorkshire Post* on the day following Corelli's death, "When Marie Corelli's early environment is remembered the miracle is not that she found a myriad of admirers for such faulty work, but that she wrote so well."

The lust for beauty and this last reference to a miracle are especially appropriate for Corelli, who endowed her public role with an aura of wonderment, sanctity, and elusiveness. And there was a secret, after all, a secret that stands ironically as a reply to the skeptics, critics, and cynics who were her enemies in the press, the "modern" people who had lost all faith in God and in human ideals. In the memoir she published six years after Corelli's death, Vyver describes a private ritual that was concealed during Corelli's life and that sheds light on the solemnity with which she viewed her vocation. As a novel went to the printers, Corelli "offered a prayer that it might carry her message to the world and bring comfort to her fellow men and women—and she pasted it, though hidden to the printer by a piece of paper over it, into each manuscript" (255). It is a true story. One of the prayers is at the Shakespeare Birthplace Trust in Stratford.

In the conclusion to his book on Corelli, Scott cites a BBC critic reviewing Bigland's biography in 1953 who suggested that her "phenomenal, astounding success—and not her birth or love affair or anything of that kind, is the real 'Mystery of Marie Corelli'" (212). Clearly for some literary reviewers this was true, hence the many allusions to her "secret." But two different types of headlines began to appear a few days after the funeral that had nothing to do with literature, variations on the following examples. The first is from the *Evening Standard* of 29 April 1924: "Secret of Marie Corelli's Birth. 'To Remain Sealed' Says Her Great Friend. A New Love Story. Father and Mother Met at Shakespeare's Grave." The second example is from the *Daily Sketch* of 28 April 1924: "Romance of Two Women: Inspiring Story of a Great Friendship."

For several weeks the words *secret, mystery,* and *romance* showed up in newspaper headlines about the dead novelist: "Marie Corelli's Secret" (*Daily Sketch,* 29 April), "Romance of Marie Corelli" (*South Wales Evening News,* 28 April), "The Corelli Mystery" (*Manchester City News,* 3 May), "Marie Corelli Dies: Guards Life Secret" (*New York Evening Post,* 21 April), "Friendship, Romance: Miss Corelli and Companion in Early Struggles" (*Evening Standard,* 28 April), "Life Companion: Romance of Two Women" (*Shields Daily Gazette,* 28 April), "The Corelli 'Mystery': Her Own Story by One Who Knew Her" (*Manchester City News,* 3 May). Not only did Corelli's family origins and her long and faithful friendship with Vyver become topics of speculation, they seem to have been conflated in the public imagination into the mystery of Marie Corelli. In earlier chapters I have addressed the way secrets, mysteries, false identities, and screened confessions operate in Corelli's fiction and in her self-mythology—which, incidentally, was successful, since many newspapers reported that she was almost fifty-nine, not sixty-nine, when she died and that she was "of mingled Italian and Scottish extraction," the adopted daughter of the "celebrated song-writer Charles Mackay" *(Evening Standard).* Still, posthumous media interpretations of her life continued to trade on her reclusiveness, and the Corelli mystery briefly teased readers of British and American newspapers and magazines.

Although there was immediate speculation about her parents and her true identity, the illegitimacy question did not show up in headlines for another twenty years. It was not until 1944, after Bullock's 1940 biography had delved into the question, that the *Daily Mail's* headline "Marie Corelli Secret Out: She Was Minnie Mills" evoked the "Secrets of the Strange Life of Marie Corelli," who "Wrote Her Way to Fame, Left a Mystery" (*Daily Mail,* 17 March 1944). Twentieth-century biographers have investigated Corelli's birth and family identity, and it is not necessary to go over that information here.[1] But I am interested in why the headline "Romance of Two Women" surfaced in 1924 and then quietly disappeared, for public attention was given to the "romance" with Vyver even before the world knew that in her will Corelli left everything to her friend. The source of biographical information for many of the clippings in Stratford may have been Sidney Walton's reminiscences in the *Yorkshire Evening News* on 22 April, only one day after Corelli's death and before the contents of the will were made public. The article bore this headline: "Marie Corelli: What Manner of Woman She Was." Most of the article concerns the deep friendship between Corelli and Vyver. Walton writes with respect and admiration for Corelli's character, yet I wonder if "manner of woman" refers to more than her gentle nature. Let me immediately say that I am not interested in proving anything about Corelli's sexuality; I am aware of the liability in trying to make a writer fashionable to postmodern critics by conjuring the "apparitional lesbian" (to borrow Terry Castle's term). But this lengthy excerpt from Walton is an evocative piece of writing for many reasons:

> *One of the great friendships of modern times knit together the hearts and minds of Miss Marie Corelli and Miss Bertha Vyver. The name of the one became famous the world over. The name of the other is hidden like a primrose in the gardens of Mason Croft. Together these ladies lived; sorrow and success they shared; the wine from the vineyard of life they drank from one common cup. Miss Corelli would have flamed into anger at sight or sound of the word Socialism, but in a fine human sense, she fulfilled its precepts in her friendship with Miss Vyver. Her own heart was the hearth of her comrade, and thought and love of "Marie" thrilled through Miss Vyver's veins. . . . In loneliness of soul, Miss Vyver mourns the loss of one who was nearer and tenderer to her than a sister. I hope that for the inspiration of all friends and lovers, the story of this sweet friendship may one day be told. Miss Corelli wrote many novels. I think the noblest was unwritten. It was lived. It was set to the music of long, unbroken, undiscordant love of one who shared her hearth and home. Over the fireplace in the fine, old spacious lounge at Mason Croft the initials M. C. and B. V. were carven into one symbol. And it was the symbol of life.*

Walton effectively pairs invisibilities and exhibitions: a hidden life and name behind a famous one, a personal politics behind a public disavowal, the story that has not been told and the novels that were written. There are also comprehensive but vague allusions to the two women as sisters, friends, and lovers, which is especially interesting because five days later other newspapers described Corelli and Vyver's relationship as "mother and daughter" and called Vyver Corelli's "guardian angel." As if to tie these oppositions together, Walton evokes romantic symbols of unity in the common cup, the unbroken music of love, and the sculpted crest above the fireplace with the initials M. C. and B. V., a symbol of life. The motto on the crest is "Amor Vincit." All of the newspapers that covered the funeral reported that Vyver was too ill to attend; she sent a floral wreath with the tribute, "'Amor Vincit,' to the best and purest soul I ever met on earth, whose ideals were always of the highest, from her devoted and loving friend Bertha."

Vyver and Corelli may be understood as devoted companions, sexual lovers, or romantic friends, sisters, mother and daughter, or even guardian angel and inspired genius. There are so many kinds of relationships, after all. Certainly Corelli's relationship with Vyver strengthened her faith in women's self-sufficiency and limitless capacities for achievement. "I love my own sex, and I heartily sympathize with every step that women take towards culture, freedom, advancement, and the moral and intellectual mastery of themselves," Corelli wrote in 1907 ("Man's War" 550). But just how did journalists and biographers interpret this part of the famous novelist's life, and how does the Vyver factor affect our understanding of Corelli's supposed man hating, her ostensible disgust with suffragists and progressives, and her proclaimed love for women?

The very broad subject of cultural constructions of Corelli and women can be addressed in a ruthlessly abridged survey of four biographies and memoirs published between 1901 and 1940. These works say as much about the way gender touches the culture of celebrity as they do about Corelli's secrets and are worth looking at for their suggestions, fabrications, constructs, and omissions, for clearly "what manner of woman" Corelli was involves some sifting through observations of her pose, and any biographer would need to decide what to emphasize and what to ignore. Even after her death there were some aspects of Corelli's life that still could not be treated frankly—in fact, even thirty years later, in 1955, Scott's insinuation about the relationship between Vyver and Corelli is difficult to figure out: "Who was Bertha Vyver?" he asks. "And in what capacity did she join the Mackay household in 1878? Servant, housekeeper, companion, or paying guest? Or just—friend?" (183). The need to find a category is clear, and that pause may be an approach to an unmentionable possibility. Corelli's relationships with and feelings for women were intense, complex, and contradictory. How did biographers read her?

The first biography of Corelli, by Kent Carr, was published in 1901, supposedly with her sanction. Carr's book is a miniature (about five inches by three inches) in Henry J. Drane's series Bijou Biographies of famous people. Others in the Bijou series were the Right Honorable Joseph Chamberlain, M.P., Lord Kitchener, Lord Roberts, John Burns, M.P., Lord Salisbury, and King Edward VII. The inclusion of Corelli among these conservative political luminaries is odd, to say the least; it suggests that the ideological impetus of the Bijou Biographies was to promote Tory heroes and explains why there are such long accounts of Corelli's popularity with British soldiers fighting the Boer War. Carr's book is a pocket hagiography with a bit of literary criticism thrown in —for example, he divides Corelli's novels into three categories, "religious novels, novels of the imagination, and novels with a purpose," and offers long plot summaries of two of her most popular books, *Barabbas* and *The Sorrows of Satan* (88). On the subject of women Carr is curiously selective. He deems it important enough to write about Corelli's choice of a woman doctor, for instance: "Now, it is one thing to believe in the suitability of the medical profession for women in the abstract and quite another to stand by the belief when one's life hangs in the balance. But Miss Corelli called in Mary Scharlieb, of Harley Street, and allowed her to perform the necessary operation" (48). It is true that in 1901 Corelli's faith in a woman doctor would have seemed notable, since female physicians were considered less competent than men and even scandalous. Still, it is important that Carr records Corelli's tribute to Dr. Scharlieb, whom she called "the best and cleverest of women" (49).

Only a few pages later, however, Carr undermines whatever kind of feminist solidarity his earlier story could have evoked by writing about Corelli's allegiance to men: "Miss Corelli's supposed and reported 'hatred of men' is pure fiction. She has as many men friends as women—perhaps more" (67). The admiration for female cleverness and competence, the attachment to literary men, and the hatred of New Women are presented unproblematically—in fact, if anything is contradicted, it is Corelli's reputation as a man hater, something all the biographers seem compelled to deal with sooner or later. My favorite piece of propaganda in Carr's book, however, is about how New Zealand and Australian soldiers in South Africa came across a stray copy of *The Soul of Lilith* on the veld and tore out each page after it was read to pass along to the next man in the troop. Carr cites a letter Corelli received from a colors sergeant in the Boer War in May 1900:

(63–64)

> Now to tell you about your delightful books which were invaluable to the troops during the siege; one, "The Sorrows of Satan," was read and re-read by me, and then handed round. As many as three would be waiting to read it, so where literature was scarce, you can imagine what a blessing it was to have a book like it. We all seemed to think it the very best we ever read. Still more strange to say, I was one day strolling over the battlefields of Colenso, and I found in the trenches evacuated by the Boers two leaves of one of your famous books, "The Murder of Delicia," which I am sending to you, with a clip of Mauser cartridge, also found in the same trench about 500 yards east of Fort Wylie, and which was occupied for so long by the Boers; so that you see the Boers also read your works.

If Carr's little book is Tory hagiography, T. F. G. Coates and R. S. Warren-Bell's *Marie Corelli: The Writer and the Woman,* published in 1903, is downright chivalric. In their preface the authors explain that writing a biography of a living writer is "a most delicate literary performance" and that although their aim is to "set before the public as many particulars as possible concerning Marie Corelli the Woman—as distinct from Marie Corelli the Writer"—out of common courtesy to the novelist they can only publish a "limited number of personal minutiae" (3). Thus this authorized biography makes no pretense to tell all, and the authors accept whatever version of her life Corelli chooses to sanction. Coates and Warren-Bell's enterprise is largely to extol her fiction and defend her from mean-spirited and envious male critics. They admire both her femininity and her genius, citing at length an article by J. Cuming Walters in the *Manchester Chronicle,* which calls Corelli "a very woman, too, with a woman's likes and dislikes, a woman's feelings, a woman's impulses" (332). These feelings and impulses remain unspecified, of course, but clearly the suggestion is that her outwardly feminine manner compensates for the virulent scorn she heaps on men in all of her books.

Interestingly, though, the authors respectfully object to her ferocious attacks on masculine parasitism and faithlessness in *The Murder of Delicia*. They call it "the least worthy of all the books Marie Corelli has written. It is far too full of railing against men; it is far too one-sided and far too bitter" (209). That they are able to say this while also disputing charges of Corelli's man hating is another example of diluting, ignoring, or erasing the complexities of her position as a woman, the picture of female charm, and as a writer, vituperative, opinionated, full of feminist rage.

Bertha Vyver's *Memoirs of Marie Corelli* was published in 1930, five years after she published her friend's most emotionally revealing book, *Open Confession,* which far exceeds *The Murder of Delicia* in antimale railing. In her memoir, though, Vyver omits the story of her friend's profound attachment to Joan and Arthur Severn. The only expressions of emotion and longing that are cited verbatim in this memoir are the letters Corelli wrote to Vyver in the 1880s, when the two women were separated and Corelli was beginning to capitalize on the popularity of her first two books. "Write me as often as you can, and do not ogle that big clumsy 'Herman' too much with those eyes of yours; it is naughty. Mind you tell me all your flirtations," she wrote to Vyver (96). Corelli calls her "My own little Mamasita" and longs for the day when they will be together. "Your little wee one embraces you fondly," she writes, "and sends you dozens of tender kisses" (97). These letters take up several pages and make me wonder what Vyver intended them to suggest about Corelli. The decision to publish these playful, doting letters while conspicuously omitting *any* mention of the Severn affair and the impetus for *Open Confession* is a mystery within a mystery. It is telling that in his epilogue to Vyver's book J. Cuming Walters asks precisely the questions Vyver ignores: "If these *Confessions* were not the outcome of experience, it is not easy to account for the imagination which could give them such painful realism. They are cries of agony, of bitterness, of scorn. Can these things be dissembled? Can we be deceived by painted shadows? Are we mocked? It scarcely seems possible. The bleeding heart is bared; the sob of anguish is real. Yet, if this surmise be correct, it adds but another mystery—and the one furthest from solution—in Marie Corelli's life" (Vyver 270).

Ten years later, in 1940, George Bullock's *Marie Corelli: The Life and Death of a Best-Seller* attempted to crack the case, using watered-down psychoanalytic theory that fully reflects the sexism of the period. Vyver died in 1942, and I can only hope that at the age of eighty-eight she was too tired to read Bullock's version of Corelli's life. I have already referred to his interpretations of *Open Confession* in the previous chapter. Early in the biography he defines Corelli's neurosis, her frustration, and her prudishness: "In her shrill denunciation of men there was always to be detected in later years an itch for their approbation. . . . She looked upon the intimate relations that may result in childbirth as gross. Her young ladylike mind saw the realisation of sexual desire as a sordid obstruction to the ethereal passion for which her suburban soul yearned. . . . Brought up to date, she belongs to the 'No,-don't-let's,-it-will-spoil-everything' variety" (28–31). According to Bullock, she is an example of "retarded development," her "natural instincts" have been frustrated (210, 203). Although she had no "frigidity of feeling," she suffered from a "middle-class consciousness" about sex that "made it necessary to assert that love was more than wanting a person 'just physically'"—an assertion, I would think, many people share, even those who are *not* middle-class (34).

In Bullock's biography we hear scary echoes of the *Westminster Review* critic from 1906 who asserted that Corelli was psychologically disturbed and a sexual hysteric. Bullock writes: "While she was alive she wanted the public to think that her unmarried state was of her own deliberate choosing, and she welcomed the opinion that she was a 'man-hater'" (219). This contradicts the authorized biographies, written while Corelli was alive and famous, which insisted on her warm friendships with men, and Vyver's memoir is full of anecdotes about literary men who visited Mason Croft. Man hating seems to resurface, though, as a particularly offensive label, a charge that must be seriously refuted. It certainly may imply a suspicion of lesbianism, but more likely it connotes an assertive sexual pride, a vocal stance against patriarchal oppression, and, as Bullock suggests, a refusal of the roles of wife and mother. It is definitely a stigma connoting unattractive anger, resistance, and some kind of female solidarity.

It is undeniable that there is a strong current of sexual hostility in

Corelli's novels, and it is equally true that she fought the sexism of the London literary world loudly and belligerently. We are already familiar with her brand of feminism, the contradictions and the overstated claims for female sovereignty. Yet in a 1907 article, "Man's War against Woman," she seems to reshape her opinions, straining not so much for consistency as for a deep-rooted explanation for male-female hostility: "May I dare to say to my distracted, man-fighting sisters that I am just a woman like themselves and yet,—*not* a 'suffragette'?" (426). For Corelli, as we have seen, the desire to obtain the vote was a confession that women had lost their power to conquer by exciting male reverence, and thus "woman alone is at fault for the war against her" ("Man's War" 427). "Man is what woman makes him. She bears him and rears him. She is his sovereign and supreme ruler. From the first breath he draws, She and She alone possesses him," she declares ("Man's War" 427). This insistence on female sovereignty stems from a serious and bitter attempt to find the basis of sexual hostility, the cause of misogyny and male dominance—a problem that is still at the heart of feminist psychoanalysis and sociology. For Corelli woman is at fault for man's tyranny not because she is inferior but because she has agreed to feed and confirm man's ego, beginning with her maternal role in the patriarchal family:

> *if she coddles and spoils him till he imagines he is, as he asserts, her lord and master, then she has only herself to blame if he continues to "lord and master" it over her always. . . . She trains him to consider his existence the be-all and end-all of her own. . . . She begins her doting stupidity in his childhood. . . . Presently, as a perfectly natural consequence, he, as soon as he comes to years of "discretion," turns round on mothers, sisters, sweethearts, and all other relatives of the feminine gender and says, "Your place is the nursery and kitchen! Women have no business in literature, politics, or art." This is the only attitude to be expected of him after women's constant indulgence of all his little whims and tempers.*     ("Man's War" 427)

As a rudimentary and undertheorized effort to understand gender oppression, identity, and family structures, this passage bears comparison with later psychoanalytic theories by feminists such as Nancy Chodorow, Dorothy Dinnerstein, and Carol Gilligan. Dinnerstein, for instance, has written that a "naturally keen childhood fantasy-wish (lived out widely by men with the women whom they rule) is to keep female will in live captivity, obediently energetic, fiercely protective of its captor's pride, ready always to vitalize his projects with its magical maternal blessing and to support them with its concrete, self-abnegating maternal help" (169). Is it possible to interpret Corelli's man hating as her refusal to fulfill the maternal or wifely role? As breadwinner, did she want the ego stroking and the domestic support that she knew men claimed as their right without question? Recall the newspaper articles describing Vyver as a "mother" to Corelli and the letters addressed to "Mamasita" cited in Vyver's memoir. In his 1955 book Scott stated sympathetically, "It is scarcely necessary to say that had Marie Corelli searched the world, she had not found a *man* to treat her with such infinite patience and give her such a constant devotion [as Vyver]" (190). Lillian Faderman has said almost the same thing, referring to Vyver as a "proper, unreflecting Victorian wife (and mother)" and asking, "What husband would have subsumed his own existence under hers for the sake of her continuing success?" (213–14). Not only did Corelli take pride in her success and her hard work, but she bravely and gladly assumed the role of provider in the Mackay household. In letters to her father and to Vyver in the 1880s she frequently alludes to her invented persona as the ticket to economic security, promising a trip to the Highlands "if 'Marie Corelli' has any luck at all," expressing confidence that "Marie Corelli will be quite rich, and able to do all sorts of good things for her darlings," telling Vyver that "*Thelma* is your book, and the world will know that Bertha is Marie Corelli's dearest friend," and saying that "'Marie Corelli' will attain her highest ambition when she can make those she loves free from worry" (Vyver 71, 72, 74).

It is not much of an exaggeration to say that in late-Victorian and Edwardian society, only women who were actresses, singers, or celebrities, including popular novelists, could earn a large income completely on their own, without relying on legacies or the support of a working husband. Corelli insisted that she had worked hard and continuously all her life, "and I have never been indebted to any man for the least assistance or support in the making of my career. . . . I earn every pound I possess; I am a householder, paying rates and taxes, and I employ men who depend upon me for their wages, these men having a 'right' to vote, while I have none" ("Man's War" 426). Despite her financial independence, and indeed her considerable wealth and influence, some critics found it impossible to reconcile her ambition with cultural stereotypes of women's work. "In spite of her cleverness and her literary ability she was at heart the hard-headed, practical little English housewife, with a decided preference for the coin of the realm," wrote one critic in 1925 ("Housewife"). Sadly, this sounds a lot like Edmund Gosse's dismissive "that little milliner" of some twenty years before.

In the course of my research for this chapter, I have been disconcerted to find so many narrow-minded reiterations, even more than half a century after her death, so few attempts at a fresh view of Corelli's achievements. Though far from "mannish" in her personal appearance, the fact that Corelli never married made her vulnerable to attacks every bit as fearful and cruel as those leveled against sexually independent New Women. One of the most blatant accusations of "unnatural" sexuality appeared in the *Westminster Review* in 1906, under the title "A Note upon Marie Corelli by Another Writer of Less Repute":

> *She is an erotic degenerate of the subtlest type. Had she been domesticated she might have been as harmless as her foreign contemporaries. As it is she stands alone, and the woman who has lost her womanliness is diseased. We may have in her case the body, the methods, and the talents of a woman, but there are unmistakably demonstrated also the arrogance and the intense prejudices of a man. Despite her photograph, and the sentimental interviews that she has caused to be published concerning her home-life, the only term which can be honestly applied to Marie Corelli is a "man-woman." So soon as a woman begins to concern herself passionately and discontentedly with problems which are not within the normal sphere of experience she loses the most charming asset of her sex. It is only on degenerate subjects that hysterical people can make effect. A strong and healthy man looks for a woman who is above all things else womanly and kind. Marie Corelli's celibacy is a fact of wonderful psychological value.* (Stuart-Young 692)

A similar interpretation of Corelli's personality was offered in the 1920s by A. C. MacDonell, who wrote in the *Observer,* "The root of her trouble was, I think, that she was dynamically active and physically unattractive. She attained her triumphs by an immense amount of hard work and loud shouting, whereas other women attain triumphs, which were outside her reach, by simply being beautiful" (quoted in Scott 33). If it is troubling to find Bullock in 1940 repeating the same cruel suggestions as the *Westminster Review* in 1906, it is even worse to realize that in 1978, after the considerable work of feminists and social theorists, a biographer could write: "Women without men usually have overweening ambition, coupled with a ruthless determination to satisfy it. Deprived of the primitive function which is their right, they spend their lives trying to show the world that they too can achieve something. . . . The phenomenon of Marie Corelli is less a case for the literary critic than for the psychiatrist" (Masters 238–40).

Not knowing what to do with Corelli's popular success and her disregard of male critical standards, her campy femininity and her self-reliance and financial freedom, her high moral tone and her barely suppressed eroticism, these male critics fall back on female neurosis. That the "root" of Corelli's man hating, her presumed frustration, her retarded development, her appearance, or her contested sexuality was still an issue, a mystery, for journalists and for biographers in the years after her death shows how resistant a culture can be to the resourceful use of gender roles and identities, especially when the subject is a famous woman who has been lauded for her earnestness and sincerity.

The presumptuousness of modern interpreters on all the issues I have addressed in this chapter—knowledge of Corelli's private life, predictions about her work, speculations about her intimate relationships—is quietly addressed in a remarkable testimonial by someone called Mary Murfitt that appeared as a letter to the editor of the *Daily Sketch* on 8 May 1924:

> *With the passing of Marie Corelli, one feels that the general public has an unconscious resentment that she should have had the courage to live and die as an enigma.*
>
> *To people who love Marie Corelli, she speaks through her art. Her books were prophetic—history has not yet caught up with her. Yet she is described as out of date.*
>
> *One scrap of certain truth about it is that Marie Corelli, the real inner woman, was capable of inspiring and retaining a life-long friendship with one of her own sex—no mean accomplishment.*
>
> *I shall always love Marie Corelli, the mystic.*

The emotional honesty of this letter is striking when compared with so many of the other opinions about Corelli that I have cited. Although it might sound sentimental, eccentric, or even marginally fanatic, the letter is valuable evidence that readers could, and did, have faith in their deeply felt responses to Corelli's novels, regardless of critical opinion, and that some of them at least did not need to solve the "enigma" of Marie Corelli or disguise the important place her books had in their lives. Others who knew her personally may not have cared for her novels but admired the fact that she was totally and consistently herself in all she did. E. F. Benson, who modeled his character Lucia on Corelli in his series of popular Edwardian novels, wrote in 1940, "I do not know whether she is widely read today, but throughout the nineties and well into this century she produced a series of dizzy bestsellers, which she sincerely believed were masterpieces of literature. This made her very happy not only for her own sake but for the sake of the world. It is not, however, as an author I celebrate her, but because she lived, furiously and excitedly, in a bellicose romance of her own devising, which she was persuaded was real" (74).

Although this chapter has focused on opinions about Corelli from more or less experts—journalists, critics, biographers, men of letters— the impressions of Benson and Mary Murfitt call to mind the people who found her books or her life so wonderful, so amazing, and summon up novel readers' various and unpredictable passions, whether they belong to the middle class or not. And it is useful to remember that Corelli appealed across all classes, to gentlewomen, shopkeepers, artists, and intellectuals.

Nevertheless, it was a surprise to find a Corelli fan in Henry Miller. He wrote in the *New York Times Book Review* in 1976, "It is my belief that if a revival of her work is aroused it will be by young people or by the same sort of enthusiasts who made Hermann Hesse, Knut Hamsun, and Isaac Bashevis Singer." Miller is unintentionally ironic; these three writers would have been very odd company for Corelli, in that Hesse and Singer warmly admired Hamsun, whose novel *Hunger* (1890) was a seminal modernist text about a starving artist; Hamsun was also fiercely anti-democratic and unrepentantly loyal to Hitler, according to John Carey.

Still, Miller's evocation of enthusiasts and capricious readers (young people in this case) who help start literary revivals is appropriately applied to Corelli. Although my reading of Corelli has come from an academic discipline and a critical perspective, I agree with John Gross that people who enjoy reading books do not need to depend on disciplinary homes or even on the opinions of critics: "an interest in literature thrives on spontaneity, eager curiosity, the anticipation of pleasure" (315).

There are still many ways for academics, scholars, and readers to approach Corelli. In a chapter on the Edwardians in *The Rise and Fall of the Man of Letters,* Gross observes that the strength of that eminent belletrist G. K. Chesterton was that "he was unembarrassed by the childish element in art, and would no more have condescended to it than he would have condescended to an actual child" (240–41). Not being a student of Chesterton, I do not know if he ever referred to Corelli in his many essays, but I think his intellectual generosity, his optimism and social conservatism, his religious faith, and his affection for romance would have made him a generous reader of Corelli's work. In a wonderful essay of 1901 called "A Defence of Penny Dreadfuls," Chesterton argues that it is wrong to call popular literature vulgar, for "it is not vulgar intrinsically—it is the actual centre of a million flaming imaginations. . . . Literature and fiction are two entirely different things. Literature is a luxury; fiction is a necessity" (19, 21). The Chestertonian approach is, I think, a promising one in understanding Corelli: the childish element of her playful and outlandish imagination really is matched by a faith in the necessity of fiction, the desirability of myths, all of the ideals that must somehow find expression in a given culture and often in crude and marvelous forms.

# Notes

## Introduction

1. Although I often take issue with Masters's explanations of Corelli's motives and his interpretations of events in her life, I have to give credit to his construction of the facts. Although his is not a scholarly work, he is a gifted writer who tells the story in a lively manner, and his book gives a broad picture of many turn-of-the-century personalities and events. A feminist biography of Corelli by Teresa Ransom, *The Mysterious Miss Marie Corelli: Queen of Victorian Bestsellers,* was published in 1999.
2. Adaptations were made in Britain in 1917 by G. B. Samuelson Productions and, later, in 1926, by the great D. W. Griffith in the United States. In 1923 there was also some interest from Curtis Brown Ltd., which offered Corelli five thousand pounds for the film rights to *The Sorrows of Satan,* but the project apparently fell through.

## I. The Queen of Best-Sellers and the Culture of Celebrity

1. See John Stokes, *In the Nineties* (Chicago: University of Chicago Press, 1989), 146–66.
2. Established criticism in this area includes Elaine Showalter, *A Literature of Their Own* (Princeton, N.J.: Princeton University Press, 1978); Gaye Tuchman and Nina Fortin, *Edging Women Out: Victorian Novelists, Publishers, and Social Change* (New Haven, Conn.: Yale University Press, 1989); Moers, *Literary Women;* and Elizabeth Helsinger, Robin Lauterbach Sheets, and William Veeder, *The Woman Question* (Chicago: University of Chicago Press, 1983). For another view on women's participation in late-Victorian publishing, see Ellen Miller Casey, "Edging Women Out? Reviews of Women Novelists in the *Athenaeum,* 1860–1900," *Victorian Studies* 39, no. 2 (1996): 151–71.
3. Corelli wrote a long letter to the *Daily Mail* in 1897 explaining the entire transaction. She agreed to sit to Helen Donald-Smith as a personal favor to a "lady-friend" under the condition that "the picture was not to be exhibited, photographed, or in any way reproduced" without her permission. But when the picture was finished, the artist was so pleased she wished to send it to the Royal Academy. It was rejected, and out of compassion for a struggling woman artist Corelli agreed to make no objection if Donald-Smith found a gallery that would exhibit it for a short time. Corelli insisted she made no money from the exhibit: "I never should condescend to make financial profit out of my own portrait after the fashion of certain 'aristocratic' ladies and professional stage favourites. I gain nothing at all out of the transaction but the privilege of being insulted by any little paragraphist who earns 1s. 6d. or 2s. 6d. by his 'copy' for, as I said, the *lower* grades of the press."

4. See Judith Walkowitz, *City of Dreadful Delight: Narratives of Sexual Danger in Late-Victorian London* (Chicago: University of Chicago Press, 1992), 15–80.
5. See Ed Cohen, *Talk on the Wilde Side: Toward a Genealogy of a Discourse on Male Sexualities* (London: Routledge, 1993).
6. "The Marie Corelli Calendar" (London: Frank Palmer, 1913); *The Marie Corelli Birthday Book* (London: Hutchinson, 1897).
7. *The Greatest Queen in the World* (London: Skeffington and Son, 1901); *The World in Tears* (London: Robert Hayes, 1915); *A Tribute to the Grand Fleet and the Grand Fleet's Commander* (British and Foreign Sailors Society, 1917); *Is All Well with England?* (London: Jarrolds, 1917).

## II. Aestheticism in Suburbia

1. Showalter, *Sexual Anarchy,* 78–81.
2. In *Howards End,* for instance, which appeared in 1910, E. M. Forster fills out Leonard Bast's personality and class limitations by having him imagine that Margaret Schlegel is "probably one of those soulless, atheistical women who have been so shown up by Miss Corelli" (Reprint, New York: Vintage, 1921), 40–41.
3. One of the stories later published in *Cameos,* "God's Light on the Mountains," was attributed to Olive Schreiner and published in the *Pall Mall Budget* under the heading "Another 'Dream' by Olive Schreiner," with the author's portrait and autograph. Corelli seized the incident as another example of journalistic bias and wrote about it in her preface to *Cameos* in 1896: "so long as the *Pall Mall* authorities thought the story was by a woman whom they had elected to 'boom,' it was worth prominent notice; but that, on the contrary, as soon as they had learned it was by another woman, whom they were strenuously endeavouring to 'quash,' it became quite a different matter!" (London: Hutchinson, 1896), x.

## III. The Ardor of the Pen

1. To take one Victorian example, Frances Power Cobbe, in 1862, wrote: "There is little need to talk of literature as a field for woman's future work. She is ploughing it in all directions already. The one thing is to do it thoroughly, and let the plough go deep enough, with good thorough drainage to begin upon. Writing books ought never to be thought of slightly. In one sense, it is morally a serious thing, a power of addressing many persons at once with somewhat more weight than in common speech. . . . We cannot without offence neglect to *use* such a power for a good end; and if to give pleasure be the object of our book, make it at least to the reader an ennobling and refining pleasure" ("What Shall We Do with Our Old Maids?" in *Prose by Victorian Women,* ed. Sally Mitchell and Andrea Broomfield [New York: Garland, 1996], 259).

## IV. The Weltanschauung of Marie Corelli

1. Several other recent books reexamine literary modernism in ways similar to the approaches of these feminist scholars. See Jane Eldridge Miller, *Rebel Women: Feminism, Modernism, and the Victorian Novel* (Chicago: University of Chicago Press, 1997); Carola

M. Kaplan and Anne B. Simpson, eds., *Seeing Double: Revisioning Edwardian and Modernist Literature* (New York: St. Martin's Press, 1996); Maria DiBattista and Lucy McDiarmid, eds., *High and Low Moderns: Literature and Culture, 1889–1939* (New York: Oxford University Press, 1996); Lyn Pykett, *Engendering Fictions: The English Novel in the Early Twentieth Century* (London: Edward Arnold, 1995); and Lisa Rado, ed., *Rereading Modernism: New Directions in Feminist Criticism* (New York: Garland, 1994).

2. Richard L. Kowalczyk has written about Corelli's role in advancing Severn's career. See Kowalczyk, "Marie Corelli and Arthur Severn's Reputation as an Artist," *Modern Philology* 66 (1969): 322–27; "New Evidence on Marie Corelli and Arthur Severn: Some Unpublished Letters," *English Literature in Transition* 13 (1970): 27–36. For another account of the relationship, see Sheila Birkenhead, *Illustrious Friends: The Story of Joseph Severn and His Son Arthur* (London: Hamish Hamilton, 1965), 369–78.

3. Corelli returns almost compulsively to the opposition of romantic longing and modern systems of knowledge. *Love and the Philosopher* (1923), a sustained conversation between a cynical male intellectual and a romantic young woman, for example, exposes the dangerous tendency of philosophical despair when the heroine exclaims to the philosopher, "If one *thought* the things you *say,* one would commit suicide!" (68).

4. I am struck by how similar Emmanuel Levinas's theories of love and alterity are to the untheorized position of the abandoned lover in Corelli's text. In *Time and the Other* he writes, "The relationship with the other is not an idyllic and harmonious relationship of communion, or a sympathy through which we put ourselves in the other's place; we recognize the other as resembling us but exterior to us; the relationship with the other is a relationship with a Mystery." He continues: "Consequently only a being whose solitude has reached a crispation through suffering, and in relation with death, takes its place on a ground where the relationship with the other becomes possible. . . . I think the erotic relationship furnishes us with a prototype of it. Eros, strong as death, will furnish us with the basis of an analysis of this relationship with mystery" (trans. Richard A. Cohen [Pittsburgh: Duquesne University Press, 1987], 75–76).

5. Corelli sometimes sounds like Arthur Schopenhauer, whose writings were fashionable among English intellectuals at the end of the century. "At all events even the man who has fared tolerably well, becomes more clearly aware, the longer he lives, that life on the whole is a *disappointment, nay a cheat,*" writes Schopenhauer, "in other words, bears the character of a great mystification or even a fraud" (*Philosophical Writings,* trans. Wolfgang Schirmacher [New York: Continuum, 1994], 35). Some of her contemporaries noted Corelli's temperamental affinities with Schopenhauerian pessimism. Ironically, she disapproved of his work, writing to Severn, "Why do you read Schopenhauer? He is a miserable self-analyst, reasoning away every beautiful ideal in life to suit his own diseased soul. Put him aside!" (19 August 1910).

6. I have not been able to find out whether or not Yeats read Corelli, but he did visit her at Mason Croft in 1905, politely declining a ride in her gondola. See *The Letters of W. B. Yeats,* ed. Allan Wade (New York: Macmillan, 1955), 449.

7. *Paulus Antonius, A Tale of Ancient Rome* (London: Spiritual Truth Offices, 1932); *The Voice of Marie Corelli* (Manchester, U.K.: Sherratt and Hughes, 1933).

8. Corelli refers to getting tickets for *Salome* in two letters to Severn dated 12 and 13 October 1910.

## V. Who Was Marie Corelli?

1. Teresa Ransom's biography of Corelli is the latest step in literary detection: "I am still searching for clues to her real identity, and three times now have started along trails of evidence from which the vital page of records is missing. I find this quite strange" (personal correspondence with author, 22 August 1998). It would appear that the mystery of Corelli's identity is still unsolved.

# Works Cited

Acocella, Joan. "Cather and the Academy." *New Yorker,* 27 November 1995, 56–71.

Adcock, A. St. John. "Marie Corelli: A Record and an Appreciation." *Bookman* 26, no. 212 (1909): 59–78.

Alcoff, Linda. "Cultural Feminism versus Post-structuralism." In *Feminism and Philosophy: Essential Readings in Theory, Reinterpretation, and Application,* ed. Nancy Tuana and Rosemarie Tong, 435–56. Boulder, Colo.: Westview, 1995.

Angell, Roger. "Marching Life." *New Yorker,* 22–29 December 1997, 126–34.

Ardis, Ann. *New Women, New Novels: Feminism and Early Modernism.* New Brunswick, N.J.: Rutgers University Press, 1990.

Auerbach, Nina. "Magi and Maidens: The Romance of the Victorian Freud." In *Writing and Sexual Difference,* ed. Elizabeth Abel, 111–30. Chicago: University of Chicago Press, 1982.

Barthes, Roland. *A Lover's Discourse.* Trans. Richard Howard. New York: Hill and Wang, 1977.

———. "The Photographic Message." In *A Barthes Reader,* ed. Susan Sontag, 194–210. New York: Hill and Wang, 1982.

Bartky, Sandra Lee. "Toward a Phenomenology of Feminist Consciousness." In *Feminism and Philosophy: Essential Readings in Theory, Reinterpretation, and Application,* ed. Nancy Tuana and Rosemarie Tong, 396–406. Boulder, Colo.: Westview, 1995.

Basham, Diana. *The Trial of Woman: Feminism and the Occult Sciences in Victorian Literature and Society.* New York: New York University Press, 1992.

Beauvoir, Simone de. *The Second Sex.* Trans. H. M. Parshley. 1952. New York: Vintage, 1974.

Beckson, Karl, ed. *Aesthetes and Decadents of the 1890s.* Chicago: Academy Chicago, 1993.

Bennett, Arnold. *Fame and Fiction.* New York: Dutton, 1901.

Benson, E. F. *Final Edition.* London: Appleton-Century, 1940.

Bigland, Eileen. *Marie Corelli: The Woman and the Legend.* London: Jerrolds, 1953.

Bovenschen, Silvia. "Is There a Feminine Aesthetic?" Trans. Beth Weckmueller. In *Feminist Aesthetics,* ed. Gisela Ecker, 23–50. Boston: Beacon, 1986.

Brooks, Peter. *The Melodramatic Imagination: Balzac, Henry James, Melodrama, and the Mode of Excess.* 1976. New Haven, Conn.: Yale University Press, 1995.

Bullock, George. *Marie Corelli: The Life and Death of a Best-Seller.* London: Constable, 1940.

Burdett, Osbert. *The Beardsley Period: An Essay in Perspective.* 1925. Folcroft, Pa.: Folcroft Press, 1969.

Calinescu, Matei. *Five Faces of Modernity.* 1987. Durham, N.C.: Duke University Press, 1995.

Carey, John. *The Intellectuals and the Masses: Pride and Prejudice among the Literary Intelligentsia, 1880–1939.* New York: St. Martin's, 1992.

Carr, Kent. *Miss Marie Corelli.* London: Henry J. Drane, 1901.

Carroll, Raymond G. "What's Next in Literature? Opinions of Leading English Novelists." *Philadelphia Public Ledger,* 10 August 1919, Magazine section, 1–2.

Casey, Janet Galligani. "Marie Corelli and *Fin de Siècle* Feminism." *English Literature in Transition* 35, no. 2 (1992): 163–78.

Chesterton, G. K. "A Defence of Penny Dreadfuls." In *The Defendant.* London: J. M. Dent, 1901.

Christ, Carol T., and John O. Jordan, eds. *Victorian Literature and the Victorian Visual Imagination.* Berkeley: University of California Press, 1995.

Cixous, Hélène. "The Laugh of the Medusa." In *Feminisms,* ed. Robyn R. Warhol and Diane Price-Herndl, 334–49. New Brunswick, N.J.: Rutgers University Press, 1991.

Clark, Suzanne. *Sentimental Modernism: Women Writers and the Revolution of the Word.* Bloomington: Indiana University Press, 1991.

Coates, T. F. G., and R. S. Warren-Bell. *Marie Corelli: The Writer and the Woman.* Philadelphia: George W. Jacobs, 1903.

Conrad, Barnaby. *Absinthe: History in a Bottle.* San Francisco: Chronicle, 1988.

Conrad, Joseph. *The Collected Letters of Joseph Conrad,* ed. Frederick R. Karl and Laurence Davies. Vols. 1 and 2. Cambridge: Cambridge University Press, 1986.

Corelli, Marie. *Ardath: The Story of a Dead Self.* 1889. New York: Rand, McNally, n.d.

———. *Barabbas: A Dream of the World's Tragedy.* 1893. Philadelphia: Lippincott, 1895.

———. *Boy: A Sketch.* Philadelphia: Lippincott, 1900.

———. Corelli–Arthur Severn Correspondence. University Archives and Special Collections, University of Detroit Mercy.

———. Corelli–George Bentley Correspondence. Beinecke Rare Book and Manuscript Library, Yale University.

———. *Free Opinions Freely Expressed on Certain Phases of Modern Social Life and Conduct.* New York: Dodd Mead, 1905.

———. "The Happy Life." *Strand* 28, no. 163 (1904): 72–76.

———. *Holy Orders: The Tragedy of a Quiet Life.* New York: Frederick A. Stokes, 1908.

———. *Innocent: Her Fancy and His Fact.* New York: A. L. Burt, 1914.

———. "The Last Days of Edmund Yates." 4 June 1894. MS DR 777/6–49. Shakespeare Birthplace Trust, Stratford-upon-Avon.

———. Letter to William Meredith. 9 April 1905. MS DR 904/1. Shakespeare Birthplace Trust, Stratford-upon-Avon.

———. *The Life Everlasting: A Reality of Romance.* New York: Hodder and Stoughton, 1911.

———. "A Little Talk about Literature." c. 1910. MS DR 777/23. Shakespeare Birthplace Trust, Stratford-upon-Avon.

———. *Love and the Philosopher: A Study in Sentiment.* London: Methuen, 1923.

———. "Manners, Gentlemen!" *Free Lance* 1, no. 1 (1900): 12–14.

———. "Man's War against Woman." Parts 1 and 2. *Harper's Bazaar,* May 1907, 425–28; June 1907, 550–53.

———. Manuscript. MS DR 777/48. Shakespeare Birthplace Trust, Stratford-upon-Avon.

———. *The Master Christian.* New York: Dodd Mead, 1900.

———. *The Mighty Atom.* 1896. Philadelphia: Lippincott, 1900.

———. *The Murder of Delicia.* Philadelphia: Lippincott, 1896.

———. "My First Book." *Idler* 4 (1893): 239–52.

———. *My Wonderful Wife.* In *Cameos,* 177–291. 1895. Freeport, N.Y.: Books for Libraries Press, 1970.

———. *Open Confession: To a Man from a Woman.* New York: George H. Doran, 1925.

———. *Poems.* London: Hutchinson, 1925.

———. "Press Cliques." D4. Bentley Papers. Rare Book and Special Collections Library, University of Illinois at Urbana-Champaign.

———. *A Romance of Two Worlds.* 1886. New York: Hurst, n.d.

———. *The Secret Power.* New York: A. L. Burt, 1921.

———. *The Silver Domino, or: Side Whispers, Social and Literary.* London: Lamley, 1893.

———. *A Social Note on the War: Patriotism,—or Self-Advertisement?* Birmingham, U.K.: Norton and Neale, 1900.

———. *The Sorrows of Satan.* 1895. Philadelphia: Lippincott, 1896.

———. *The Soul of Lilith.* New York: American News Company, 1892.

———. "Speech to the American Ladies Club." c. 1910. MS DR 777/24. Shakespeare Birthplace Trust, Stratford-upon-Avon.

———. *Temporal Power: A Study in Supremacy.* New York: Dodd Mead, 1902.

———. *Thelma: A Society Novel.* 1887. New York: Hurst, n.d.

———. "The Time of Our Lives: Our Women in War." c. 1914–18. MS DR 777/47. Shakespeare Birthplace Trust, Stratford-upon-Avon.

———. *The Treasure of Heaven: A Romance of Riches.* New York: Dodd Mead, 1906.

———. *Vendetta, or: The Story of One Forgotten.* 1886. New York: Hurst, n.d.

———. "Whitefriars Club Speech." May 1901. MS DR 777/13. Shakespeare Birthplace Trust, Stratford-upon-Avon.

———. "The Woman's Vote: Nature versus Politics." c. 1918. MS DR 777/32. Shakespeare Birthplace Trust, Stratford-upon-Avon.

———. "A Word about 'Ouida.'" *Belgravia* 71 (March 1890): 362–71.

———. *Wormwood.* New York: A. L. Burt, 1890.

———. *The Young Diana: An Experiment of the Future.* New York: George H. Doran, 1918.

———. *Ziska: The Problem of a Wicked Soul.* New York: Stone and Kimball, 1897.

Curtis, Gerard. "Dickens in the Visual Market." In *Literature in the Marketplace: Nineteenth-Century British Publishing and Reading Practices,* ed. John O. Jordan and Robert L. Patten, 213–49. Cambridge: Cambridge University Press, 1995.

Cvetkovich, Ann. *Mixed Feelings: Feminism, Mass Culture, and Victorian Sensationalism.* New Brunswick, N.J.: Rutgers University Press, 1992.

Debord, Guy. *The Society of the Spectacle.* New York: Zone, 1994.

DeSalvo, Louise. *Virginia Woolf: The Impact of Childhood Sexual Abuse on Her Life and Work.* Boston: Beacon, 1989.

Dinnerstein, Dorothy. *The Mermaid and the Minotaur: Sexual Arrangements and Human Malaise.* New York: Harper and Row, 1976.

Dowling, Linda. *The Vulgarization of Art: The Victorians and Aesthetic Democracy.* Charlottesville: University Press of Virginia, 1996.

Dyos, H. J. *Victorian Suburb: A Study of the Growth of Camberwell.* London: Leicester University Press, 1966.

Eagleton, Terry. "The Flight to the Real." In *Cultural Politics at the Fin de Siècle,* ed. Sally Ledger and Scott McCracken, 11–21. Cambridge: Cambridge University Press, 1995.

———. *The Ideology of the Aesthetic.* London: Basil Blackwell, 1990.

Ellmann, Richard. *The Identity of Yeats.* New York: Oxford University Press, 1964.

———. *Yeats: The Man and the Masks.* New York: Dutton, 1948.

Faderman, Lillian. *Surpassing the Love of Men.* 1981. New York: Quality Paperback Book Club, 1994.

Felman, Shoshana. *What Does a Woman Want? Reading and Sexual Difference.* Baltimore, Md.: Johns Hopkins University Press, 1993.

Felski, Rita. *Beyond Feminist Aesthetics: Feminist Literature and Social Change.* Cambridge, Mass.: Harvard University Press, 1989.

———. *The Gender of Modernity.* Cambridge, Mass.: Harvard University Press, 1995.

Feltes, N. N. *Literary Capital and the Late Victorian Novel.* Madison: University of Wisconsin Press, 1993.

Freedman, Jonathan. *Professions of Taste: Henry James, British Aestheticism, and Commodity Culture.* Stanford, Calif.: Stanford University Press, 1990.

Freeman, Barbara Claire. *The Feminine Sublime: Gender and Excess in Women's Fiction.* Berkeley: University of California Press, 1995.

Gagnier, Regenia. *Idylls of the Marketplace: Oscar Wilde and the Victorian Public.* Stanford, Calif.: Stanford University Press, 1986.

Gardiner, Judith Kegan. "On Female Identity and Writing by Women." In *Writing and Sexual Difference,* ed. Elizabeth Abel, 177–92. Chicago: University of Chicago Press, 1982.

Gilmore, Leigh. *Autobiographics: A Feminist Theory of Women's Self-Representation.* Ithaca, N.Y.: Cornell University Press, 1994.

Goldring, Douglas. "Clever Novels." In *Reputations: Essays in Criticism,* 171–81. New York: Thomas Seltzer, 1920.

Gosse, Edmund. *Questions at Issue.* New York: D. Appleton, 1893.

Gross, John. *The Rise and Fall of the Man of Letters: English Literary Life since 1800.* 1969. Chicago: Ivan R. Dee, 1992.

Grossmith, George, and Weedon Grossmith. *The Diary of a Nobody.* 1892. London: Everyman, 1992.

Hamilton, Walter. *The Aesthetic Movement in England.* 1882. New York: AMS, 1971.

Hichens, Robert. *The Green Carnation.* New York: D. Appleton, 1894.

Hoare, Philip. *Oscar Wilde's Last Stand: Decadence, Conspiracy, and the Most Outrageous Trial of the Century.* New York: Arcade, 1998.

Hobman, D. L. "Books in General." *New Statesman and Nation,* 2 August 1947, 93–94.

Honey, Maureen. "The Confession Formula and Fantasies of Empowerment." *Women's Studies* 10 (1984): 303–20.

"Housewife." c. 1925. DR 777/125. Shakespeare Birthplace Trust, Stratford-upon-Avon.

Hunt, Violet. *A Hard Woman: A Story in Scenes.* New York: D. Appleton, 1895.

Huyssen, Andreas. *After the Great Divide: Modernism, Mass Culture, Postmodernism.* Bloomington: Indiana University Press, 1986.

Jackson, Holbrook. *The Eighteen Nineties.* 1913. New York: Capricorn, 1966.

Jameson, Fredric. "Imaginary and Symbolic in Lacan: Marxism, Psychoanalytic Criticism, and the Problem of the Subject." In *Literature and Psychoanalysis: The Question of*

*Reading, Otherwise,* ed. Shoshana Felman, 338–95. Baltimore, Md.: Johns Hopkins University Press, 1982.

Jones, Ann Rosalind. "Writing the Body: Towards an Understanding of *l'écriture féminine.*" In *Feminisms,* ed. Robyn R. Warhol and Diane Price-Herndl, 357–70. New Brunswick, N.J.: Rutgers University Press, 1991.

Jordan, John O., and Robert L. Patten, eds. *Literature in the Marketplace: Nineteenth-Century British Publishing and Reading Practices.* Cambridge: Cambridge University Press, 1995.

Kappeler, Susanne. *The Pornography of Representation.* Minneapolis: University of Minnesota Press, 1986.

Kershner, R. B. "Joyce and Popular Literature: The Case of Corelli." In *James Joyce and His Contemporaries,* ed. Diana A. Ben-Merre and Maureen Murphy, 52–58. New York: Greenwood, 1989.

———. "Modernism's Mirror: The Sorrows of Marie Corelli." In *Transforming Genres: New Approaches to British Fiction of the 1890s,* ed. Nikki Lee Manos and Meri-Jane Rochelson, 67–86. New York: St. Martin's, 1994.

Kranidis, Rita. *Subversive Discourse: The Cultural Production of Late Victorian Feminist Novels.* New York: Macmillan, 1995.

Kristeva, Julia. "Women's Time." In *The Kristeva Reader,* ed. Toril Moi, 188–213. New York: Columbia University Press, 1986.

Lambourne, Lionel. *The Aesthetic Movement.* London: Phaidon, 1996.

Lawrence, Arthur H. "Miss Marie Corelli." *Strand* 16, no. 91 (1898): 17–26.

Lawrence, D. H. *Women in Love.* 1921. Harmondsworth, U.K.: Penguin, 1984.

Leavis, Q. D. *Fiction and the Reading Public.* London: Chatto and Windus, 1932.

Ledger, Sally. *The New Woman: Fiction and Feminism at the Fin de Siècle.* Manchester, U.K.: Manchester University Press, 1997.

Linton, Eliza Lynn. "Literature: Then and Now." *Fortnightly Review* 47 (1890): 517–31.

Macherey, Pierre. *A Theory of Literary Production.* Trans. Geoffrey Wall. London: Routledge and Kegan Paul, 1978.

Mangum, Teresa. "Style Wars of the 1890s: The New Woman and the Decadent." In *Transforming Genres: New Approaches to British Fiction of the 1890s,* ed. Nikki Lee Manos and Meri-Jane Rochelson, 47–66. New York: St. Martin's, 1994.

Masters, Brian. *Now Barabbas Was a Rotter: The Extraordinary Life of Marie Corelli.* London: Hamish Hamilton, 1978.

McDonald, Peter D. *British Literary Culture and Publishing Practice, 1880–1914.* Cambridge: Cambridge University Press, 1997.

Miller, Henry. "Marie Corelli: A Recommendation." *New York Times Book Review,* 12 September 1976, 55.

"Miss Marie Corelli: A Character Study by a Reader of Books." *Daily Mail,* 2 August 1906, 5.

Moers, Ellen. *Literary Women.* 1963. New York: Oxford University Press, 1977.

Murray, David Christie. *My Contemporaries in Fiction.* London: Chatto and Windus, 1897.

Nelson, Carolyn Christenson. *British Women Fiction Writers of the 1890s.* New York: Twayne, 1996.

"New Novels." *Academy,* 30 December 1893, 583–84.

Orwell, George. *Coming Up for Air.* 1939. Harmondsworth, U.K.: Penguin, 1967.

Polhemus, Robert M. *Erotic Faith: Being in Love from Jane Austen to D. H. Lawrence.* Chicago: University of Chicago Press, 1990.

Poovey, Mary. "Speaking of the Body: Mid-Victorian Constructions of Female Desire." In *Body/Politics: Women and the Discourses of Science,* ed. Mary Jacobus, Evelyn Fox Keller, and Sally Shuttleworth, 29–46. London: Routledge, 1990.

Purcell, L. Edward. "*Trilby* and Trilby-Mania: The Beginning of the Bestseller System." *Journal of Popular Culture* 11 (1977): 62–76.

Pykett, Lyn. *The "Improper" Feminine: The Women's Sensation Novel and the New Woman Writing.* London: Routledge, 1992.

Rich, Adrienne. "Jane Eyre: The Temptations of a Motherless Woman." In *On Lies, Secrets, and Silence: Selected Prose, 1966–1978,* 89–106. New York: Norton, 1979.

Robinson, Henry Peach. "Idealism, Realism, Expressionism." In *Classic Essays on Photography,* ed. Alan Trachtenberg, 91–98. New Haven, Conn.: Leete's Island Books, 1980.

Sadleir, Michael. "Mary Mackay." In *Dictionary of National Biography, 1922–1930,* ed. J. R. H. Weaver, 539–42. London: Oxford University Press, 1937.

Salmon, Richard. "Signs of Intimacy: The Literary Celebrity in the 'Age of Interviewing.'" *Victorian Literature and Culture* 25, no. 1 (1997): 159–77.

Samuel, Horace B. *Modernities,* 114–33. New York: Dutton, 1914.

Scheick, William J. *The Ethos of Romance at the Turn of the Century.* Austin: University of Texas Press, 1994.

Scott, William Stuart. *Marie Corelli: The Story of a Friendship.* London: Hutchinson, 1955.

Shaw, George Bernard. *The Matter with Ireland,* ed. Dan H. Laurence and David H. Greene. New York: Hill and Wang, 1962.

Shires, Linda M. "The Author as Spectacle and Commodity: Elizabeth Barrett Browning and Thomas Hardy." In *Victorian Literature and the Victorian Visual Imagination,* ed. Carol T. Christ and John O. Jordan, 198–212. Berkeley: University of California Press, 1995.

Showalter, Elaine. "Feminist Criticism in the Wilderness." In *Writing and Sexual Difference,* ed. Elizabeth Abel, 9–36. Chicago: University of Chicago Press, 1982.

———. *Sexual Anarchy: Gender and Culture at the Fin de Siècle.* New York: Viking, 1990.

———, ed. *Daughters of Decadence: Women Writers of the Fin-de-Siècle.* New Brunswick, N.J.: Rutgers University Press, 1993.

Sinfield, Alan. *The Wilde Century: Effeminacy, Oscar Wilde, and the Queer Moment.* New York: Columbia University Press, 1994.

Smith, Betty. *A Tree Grows in Brooklyn.* 1943. New York: Perennial Library, 1967.

Snitow, Ann Barr. "Mass Market Romance: Pornography for Women Is Different." *Radical History Review* 20 (spring/summer 1979): 141–61.

Sontag, Susan. *On Photography.* New York: Farrar, Straus, Giroux, 1977.

Spender, J. A. *The New Fiction and Other Papers.* 1895. London: Garland, 1984.

Stead, W. T. "'The Sorrows of Satan'—and of Marie Corelli." *Review of Reviews* 12 (July–Dec. 1895): 453–64.

Steiner, Wendy. *The Scandal of Pleasure.* Chicago: University of Chicago Press, 1995.

Stetz, Margaret Diane. "Life's 'Half-Profits': Writers and Their Readers in Fiction of the 1890s." In *Nineteenth-Century Lives: Essays Presented to Jerome Hamilton Buckley,* ed. Laurence S. Lockridge, John Maynard, and Donald D. Stone, 169–87. Cambridge: Cambridge University Press, 1989.

Stuart-Young, J. M. [Peril, pseud.]. "A Note upon Marie Corelli by Another Writer of Less Repute." *Westminster Review* 167 (1906): 680–92.

Stutfield, Hugh E. M. "Tommyrotics." *Blackwood's* 157 (1895): 833–45.

Symons, Arthur. *Selected Letters, 1880–1935,* ed. Karl Beckson and John H. Munro. Iowa City: University of Iowa Press, 1989.

———. *The Symbolist Movement in Literature.* 1899, 1908, 1919. New York: Dutton, 1958.

Thomas, Ronald. "Making Darkness Visible: Capturing the Criminal and Observing the Law in Victorian Photography and Detective Fiction." In *Victorian Literature and the Victorian Visual Imagination,* ed. Carol T. Christ and John O. Jordan, 134–68. Berkeley: University of California Press, 1995.

Thompson, F. M. L. "The Rise of Suburbia." In *The Victorian City: A Reader in British Urban History, 1820–1914,* ed. R. J. Morris and Richard Rodger, 149–80. London: Longman, 1993.

Twain, Mark. *The Autobiography of Mark Twain.* 1917. New York: Harper, 1959.

Vyver, Bertha. *Memoirs of Marie Corelli.* London: Alston Rivers, 1930.

[Ward, Mrs. Humphry]. "The Looker-On." *Blackwood's Edinburgh Magazine,* December 1895, 914–15.

Watts, Carol. "Releasing Possibility into Form: Cultural Choice and the Woman Writer." In *New Feminist Discourses,* ed. Isobel Armstrong, 83–102. London: Routledge, 1992.

Weeks, Jeffrey. *Sexuality and Its Discontents: Meanings, Myths, and Modern Sexualities.* London: Routledge, 1985.

Weir, David. *Decadence and the Making of Modernism.* Amherst: University of Massachusetts Press, 1995.

Wells, H. G. *The Literary Criticism of H. G. Wells.* Ed. Patrick Parrinder and Robert Philmus. Sussex, U.K.: Harvester, 1980.

West, Rebecca. *The Strange Necessity.* London: Jonathan Cape, 1928.

Wilde, Oscar. "The Decay of Lying." 1889. In *Oscar Wilde,* ed. Isobel Murray, 215–40. Oxford: Oxford University Press, 1989.

———. *The Letters of Oscar Wilde.* Ed. Rupert Hart-Davis. London: Harcourt Brace, 1962.

———. "Pen, Pencil and Poison." 1891. In *The Artist as Critic: Critical Writings of Oscar Wilde,* ed. Richard Ellmann, 320–40. Chicago: University of Chicago Press, 1969.

Woolf, Virginia. *A Writer's Diary.* New York: Harcourt Brace Jovanovich, 1953.

Zwerdling, Alex. *Virginia Woolf and the Real World.* Berkeley: University of California Press, 1986.

# Index

# Victorian Literature and Culture Series